TEACHER EDUCATION IN THE NINETIES:

TOWARDS A NEW COHERENCE

Vol. II WITHDRAWN FROM STOCK

Edited by

John Coolahan

Papers from
The 15th Annual Conference of
The Association for Teacher Education in Europe (ATEE),
Mary Immaculate College of Education, Limerick, Ireland, 1990.

ISBN — 0-9518060-1-7
(Set) ISBN — 0-9518060-2-5

Printed in the Republic of Ireland
by
The Leinster Leader, Naas, Co. Kildare.

Cover Design, Bill Bolger.

Published for the ATEE
by
Mary Immaculate College of Education, Limerick.

CONTENTS

ii

ENERGY AS A STARTING POINT TO AVOID CONCEPTUAL PROBLEMS IN INTRODUCTORY ELECTRICITY EDUCATION

Pieter Licht

Department of Science Education,
Free University Amsterdam, The Netherlands

Introduction

This paper gives an outline of a part of a teaching programme on the concepts of electric energy, voltage and current. The whole programme is intended for use throughout secondary education. Elements of this programme have already been partly tested in school practice. It introduces a sequence of ideas and concepts different from the one normally followed and places more emphasis on some aspects which normally are treated briefly or never at all. The proposed changes arise from research findings on students' ideas about, and their understanding of, electricity. The part of the teaching programme which is discussed here concerns the first two lesson blocks out of six blocks in total. In these two blocks, the concept of energy is chosen as a starting point for electricity education. Firstly, in the next sections I will describe both the whole teaching programme and the first two blocks in more detail. Secondly, I will present the main research findings on the students' cognitive and affective results based on their working in these two blocks and arrive at some conclusions and implications for education.

The history of the teaching programme

Elsewhere we have reported on a test instrument which traces persistence of alternative conceptions among students (Licht & Thijs, 1990). The construction of clusters of questions which deal with the same physical concepts in several contexts has the benefit of contributing to the identification and fairly precise categorisation of errors and conceptual difficulties among students. It would appear that they do not make incidental mistakes, but show patterns of conceptual difficulties and ways of reasoning. Based on the test results, students can be characterised conceptually. Furthermore, the statistical reliability of this characterisation increases throughout secondary education. This means that the students in higher forms use alternative conceptions more consistently than the students in lower forms. Although the former may resort less frequently to alternative conceptions than the latter, they do so in a more coherent way. This research finding offered me an explanation for the results of my previous research, concerning the lack of learning success among students in the lower forms of secondary education with respect to the concepts of voltage and current. Although they had had 20 to 25 lessons on the topic of electricity, they still demonstrated vague ideas about the differences and the relations between voltage and current. In these lower forms a teaching strategy was applied in which an explicit confrontation took place between the students' own intuitive ideas and the scientific concepts of voltage and current (Licht, 1987). Although immediately after the lesson series the cognitive results were quite positive, five months later the results were disappointing. Most students showed their alternative ways of reasoning and a lack of discrimination between the concepts of voltage and current in much the same way as before the lesson series. The explicit confrontation approach seemed to be not very effective among relatively young students with their rather unstable alternative ideas. Therefore, in the next section an outline is presented of a teaching programme in which the use of a confrontation approach is restricted to the higher forms of secondary education and in which I try, as much as possible, to adapt the content of physics in the lower forms to the intuitive ideas of the students concerned.

Outline of the whole teaching programme on electricity

The programme I propose for teaching the key concepts of electricity, i.e. electric energy, voltage and current, consists of six successive blocks. The information covered in the first three blocks is normally treated briefly and some parts of it never at all in the Netherlands. Instead of doing what is commonly done at the start of teaching electricity — measuring current and voltage and almost immediately after that working with these concepts in a formal and mathematical way — the first three blocks of the programme deal with a phenomenological introduction to the topic, with qualitative reasoning about changes in electric circuits and with a dynamical, microscopic model to represent voltage, current and electric energy. The programme consists of six blocks which can be labelled in the following way:

block 1   a phenomenological orientation concerning the relative brightness of bulbs and the relative speed of electric motors

block 2   a *qualitative macroscopic* treatment, including the concepts of electrical energy, current and voltage

block 3   a *qualitative microscopic* treatment, including the relation between the macroscopic concepts of electrical energy, current and voltage and the microscopic concepts of moving electrons and quasi-static electron densities (Licht, 1990a)

block 4A   a *quantitative macroscopic* treatment in the context of "electricity in the household," including the concepts of electrical energy, power, current, voltage and resistance, and a process of thinking back and forth between macroscopic and microscopic concepts (Licht, 1990b)

block 4B   a *quantitative macroscopic* treatment in the context of "the production, transport and consumption of electrical energy," including the concepts in the domain of electromagnetism, and the process of thinking back and forth between macroscopic and microscopic concepts

block 5   a *quantitative macroscopic* treatment in the context of "lightning and thunderstorms," including the theoretical concepts of electric field, potential, the potential and kinetic energy of electrons, and the process of thinking back and forth between these concepts and the macroscopic concepts from block 4A and block 4B.

Table 1 shows the form in which each block is to be dealt with, the type of students for whom each block is intended (low, middle or high ability students), the blocks for which there are already some research findings available (extensive : ++; preliminary: +; none:-) and the number of lessons planned for each block.

TABLE 1 — The six blocks in secondary education

Block	Form	Type of students	Research findings	Number of lessons
1	2	1/m/h	+	5
2	2	1/m/h	+	10
3	3	m/h	+	12
4A	4	h	++	15
4B	5	h	-	15
5	5	h	+	15

I will now present the information on the blocks 1 and 2 into more detail.

Block 1 : a phenomenological orientation

During this block students discover regularities in electric circuit phenomena, by varying the number and the position of the batteries in a circuit and the number of (parallel -) connected bulbs and/or electric motors. The language spoken during this block does not include physics terms like "energy" or "current." Students are invited by the teacher to give their arguments in terms of the relative brightness of bulbs or the relative speed of electric motors. Also the word "task" is introduced, to express the idea that the battery or the power supply "has to do a job." A battery's task is heavier when instead of one bulb two bulbs are connected in parallel to the battery, because the total amount of light production is greater. The task for a battery in a Walkman is lighter if you play it soft instead of loud. A power station's task is heavier when more houses and schools are connected, etc. The intention behind using the word "task" is to adapt the language of the teacher and the textbook to the intuitive language of the students and to pave the way for the concept of energy through discrimination between heavy and light tasks. In block 2 it is then possible to introduce the concept of energy as "what is needed to carry out a certain task." At the start of block 1 we do not restrict the term "task" to electrical contexts. Also car engines, windmills or matches are included as objects which may carry out a job. The electrical contexts are restricted to parallel-connected components such as lamps and electric motors. In these contexts students are supposed to discover the regularity that "the more components are connected in parallel the heavier the task will be."

Although this orientation block is certainly context-bound and the regularities in phenomena are not expressed in terms of physics concepts, it nonetheless offers a coherent and worthwhile intermediate step for all students in form 2. Most of the regularities found in students' practicals with batteries and parallel-connected bulbs can be transferred to the household situation with power-points and parallel-connected electrical devices, and thus be made relevant to daily life.

Block 2: a qualitative macroscopic treatment

In this block it seems possible to avoid some of the conceptual difficulties concerning voltage and current as they have been traced in several research projects (McDermott & van Zee, 1985; Shipstone, 1985; Kuiper et al, 1985; Shipstone et al, 1988; Licht, 1990b), by choosing the energy concept as an entrance to the cluster of key concepts in electricity. The energy concept is supposed to be more closely related to the observations during the phenomenological orientation than the concepts of voltage and current. Also, the concept of energy is supposed to be better adapted to the students' need to express themselves in terms of "something that is used up" in a bulb or apparatus than the concepts of voltage and current. However, the concepts of voltage and current, on which most research studies report, should not be postponed completely until the next blocks. The concept of current can be introduced as a tool for the transportation of electrical energy from the battery to the bulb, or generally, from the electrical energy "producer" to the electrical energy "consumer." One reason for not postponing the concept of current is that students ask questions about the difference between energy and current. A second reason is that the fact that energy transportation requires a closed circuit can only be understood in terms of a circulating current, even though the energy moves unidirectionally from "producer" to "consumer." Using a home central-heating system as an analogy for an electric circuit seems to be intelligible for most students in the mixed ability group, at least if such a system is presented on video — not all the students are familiar with or able to recognise the features of a central-heating system (figure 1).

FIGURE 1 — The analogy between a central heating system and an electrical circuit

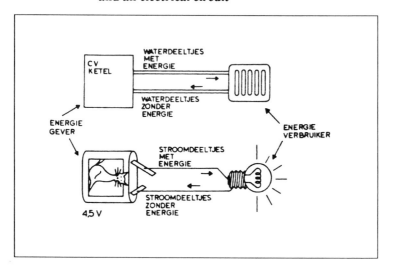

The meaning of the concept of voltage is restricted to the labels used on batteries or voltage sources. The label gives information on the (relative) amount of energy the supply is able to give when it is connected to a certain electrical device. A supply of 220 volt connected to a lamp produces more electrical energy than a supply of 12 volt connected to the same lamp.

The regularities found during this block can be expressed by statements like: "the more bulbs are connected in parallel, the more energy is used up in the bulbs and thus the more energy is produced in the battery," or like "the more batteries are connected in series, the more electrical energy is used up in a bulb and thus the more electrical energy is produced in the batteries." We call statements of this type "functional relationships." By this we mean that they summarise qualitatively the dynamics of the interdependence of objects and variables in a circuit.

The main messages from this block, as far as the physics contents is concerned, are:

1.   The heavier the task, the more electrical energy is "consumed" *and thus*

2.   the more electrical energy is "produced" by the power supply.

3.   Energy is transported by the current. So, electrical energy is "used up" for the task and current is not.

4.   The more volts are mentioned on a power supply the more energy this supply is able to give a certain electrical device.

The evaluation of the cognitive results of the students is focused on these four main messages. Teaching materials which fit into this block could serve as a worthwhile end-point for all students who will not go on studying science after the age of 15.

The sample and the set-up of the research

A group of 204 students (106 male, 98 female) in ten form 2 classes (14 year old students) at two different schools took part in the lessons on the blocks 1 and 2. One school for middle and high ability students participated with one physics teacher and two classes, the other school participated with four teachers and eight mixed ability classes. In this school, three out of these four teachers were qualified in another science subject other than physics.

The research on block 1 was of a qualitative and exploratory nature. Classroom observations of some lessons, discussions with teachers and the notes of some students should give us an impression of the possibilities of the chosen approach. The research on block 2 was of a quantitative and verifying nature. A multiple choice test with 29 questions was constructed, mainly dealing with the four main content issues of block 2 as mentioned above. For most questions two versions were made, a so-called school context version (SC) including batteries and bulbs, and a life context version (LC) including a 220 volt power-point, lamps and/or other electrical household devices (see Figure 2). the same test was used five times in the following set-up:

after 4 lessons :   a subtest of 13 questions, mainly dealing with the "consumption" of electrical energy by bulbs, lamps and electrical devices

after 8 lessons :   a subtest of 16 questions, mainly dealing with the "production" of electrical energy and the discrimination between electrical energy and current

after 12 lessons :   the whole test of 29 questions

after 4 months :   the whole test again.

Although we started with 207 students, the results on all tests are available for 144 students (76 male; 68 female) only. I restrict myself to the data concerning them, because my main interest lies in the progression of conceptual understanding among the students. After the course on electricity as presented in blocks 1 and 2, all students involved in this study went on to another topic in physics which had no relation to the topic of electricity. So, the post-test results after four months are not based on another course on electricity during this period.

FIGURE 2 — Two versions of a test question : a School-world version and a Life-world version

The School-world version (SC)

The Life-world version (SC)

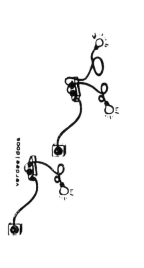

We connect two bulbs L_1 and L_2 to a battery. Both bulbs shine with equal brightness. Then we take bulb L_2 out of its socket. Bulb L_1 still shines with the same brightness

We connect a lamp to a distribution-box. The box is connected to a power-point. Then we add a second lamp. The first lamp still shines with the same brightness. Both lamps shine with equal brightness

Compare the amount of electrical energy used in 1 minute by the two bulbs with the amount used by one bulb in 1 minute, etc.

Compare the amount of electrical energy used in 1 minute by one lamp with the amount used by the two lamps in 1 minute, etc.

Some qualitative findings from block 1

The results on the phenomenological orientation are positive in the sense that teachers can continue talking and discussing with their students. This means that teacher-students discussions are possible without the existence of a steadily growing gap between the language used by the teacher and the language used by the students. Basing themselves on their notes almost all students (more than 90%) give correct arguments, in familiar as well as in unfamiliar contexts, in terms of heavy and light tasks and in terms of the relative amount of production of a certain "activity," such as light, motion or heat. The teachers are pleased about the fact that both male and female students remain motivated about the topic, not only during lessons but apparently also during their homework. Generally all homework tasks were made. On the basis of discussions with the participating teachers one can conclude that the threshold for students' participation is not as high as it was before. It is worth noting that especially the non-physics teachers prefer the phenomenological approach, probably because it can be adapted more easily to their own way of reasoning about electric circuits.

Some quantitative findings from block 2

During block 2 the multiple choice test was administered five times to get an impression of the possible progression of students' understanding.

In Table 2a the percentages of correct answers are presented for all questions dealing with a comparison of the amount of electrical energy "used" for two different tasks. For instance, in a question about 1 bulb (School Context), a bulb which shines bright is compared to another bulb which shines less bright; in the question about 2 lamps (Life Context) one lamp is compared to the situation with the same lamp to which a second lamp is added (see also Figure 2); energy "consumption" of a radio is compared while playing in a sound and a less sound way. The results before teaching show that the majority of the students already have correct intuitive ideas, at least in the contexts concerning bulbs and lamps. It looks as if the "energy-path" is paved the way we hoped for in using the concept of

TABLE 2a — Percentages of correct answers on "the heavier the task the more electrical energy is "consumed"" (N=144)

Question About		2 weeks Before Teaching	After Four Lessons	After Eight Lessons	After Twelve Lessons	After Four Months
1 bulb	(SC)	75	89	—	100	97
1 lamp	(LC)	60	91	—	98	95
A radio	(LC)	44	86	—	98	96
2 bulbs	(SC)	68	84	—	97	93
2 lamps	(LC)	65	83	—	94	93
2 devices	(LC)	43	86	—	90	90
MEAN %		59	87	—	96	94

TABLE 2b— Percentages of correct answers on "the heavier the task the more electrical energy has to be "produced"" (N=144)

Question About		2 weeks Before Teaching	After Four Lessons	After Eight Lessons	After Twelve Lessons	After Four Months
1 bulb	(SC)	39	—	89	95	92
1 lamp	(LC)	45	—	89	98	92
A radio	(LC)	34	—	88	92	87
2 bulbs	(SC)	37	—	84	92	91
2 lamps	(LC)	31	—	92	97	90
2 devices	(LC)	31	—	82	95	93
MEAN %		36	—	87	95	91

TABLE 3 — Percentages of correct answers on "the discrimination between electrical energy and current" (N=144)

Question About	2 weeks Before Teaching	After Four Lessons	After Eight Lessons	After Twelve Lessons	After Four Months
A battery contains current (NO)	43	47	52	60	56
A battery contains energy (YES)	88	92	91	98	96
Current provides the transportation of electrical energy (YES)	55	—	75	85	82
Only in a closed circuit a bulb uses electrical energy (YES)	59	95	—	100	97
Only in a closed circuit a battery provides electrical energy (YES)	53	71	—	89	86
Passing through a bulb, current is conserved (YES)	37	—	67	88	80
Passing through a bulb, electrical energy is "consumed" (YES)	55	—	72	89	95

"task" during block 1. The greatest progression in understanding takes place after the first four lessons, in which the step is taken from "task" to "energy." It is evident that most students are able to take this step and even show some progress in their understanding at the end of the lesson series. However, the most striking results appear on the post-test, which has been administered after four months. From these it is clear that there is hardly any decrease in understanding. These results are in no way comparable to the results of my previous research on voltage and current (Licht, 1987). Of course, the results presented here deal with a topic which seems to be less difficult. However, what is more important is that the results may be seen as a first sign of a path through the topic of electricity, which is accessible to almost all students.

In Table 2b the percentages of correct answers are presented in relation to a comparison between the amount of electrical energy "produced" for two different tasks. What is remarkable is that before teaching, about 40% of the students state that more energy has been used up for a certain task in comparison to another task, whereas at the same time they state that the amount of energy "produced" stays the same for both tasks, or is sometimes even less for the heavier task. But after eight lessons this discrepancy has vanished completely, and a very stable correct idea develops, which is retained for at least a period of four months. Although at the start of block 2 the results were lower than we had expected on the basis of previous interviews with students, the idea of a balance between the "consumption" and the "production" of electrical energy seems understandable for almost all students.

In Table 3 the percentages of correct answers are presented with respect to the questions dealing with the discrimination between electrical energy and current. Almost all sentences in Table 3 are rephrased, because in the test I used more indirect ways to find out whether students discriminate sufficiently between electrical energy and current. As could be expected from the results in Tables 2a and 2b, all questions dealing with energy were answered correctly by almost all students, at least after 8 to 12 lessons. The results concerning the questions dealing with the concept of current are relatively low at the start and lay behind both till the end of the lessons series and after four months. The same holds for the results concerning the concept of voltage. Although the results concerning current and voltage are lower than we had hoped for, one still can not say that what has been gained in the area of energy has been lost in the area of voltage and current.

Two weeks before the teaching programme starts there are significant differences between the answers given by female and male students on almost all questions. The scores of the male students are better. These differences disappear completely during the programme. In the same way the (significant) differences in scores between both schools disappear during the programme.

Some affective findings from block 1 and 2

I also administered a questionnaire to find out the students' opinion on the topic of electricity and their experiences during the lessons. Although about 50% (N=195) of the students state that the topic is difficult, most of them state that they find the topic interesting (77%), that they like the topic (60%) and that they learn a lot from it (94%). More than 80% of the students are (very) positive about the lessons, i.e. about their practicals, the cooperation with their fellow students and the teacher-independent approach. However, 75% of the students agree they had to ask the teacher frequently for help during the lessons. Between 75% and 85% of the students are positive about the text book, i.e. about the clarity of explanation (76%), the clarity of what is important or not (81%), and the level and the content of the questions (81% respectively 75%). There are no (significant) differences in opinions and experiences between female and male students, except for the questions on their appreciation of the topic (more male than female students) and on the need for help from the teacher (more female than male students).

Conclusions and implications for teaching

Based on physics education research, a science curriculum must provide a gradual progression towards more abstract and more powerful concepts. However, each level of conceptual understanding has to provide a coherent collection of rules and regularities which is relevant to pupils. The outlined teaching programme in the domain of electricity seems to be a possible example of the use of these hierarchical levels. So far, the research results show that the energy concept as a starting point for electricity education provides both the students and the teachers with a passable path through the cluster of key concepts. Other results, not presented in this paper, show that a microscopic model can serve as an effective tool for qualitative reasoning about electric circuits during block 3 of the programme, without negative interference with the next blocks (Licht, 1990a).

The implications of this new approach concern especially the changes required from the teachers to cope with it in the planned way. It took quite some time before I was fully aware of the changes which have to take place among the teachers. They have to change:

1.   their subject matter language, certainly at the beginning of the teaching sequence;

2.   their pace concerning the introduction of formal relations. They have to postpone these relations until students have discovered some patterns within the phenomena and have formulated the regularities in their own words;

3.   their view on what is important to know for students and what is not in the light of the relevance of certain aspects to daily life situations;

4.   their view of their own subject matter knowledge, because it is not very common among physics teachers to conceive an electric circuit as mainly a very sophisticated way of energy transportation.

From all these required changes it is evident that teachers have to be guided by means of inservice activities if they are willing to introduce this new teaching programme.

Until now, I have worked with a group of ten teachers. We met at least once a month and discussed new teaching materials and their classroom experiences. My expectations of the results and opinions of students are low, if teachers are going to introduce the new teaching materials in their physics lessons guided only by a written teacher guide. In my opinion, it is impossible to achieve the required changes among teachers without intensive discussions within a group of fellow teachers, curriculum developers and educational researchers. I almost needed one year to make clear to the teachers what the intentions of the programme are and what kind of role they are asked to play during their lessons. It is only through the discussions on the concrete teaching materials and on their (different) experiences with these materials, that the intentions became more clear to the participating teachers. In fact, the teachers needed the same kind of gradual conceptual progression or, even sometimes, conceptual change as their students did, with respect to their own intuitive ideas on the effectiveness of certain learning and teaching approaches and their view on physics itself. As a result of my experience of this one year my doubts have grown about teachers "learning" how to teach in a more constructivistic way, by just participating in a workshop on this topic. If we fail to see teachers as constructors of their own knowledge on the basis of their own experiences and regularities discovered during their classroom teaching, the implementation of a more constructivistic teaching approach will certainly not succeed.

338

REFERENCES

Kuiper, J., Dulfer, G.H., Licht, P., Thijs, G.D. (1985)
Students' Conceptual Problems in the Understanding of Simple Electric Circuits. Internal Report, Free University, Amsterdam.

Licht, P. (1987)
A strategy to deal with conceptual and reasoning problems in introductory electricity education. In : J. Novak, *Proceedings of the second international seminar on misconceptions and educational strategies in science and mathematics,* Vol.2, 275-285. Cornell University, Ithaca, U.S.A.

Licht, P. & Thijs, G.D. (1990)
A method to trace coherence and persistence of preconceptions. *International Journal of Science Education* (in press).

Licht, P. (1990a)
A microscopic model for a better understanding of the concepts of current and voltage. In : P. Lijnse et al (eds), *Relating Macroscopic Phenomena to Microscopic Particles : a central problem in secondary Science Education.* Proceedings of an International Seminar. Rijks-Universiteit Utrecht, Utrecht, The Netherlands (in press).

Licht, P. (1990b)
Diagnosis of pupils' preconceptions with a multiple choice test and the effects of its use in a teaching strategy. *European Journal of Teacher Education* (in press).

McDermott, L. & Zee, E. van (1985)
Identifying and Addressing Student Difficulties with Electric Circuits. In : R. Duit et al (eds), *Aspects of Understanding Electricity,* 39-48, IPN, Kiel (BRD).

Shipstone, D.M. (1985)
On Childrens' Use of Conceptual Models in Reasoning about Electricity.   In : R. Duit et al (eds), *Aspects of Understanding Electricity,* 73-82, IPN, Kiel (BRD).

Shipstone, D.M., Rhöneck, C. von, Jung, W., Kärrquist, C., Dupin, J.J., Joshua, S. & Licht, P. (1988).   A Study of Students' Understanding of Electricity in five European Countries. *International Journal of Science Education,* 10, (3), 303-316.

TRAINING TEACHERS TO USE
CONCEPTUAL CHANGE STRATEGIES : THE CASE
OF IONIZING RADIATION

H.M.C. Eijkelhof, C.W.J.M. Klaassen and P.L. Lijnse

Centre for Science and Mathematics Education
University of Utrecht, The Netherlands

Several authors have recognised that the initial training of teachers should draw attention to the typical ideas which pupils bring to particular topics, to the prevalence of these views (Cosgrove and Osborne, 1985), and to the role played by pupils' existing knowledge in understanding new material (Hewson and Hewson, 1988). However, at least in Europe, there does not appear to be much experience of courses of this type (Licht et al, 1990). In this paper we restrict ourselves to teacher training in the field of dealing with preconceptions about ionizing radiation.

In the Netherlands, the topic of radioactivity was traditionally taught only in senior high school. A recent trend in this country is to include the topic in the syllabuses at junior secondary level, using the argument that all pupils should have some basic knowledge about the risks of ionizing radiation. Two problems have arisen from the introduction of this topic. Firstly, many teachers have no experience of teaching this topic so inservice training is required. Secondly, recent studies in our group have shown that relating the physics of ionizing radiation to applications and risks evokes a number of lay-ideas which seem to be resistant to change by present educational strategies (Eijkelhof, 1990), probably because they are part of life-world thinking about radioactivity and ionizing radiation (Eijkelhof and Millar, 1988; Lijnse et al, 1990).

In this paper we will first summarise the main findings about pupils' lay-ideas in this field and identify criteria for a new educational strategy to deal with these ideas. Then we will describe our experiences in teacher training. Finally we will discuss some implications of our findings.

Pupils' ideas about radioactivity

Based on a Delphi-study with radiation experts, an analysis of news reports, questionnaires and interviews with pupils and classroom observation (Eijkelhof, 1990), we have concluded that the framework of many pupils and other lay-people concerning radioactivity and ionizing radiation, can be characterised as follows:

(a)   anything associated with radioactivity is seen as dangerous: there appears to be a widespread fear of radioactivity (Weart, 1988). This fear seems to take precedence over "rational" analyses of situations and contexts;

(b)   the use of one undifferentiated "radiation" concept; no distinction is made between the concepts of radiation and radioactive material;

(c)   "radiation" is considered to be conserved after absorption; no distinction is made between the concepts of contamination and irradiation.

It was shown that a number of lay-ideas which fit this framework are quite resistant to change through current teaching practices. Possible explanations are that these three ideas support each other, are part of common culture, seem to "work" in daily life, are reinforced by the press and other media, and are not adequately addressed in physics education. Recent research in our group has indicated that Dutch school children from the middle and lower ability bands particularly have severe difficulties with the micro-level explanation of radioactive phenomena, which is prominent towards the beginning of most treatments of the topic (Klaassen et al, 1990).

A new strategy for teaching the topic of radioactivity

Based on the findings described above and in the light of the constructivist approach of Driver (1986, 1988), Redeker's (1985) views about the difference between lifeworld ideas and physics, and the work of Ten Voorde (1977), who emphasises starting with empirical activities, postponing theory and making use of productive discussions, we developed a new teaching sequence for use with pupils between 14 and 19 years of age (Millar et al, 1990). The explicit aim of this strategy is to help pupils make the following basic distinctions:

(a)   between the risks of open and closed sources, and of high and low activity;

(b)   between the concepts of radiation and radioactive matter;

(c)   between the absorption of radiation and the storage of radioactive matter.

Characteristics of the new learning strategy are:

- eliciting pupils' prior understandings;
- differentiating between terms and emphasising accurate use of terminology;
- starting with phenomenological and macroscopic aspects and introducing microscopic aspects only later in the course;
- avoiding "enforced" learning; reconstruction of meanings can be promoted but not enforced.
- using group discussions: this enables pupils to exchange ideas and to negotiate about meanings.

At present, three modules have been constructed independently, based on the new strategy: one in the U.K. for use within the new National Curriculum, and two in the Netherlands for use in junior and senior physics classes.   These modules were all constructed in close cooperation between researchers and teachers. In the next section we will report some of our experiences in training teachers to develop and use these new modules.

Experiences with the training of teachers

In earlier studies on this topic (Eijkelhof, 1990), we found that physics teachers were in general not familiar with pupils' prior ideas and with the kinds of learning problems we identified.

Teachers often underestimated these problems until they used our questionnaires, which showed that even their sixth form pupils had these lay-ideas. This is not surprising as almost no research had previously been published about pupils' ideas in this field.

Two years ago we found that a Dutch unit which used part of the new teaching strategy (emphasising the distinction between source, radiation and receiver) was not very successful with pupils of lower ability. The teachers expected success and were discouraged when pupils' prior ideas appeared resistant to their teaching approach. These teachers underestimated the strength of pupils' prior ideas and were not sufficiently familiar with constructivist approaches to teaching and learning. At that time we as researchers started to doubt the usefulness of starting with a microscopic description and explanation of radioactive phenomena.

In developing the two new Dutch units based on the full new strategy we decided to cooperate closely with teachers. In this section we first describe (A) the experiences with training a teacher for less able pupils who was strongly involved in writing and experimenting with the new materials. Then we will outline (B) some experiences with other teachers.

(A)   Inservice training of one teacher

The teacher (T) involved was 44 years old and had about eighteen years experience of teaching physics to less able pupils in an urban school. He had taught the new topic of radioactivity only once before. The researcher involved (R) was a 29 year old PhD student with a teaching certificate but with no teaching experience outside his initial teacher training. Before starting the writing and experimenting with the new materials an intensive inservice training programme (INSET) of eleven two hour sessions was given by R. Aims of the INSET were:

- to familiarise T with research results;
- to familiarise R with the teaching style of T;
- to develop a common language about teaching and learning in order to lay a foundation for further cooperation.

T and R prepared themselves for the meetings by doing some homework. Some examples of this homework were: analysing transcripts of interviews with pupils and protocols of dialogue in lessons, analysing the results of questionnaires, studying similarities and differences between teaching materials on the topic in question, and carrying out a small questionnaire study in one of the classes at T's school. In the period when the meetings were held, R visited T's lessons regularly. In each of the meetings a particular topic was discussed. Examples of these topics were: the aims of this INSET, scientific ideas and pupils' ideas about particles and molecules, arguments for and against using "particles" in the teaching of radioactivity, characteristics of pupils' ideas about radioactivity, the usefulness of specific basic scientific knowledge for understanding applications of ionizing radiation, and teaching in a constructivist way. Finally T wrote a report about his reactions to this INSET.

During the sessions it became clear that T and R approached the discussions from a different perspective and with different experiences. It took time to become acquainted with these differences. The discussions were deliberately held in such a way that both perspectives were taken seriously and were felt to be of equivalent value in making decisions about the curriculum materials.

The visits to lessons seemed to be very useful. In this way R became familiar with T's teaching style and was able to use examples from T's lessons on other topics to illustrate R's ideas about teaching. At the same time, T was encouraged to try out some new teaching methods which were evaluated and discussed in the meetings.

According to T, his main personal learning experiences were:

- he was stimulated to reflect on his own teaching style;
- he was shocked by the particle ideas of his own pupils;
- he gained insight into common pupils' ideas about the particulate nature of matter and about radioactivity;
- his attitude towards teaching changed: he was more willing to take pupils' ideas into account by listening to pupils and by postponing the presentation of the "correct" scientific view, he gave pupils more opportunities to experience and

describe phenomena and made less use of a didactic style of teaching.

The main learning outcomes for R were of a different nature:

- he learned to specify the learning strategy which he had initially in mind, continuously encouraged by T to modify his book knowledge on teaching;
- he realised the importance of reflective moments in a series of lessons;
- he was stimulated to clarify the aims of the series of lessons for pupils.

(B)   Other experiences with teachers

After the INSET described above, T and R ran three workshops on the teaching of radioactivity with teachers of less-able pupils. These teachers:

- appeared to be hesitant to teach the topic, even though it is now part of the examination syllabus for these pupils;
- were not very familiar with the physics of the topic as often it had not been part of their training;
- held a number of the same lay-ideas as have been found with pupils; these ideas were at first not expressed freely, but this changed as soon as they realised that they were not the only ones holding these ideas;
- expressed considerable interest after the workshops to take a course in which both content and teaching implications would be discussed.

From the interviews with physics teachers in senior high school it appeared that they are very experienced in teaching the topic of radioactivity and have fewer lay-ideas themselves. However, they are not familiar with the existence of these lay-ideas and do not know how to deal with these ideas in their teaching.

Discussion

What recommendations could be based on our experiences

to date with teacher training as regards promoting conceptual change in the field of ionizing radiation?

In our view a teacher training course should include the following three aims:

(a)   teachers should realise that pupils have particular ideas and ways of reasoning about radioactivity and radiation which influence learning;

(b)   teachers should become familiar with the most frequent and persistent lay-ideas of pupils in this field;

(c)   teachers should be encouraged to consider and use teaching strategies which take the existence and persistence of these lay-ideas into account.

Useful elements of such a course would appear to be:

- discussing pupils' ideas taken from the results of questionnaires and interviews;
- analysing protocols of dialogue;
- carrying out small studies in teachers' own classes, using questionnaires and interviews;
- discussing and practicing activities in which pupils are stimulated to bring up their own ideas and to confront these with the scientific ideas, for instance by studying quotations from the press media and from other pupils.

Our research on the effects of the proposed new learning strategies will continue in the coming years. It is expected that some of the results of these studies will have further implications for teacher training, especially as regards the usefulness of some teaching activities which aim to promote conceptual change.

347

REFERENCES

Cosgrove, M., Osborne, R. (1985)
Lesson frameworks for changing children's ideas. In :
*Learning in Science. The implications of children's
science,* Osborne, R., Freyberg, P. (eds). Auckland :
Heinemann, 101-111.

Driver, R., Oldham, V. (1986)
A constructivist approach to curriculum development in
science, *Studies in Science Education,* 13, 105-122.

Driver, R. (1988)
Changing conceptions, *Tijdschrift voor Didactiek der ß-
wetenschappen,* 6, 3, 161-198.

Eijkelhof, H.M.C., Millar, R. (1988)
Reading about Chernobyl : The public understanding of
radiation and radioactivity, *School Science Review,* 70, 251,
35-41.

Eijkelhof, H.M.C. (1990)
Radiation and Risk in Physics Education, Doctoral
Dissertation. Utrecht : CDß-Press.

Hewson, P.W., Hewson, M.G.A.'B. (1988)
An appropriate Conception of Teaching Science : A View
from Studies of Science Learning, *Science Education,* 72,
5, 597-614.

Klaassen, C.W.J.M., Eijkelhof, H.M.C., Lijnse, P.L. (1990)
Considering an alternative approach to teaching
radioactivity. In : P.L. Lijnse et al (eds), *Relating
Macroscopic Phenomena to Microscopic Particles.* Utrecht
: CDß-Press, 304-315.

Licht, P., Eijkelhof, H.M.C., Boschuizen, R., Bouma, J. (1990)
Results of an international inventory of experiences with
pre- and inservice education on pupils' preconceptions. In :
13a. Conferencia de l'ATEE, Aportacions, R. Jordana (ed),
Brussels : ATEE, 317-337.

Lijnse, P.L., Eijkelhof, H.M.C., Klaassen, C.W.J.M.,
Scholte, R.L.J. (1990)
Pupils' and mass-media ideas about radioactivity,
International Journal of Science Education, 12, 1, 67-78.

Millar, R., Klaassen, K., Eijkelhof, H. (1990)
Teaching about radioactivity and ionizing radiation : an
alternative approach, *Physics Education,* in press.

Redeker, B. (1985)
The difference between the lifeworld of children and the
world of physics : a basic problem for teaching and learning
mechanics. In : *The many faces of teaching and learning
mechanics,* P.L. Lijnse (ed). Utrecht : WCC, 77-95.

Voorde, H.H. ten (1977)
Verwoorden en verstaan, Doctoral Dissertation. Den Haag
: SVO.

Weart, S.R. (1988)
Nuclear Fear : A History of Images. Cambridge (Mass.) :
Harvard University Press.

RESEARCH INTO CHILDREN'S UNDERSTANDING ABOUT FOOD: WHAT ARE THE IMPLICATIONS FOR TEACHING?

Sheila Turner

Department of Science Education
University of London Institute of Education

The study described in this paper is part of an ongoing programme of research which is investigating the ideas and understandings which children of five to twelve years have about food, including the way in which they classify food and the reasons for their food choices. The research is closely linked to inservice provision for primary teachers in science education where teachers are involved as active participants in research and curriculum development. An important dimension of the research is its role in the professional development of teachers. One of the aims is to provide contexts in which teachers can review and update their own ideas about food and diet, as well as permitting debate and reflection about teaching strategies and curriculum development in science and health education.

During the past two decades there has been considerable research into children's understanding in science; much of this research has focused on the ideas which children have which are different from those of scientists. The importance of finding out what understandings children already have before teaching topics has gained credence from the findings of research projects such as the Learning in Science Project (Osborne and Freyberg, 1985) and the Children's Learning in Science Project (Brook and Driver, 1984). It appears that the ideas which children bring from their everyday experience to the classroom are strongly held, resistant to change and may impede learning. Cosgrove and Osborne (1985) have suggested that if children's conceptions are to be modified, teaching approaches must permit opportunities for ideas to be challenged.

There has been little research of children's understanding about food and diet. Holland's (1979) investigation into the ways in which children of 8 to 10 years classify food items indicated how important home background was in determining whether the classification system used was context independent or based on practical experience. The work of Newsome (1983) with secondary pupils in London schools, provided further evidence about the types of classification system used by young people. A striking finding of her study was that only a minority of pupils interviewed used the food classification system which they had been taught even when the grouping system used was one designed to help pupils with meal planning, rather than a more "traditional" nutrient grouping system. Work with primary school children in the U.S.A. (Contento and Michela, 1981) and in the Netherlands (Edema, 1985) supports Newsome's finding that classification systems taught in schools are rarely used by pupils when they are allowed to group foods according to choice. The research by Contento and Michela (1981) also indicated that children of 5 to 11 years had little understanding of nutrients. The research findings suggest that the food systems used for teaching are not fully understood by pupils or are perceived not to be relevant — what is taught does not become part of what Barnes (1976) has termed "action knowledge."

Information gained about children's ideas has evident relevance for classroom practice. However, before changes in teaching practice occur teachers need to be convinced of the usefulness of research findings. Attempts to bridge the perceived gap between "research" and classroom practice are not new in educational research. They are the basis of what is termed action research, which Cohen and Manion (1986) described as involving the investigation of particular contexts, with practitioners and researchers working together as a team. The ultimate goal of such research is to improve teaching practice.

Research into children's ideas about food and diet

The action research described in this paper has three major objectives:

1.   To investigate children's knowledge and understanding of food and diet in relation to food choice.

2.   To study ways in which primary school teachers can be helped to use the findings of research as a basis for teaching about food and diet.

3.   To help teachers to develop strategies for assessing and monitoring the progress of their pupils.

The research is relevant to science as a core subject in the National Curriculum in England and Wales and assessment at ages 7 and 11 (DES, 1988 and DES, 1989). Knowledge of children's ideas about food, however, has an importance which extends beyond the demands of the National Curriculum in science. It impinges on many areas of the curriculum and also has importance for cross curricular subjects, most notably health education.

An important dimension of the research is its role in the professional development of teachers. Firstly, it provides contexts in which teachers can review and update their own ideas about food and diet. Secondly, it encourages debate and reflection about teaching strategies and curriculum development. The writing of reports based on investigation of children's ideas is a further vital ingredient of the strategies employed to enable teachers to become more reflective practitioners of the type identified by Schon (1987).

The sixty teachers who have been involved in the research were part-time students in the Science Education Department at the Institute of Education during 1988-90. Most have responsibility for science in their school and are thus in a position to influence curriculum change and development. The Institute research programme had five main elements:

1.   An introductory session which provided background information about the research. Teachers tried out the interview schedules themselves, raised questions and modified materials to suit the needs of their own pupils;

2.   Work in school interviewing three children individually;

3.   A reporting and feedback session at the Institute;

4.   Writing of reports by teachers;

5.   Feedback to teachers including a written report, based on analysis of the results and reports of the whole group, and discussion of the implications for teaching of their findings.

These five elements were linked to other parts of the course, including planning and teaching science based topics, assessment of pupils and sessions on health education.

The interviews with the children were structured and designed to find out:

—   what types of food children choose,

—   why they make the choices they do,

—   how they group foods,

—   what understanding children have of specific nutrients,

—   the reasons children give for eating food.

The interview framework was designed to enable results to be analysed but also to permit more extended discussion. It was particularly important that the children being interviewed did not feel that the activities were a "test."   The activities also had to be appropriate for teachers to use with pupils from five to twelve years of age and be manageable in terms of time.

The interviews centred around three activities, two of which involved using thirty cards with outline pictures of food. The pictures included a range of foods, including fruit and vegetables, cereals, pulses, meat and dairy produce. Initially children were shown the cards, allowed to handle them and encouraged to talk about the foods. The name given to the food by the child was accepted — many children, for example, interpreted the picture of a bread roll as a hamburger.

In the first activity children were asked to place the pictures into groups, and the reasons for the groupings were elicited. They were then asked to select foods for meals plus snacks using the cards as a basis for the selection; the children could choose additional foods or drinks if they wanted. In the final activity cards with the names of nutrients, such as sugar, salt, vitamins, were used to initiate discussion to find out what children knew about individual nutrients. The children were also asked why they thought that they needed to eat food.

Results and discussion

The reports written by teachers based on their interviews, allied to group and individual discussions, provided the main source of information about children's — and teachers' — ideas about food and diet. The reports and discussions also enabled teachers to clarify their ideas and to reflect on practice. The important learning outcomes and issues which teachers identified can be divided into five categories:

1. Children's knowledge and understanding about food and diet.

2. Children's general scientific knowledge and understanding and skills.

3. Teacher knowledge and understanding concerning food and diet.

4. Implications for teaching.

5. The teacher as researcher.

1. Children's knowledge about food

This topic formed the main focus of the teachers' written reports and provided both qualitative and quantitative data about children's understanding. In this paper it is only possible to give a brief outline; more detailed results are discussed elsewhere (Turner, 1990). The majority of the children interviewed (66%) of all ages, used a mixture of food groupings which included some form of food classification allied to a system where associated foods, e.g. bread and cheese, were grouped together.   The foods most commonly classified were fruit and vegetables, followed by sweets.   A third of the children used a meal grouping system, although many foods grouped in pairs, e.g. chicken and rice, could be interpreted as what is eaten together as part of a meal.   Pupils below the age of eight were most likely to use groupings such as like/dislike, colour, shape, taste, texture.   Dairy and healthy/unhealthy groupings were only used by pupils aged eight years or above.   It was rare for children to use food classification systems which they had been taught.

Some teachers expressed disappointment that their pupils' food choices for meals were so sensible and ordinary!   Cereal and/or bread/toast was the breakfast chosen by all but four of the children interviewed.   The majority of the children made choices based on the pictures, or their interpretations of the pictures.   Few children extended the foods chosen to other food items, e.g. pizzas.   In the majority of cases children chose the foods they did because they were the foods normally eaten at home and/or because they were liked or favourite foods.   Children were on occasions very perceptive about their choices, for example R (aged 8 years), in giving reasons for choosing beefburger and chips for supper, explained: "if you fry it, it isn't good for you, but if you like it, you want it."

It was evident that children's understanding of nutrients was frequently more limited than teachers expected.   Most children had heard of sugar, salt, fat, and vitamins and many could give a reasonable working definition of sugar, fat and salt, e.g. salt as small white crystals.   Knowledge of other nutrients was more problematic. The idea of vitamins as tablets/pills was widespread; over 50% of children defined vitamins in this way.   The values attached to nutrients were also significant; vitamins were equated with health or as being good for you, whereas sugar and fat were bad for you.

All of the teachers recognised the importance of establishing and utilising the prior knowledge that children possessed.   Many of them commented on how much some children, including five and six year olds, understood about what they ate and why they ate particular foods. The knowledge that children had was discussed in relation to home background, which appeared to be more significant than knowledge gained in school. Many younger children in explaining why they ate particular foods stated that it was eaten because their parents said it was good for them. Children with specific dietary requirements, such as diabetics, were particularly well informed about the relationship between diet and health. Most children appreciated the need for variety in their diet and this was reflected in their meal choices. In their reports, the teachers related the children's ideas both to their own experience and the work of others, in particular that reported by Osborne and Freyberg (1985). The discussions on occasions included examination of ideas relating to the properties of foods, such as taste, as well as those linked to specific nutrients, for example, M. (six years) reveals that her concept of "sweet" is not that of her teacher:

> "During a tasting experiment M. may have described a certain food as being sweet. Because she would be using an acceptable term I would have assumed that she meant something tasted sugary. However, as a result of the interviews I know that she may not mean that at all."

> The idea of "sweet" things including crisps or chips was common to all age groups and is possibly linked to the concept of "nice tasting."

2. Skills and understanding

All the teachers included discussion of skills and understanding which were applicable to the whole of science and health education. The ability to classify and identify similarities and differences was commented on by most teachers. Sorting objects into sets is a common activity in primary education. The majority of teachers, including those working with 5-6 year olds, indicated that when they began the first activity they felt confident that pupils would have no difficulty in placing the pictures of foods into groups as a result of previous experience of grouping objects. In many instances this activity revealed that even some eleven year olds found this grouping activity difficult, not because of the nature of the task, but because of their inability to transfer the skills they had gained elsewhere to this new situation. Younger pupils were more likely to find the task difficult. One teacher wrote about a six year old: "Her sorting experience (i.e. prior experience) must be limited to sorting into groups which are the same rather than into groups whose elements are different but have a common link." A way of overcoming this difficulty was also suggested: " We could make a collection of all the items they have grouped as vegetable or fruit and compare the items in each group. How are they different or similar?"

Some teachers recognised that when they studied pupils' food groupings in more detail what appeared to be random groupings could be interpreted as a common sense view of foods which could be eaten together. The difficulties of grouping and the importance of giving children opportunities to look for similarities, as well as differences, were highlighted by many teachers: "The children (8-9 years) seemed to realise that some foods could fit into several groups and the group they finally selected was not always the most useful...." Children "found it difficult to decide exactly which were the important similarities...."

3. Teacher knowledge

Many of the teachers indicated that they themselves had learned more about food and diet as a result of interviewing children. Discussions at the institute, both prior to and after the interviews, led to individuals raising questions that they wanted answered about food and health. The questions were used as starting points for further study during the course. Comments such as the following were common:

> "In doing the tests I realised how much I didn't know about food!" "I realised how limited my knowledge of food was, together with what we need and why."

The very nature of the activity had caused teachers to review their own ideas and understanding. Some indicated that they now had greater awareness of what was meant by "healthy eating." Some teachers expressed surprise at the level of children's awareness of health and diet in relation to their own:

> "I also discovered that my own choices of food for meals would not, subject to similar analysis, produce very different comments from the children's."

This remark is significant and poignant.   It reflects our common experience and can be linked to the constraints, including the social, economic and cultural factors, which influence our choice of food in the same way as the children we teach.

4. Implications for teaching

Teachers recognised that the results had implications for all their teaching, not just food based topics.   Many of them reported that they had found the activity of finding out what children understood particularly helpful and would use the strategy as a starting point in the future.   One teacher wrote: "One-to-one discussion with children about their ideas, or carefully observing a child performing an investigation is particularly valuable as it has implications for more meaningful learning."   Another concluded: "The object of this study was to discover some of the ideas children might hold concerning food and diet.   The implications of the resultant observations were more far reaching.   ...How much more effective and enjoyable teaching is when children are encouraged to express their ideas ... and to feel accepted for their own opinions".

Issues identified by teachers as important for teaching included:

(a)   The importance of really **listening** to what pupils say, "even if they were not what you were expecting."

(b)   The range of development even within the small sample of children interviewed from each class — which was often greater than anticipated.   A very significant outcome for many was that children did not always perform according to expectation.

(c)   Observing one child is a means of developing the skills needed for observing larger groups in a class. Such skills are particularly important in the context of assessment.

(d)   The need for continuity and progression is widely recognised. However, there are concerns that neither is being achieved. If progression is to be achieved it is important to build on the knowledge that children already have in a planned way.

(e)   The importance of discussion in learning, both discussion between pupils and between teacher and pupil.

(f)   The choice of activities, of a type identified by one person as meaningful activities. It is important to "concentrate on ideas that they can experience, for example, grouping of foods."

(g)   The need to work flexibly to accommodate children's interests and to develop their thinking.

Some teachers also reported on how they had extended the task or planned to utilise the findings from the interviews in subsequent work with their pupils.

5. The teacher as researcher

Many teachers commented on the difficulty they experienced in acting as a researcher, a role with which they were unfamiliar. Some saw themselves as "testers" rather than researchers. Many wanted to extend the activity so that it became a teaching situation. They found it difficult to stand back and not to make comments or to provide "answers." "I felt unsure as to what extent to intervene and I feel that I did not always ask enough questions."

The use of a tape recorder during the interviews was particularly useful in helping teachers to listen and to analyse the interaction with the child more critically:

"I have realised that if the responses given by the children were acceptable to my own ideas and understanding, then I did not question further."

A significant outcome of the research was the increased sensitivity of teachers to the value of children's ideas and their ability to discern and analyse those ideas when teaching larger groups of children. It was evident that background reading, in particular ideas from the Learning in Science Project (Osborne and Freyberg, 1985), was particularly helpful in enabling teachers to appreciate the strength of children's ideas and the resistance of these to change through teaching.

Summary and outcomes

The research by teachers into children's ideas has had measurable effects on their teaching and attitudes. They have extended their own knowledge, in an area of science and health education where few have expertise and many lack confidence. The insights gained from the interviews caused them to consider teaching strategies and learning outcomes in a more analytical way and to plan more appropriate learning activities. In the term following the interviews they experimented with new teaching strategies, including challenging children's ideas and, as a result of their increased confidence, allowed children to take greater responsibility for their own learning.

The strategy of interviewing individual pupils has proved an effective method of helping teachers to appreciate the range of understandings held by pupils in a class. The teachers considered that the activities in which they had engaged had enabled them:

(a)   to evaluate the learning experiences they provided for children;

(b)   to diagnose strengths and weaknesses of individual pupils;

(c)   to modify teaching to match pupils' learning.

All of the points noted above are prerequisites for successful diagnostic assessment and for developing programmes of work best suited to the needs of individual pupils.

Teachers have gained insights into the nature of educational research and have begun to identify research findings which might have implications for their own teaching. It is also evident that they have a greater understanding of the role of the reflective practitioner (Schon, 1987). I would argue that becoming more reflective practitioners is an important element in the continuing professional development of teachers.

The short term outcomes suggest that the objectives outlined in the introduction to this paper are being achieved. Further monitoring will be required to gauge the long term effect on practice, including the extent to which the curriculum initiatives developed during the study become a part of normal teaching strategies.

Acknowledgments

I should like to express my thanks to all those teachers and pupils who have participated in this study.

REFERENCES

Barnes, D. (1976). *From Communication to Curriculum*. Penguin Books : England.

Brook, A. and Driver, R. (1984). *Aspects of Secondary Students Understanding of Energy : Full Report*. Children's Learning in Science Project, Centre for Studies in Science and Mathematics Education, University of Leeds.

Cohen, L. and Manion, L. (1986). *Research Methods in Education*. Croom Helm : London.

Contento, I.R. and Michela, J.L. (1981). "Spontaneous Classification of Foods by Children at Varying Cognitive Development Levels." Paper presented at the Annual Meeting of the Society for Nutrition Education, San Diego, August, 1981.

Cosgrove, M. and Osborne, R. (1985). "Lesson frameworks for changing children's ideas" in Osborne, R. and Freyberg P. (eds). *Learning in Science — the implications of children's science*. Heinemann, Auckland, London.

D.E.S. (1988). *Report by the Task Group on Assessment and Testing*. H.M.S.O. : London.

D.E.S. (1989). *Science in the National Curriculum*. H.M.S.O. : London.

Edema, J. (1985). "A sociological approach to nutrition education in elementary schools in the Netherlands" in Turner, S. and Ingle, R.B. (eds). *New Developments in Nutrition Education*. Nutrition education Series No.11. Unesco : Paris.

Holland, J. (1979). "Social class and changes in orientations in meanings" Sociological Research Unit. Unpublished paper of the Institute of Education, University of London.

Newsome, S. (1983). "The Design of Nutrition Education Programmes for multi-ethnic classrooms with special reference to the food beliefs and behaviour of adolescents." M.Phil Dissertation, Institute of Education, University of London.

Osborne, R. and Freyberg, P. (eds) (1985). *Learning in Science — the implications of children's science.* Heinemann : Auckland, London.

Schon, D.A. (1987). *Educating the Reflective Practitioner.* Jossey-Bass : San Francisco.

Turner, S.A. (1990). "'We eat it sir, so it must be a food' — an investigation of children's understanding about food" (in preparation).

OVERCOMING MISCONCEPTIONS RELATED TO THE CONCEPTS UNDERLYING THE SCIENCE PROCESSES

Pinchas Tamir

Hebrew University, Jerusalem

Although hundreds of studies have been performed to evaluate the outcomes of the inquiry oriented curricula, we do not have sufficient information about the ways by which specific instructional approaches have been actually employed. For example, how many teachers have actually used invitations to inquiry? How have teachers integrated laboratory work with concepts learning? How well has student assessment been matched to the inquiry approach? How effective is the inquiry approach in dealing with students' preconceptions and misconceptions?

There is no doubt that the laboratory should play an important role in science teaching. Most educators would agree with White (1988, p.186) that "it gives science teaching a special character, providing for many teachers and their students liveliness and fun that are hard to obtain in other ways. That character is almost sufficient alone to justify the high capital and recurrent costs of laboratories."

However, the literature is full of disappointments regarding current practice in most school laboratories. For many students the laboratory experiences may be characterised as "hands on, minds off" (e.g. Moreira, 1980; Tasker, 1981; Friedler & Tamir, 1984; Novak & Gowin, 1984). There is some evidence that even for exemplary teachers the lack of sufficient content knowledge to explain observed phenomena may result in "a sowing of seeds for the development or reinforcement of misconceptions" (Tobin & Fraser, 1990, p.19).

How can meaningful active inquiry be attained? How can we facilitate "hands on minds on" learning experiences? The key to the answer to this question (as to many other questions related to meaningful learning) is the teacher. Hence, the purpose of the article is twofold:

1.   To describe selected instructional approaches that seem to have the potential for achieving the goal of providing students with meaningful inquiry experiences, especially in the laboratory.

2.   To offer practical suggestions regarding the incorporation of these approaches into preservice and inservice teacher education. The following approaches will be described: explicit teaching of inquiry skills; Vee diagrams; White's procedure; the learning cycle; the use of inquiry process tests; analysis of students' answers to questions involving the application of inquiry skills.

THE INSTRUCTIONAL APPROACHES

Explicit teaching of inquiry skills

An inquiry-oriented laboratory lesson is very demanding. Students working in such a lesson are assumed to have acquired:

(a)   functional knowledge of relevant content;

(b)   proficiency in laboratory techniques (e.g. use of the microscope, pipetting);

(c)   inquiry skills (e.g. observing, formulating hypotheses, making inferences, reporting of results).

Moreover, they should be able to apply each and all of these to the problem under investigation. One way to deal with the apparent overload imposed on the students under these circumstances is to make sure that they have basic command of each component before having to apply all of them simultaneously to solve a particular novel problem. To this end two instructional sequences have been developed: a series of invitations to inquiry (Schwab, 1963) and a module entitled "Basic concepts of scientific research" (Friedler & Tamir, 1986).

The common rationale for these two sequences is that inquiry skills are not acquired "in passing" as a by-product of learning a body of knowledge in the regular syllabus (APU, 1984). Lack of knowledge and possession of misconceptions regarding the concepts which underlie process and inquiry skills are quite common, and specially focused instruction is necessary in order to develop the knowledge and understanding which are pre-requisite for meaningful application of these inquiry skills. Two instructional sequences developed for this purpose as described below:

(a) Invitations to inquiry
The invitations to inquiry are potentially very powerful instructional tools. They have been in existence for more than 30 years. Some of them have been supported by short films or by slides. For reasons unknown to the author, their actual use in classrooms have been limited. Detailed description of the particular invitations and how to teach them may be found in Schwab (1963, pp.45-106).

(b) Basic concepts of scientific research (The Module)
Four major stages can be identified in any investigation: planning, performance, data processing, applications and implications (Tamir and Lunetta, 1978). Since serious difficulties were found with regard to inquiry skills at the planning stage, a module was developed to teach these skills and the concepts which underlie them. This module was found to be suitable for helping students in designing experiments in contexts other than the laboratory as well. It was found to be especially effective with 11th grade students (Friedler & Tamir, 1986; Tamir, 1990).

The module consists of a student text and a teachers' guide. The student text includes six chapters. The first chapter presents a brief historical-philosophical account of the nature and development of scientific knowledge, in order to provide a general framework and explain the emergence of the concepts "problem," "hypothesis," "deduction," and "experiment." The next four chapters deal with the four concepts just mentioned. The last chapter requires the student to integrate what has been learned in previous chapters by actually analysing and designing complete investigations.

Each chapter opens with a theoretical account followed by mental and practical exercises (see Appendix for examples). Special attention was given to ensuring that the content of the exercises was familiar enough so that it does not constitute a barrier to the students, thus allowing them to concentrate on the processes and their underlying concepts, namely, problem, hypothesis, deduction, and experiment. Related concepts such as assumption, control, and replication are highlighted as well.

The exercises are organised sequentially in two ways:

1.   In each exercise the student starts with simple questions related to everyday experiences, moves on to more difficult questions which require analysis, and culminates with actually solving scientific problems utilising synthesis and evaluation.

2.   Most exercises are "dry," that is, the student is asked to think and write with no manipulation of equipment or organisms. Manipulation is incorporated into the final exercises. There are two reasons for this:

   (a)   the module is designed for advanced students (grades 11 and 12 — ages 17-18), who have had practical laboratory experience in their previous courses and do not need additional concrete props. Hence they can proceed more quickly without investing time in actual performance;

   (b)   it has been found that often the requirements imposed by the actual performance create a heavy "overload" on the functional memory. Reducing this overload during the early stages may facilitate learning (Johnstone and Wham, 1982). Of course, the actual performance which contributes to the unique nature of the practical mode (Tamir, 1975) is not left out. In the concluding assignments the students are required to synthesise, integrate, and apply what they have learned in solving novel problems by actually carrying out investigations in the laboratory. Some examples of exercises appear in Appendix 1.

The module not only explains and develops inquiry skills but also attempts to provide a realistic view of the nature of scientific research. It is emphasised that scientific research does not aim at discovering the absolute truth, that scientific knowledge is tentative, and that different scientists employ different methods. The fact that scientists often use the same skills and follow similar procedures to test their ideas does not imply the existence of one unified and rigid "scientific method."

The teachers' guide explains the aims and the rationale, but does not contain suggestions on "how to teach" since it has been anticipated that different teachers will use the module in different contexts and no one set of specific suggestions will necessarily be adequate. However, the teachers' guide does provide general guidelines and possible answers to the questions which appear in the student text. The module can be used in various ways. For instance, the teacher may assign the theoretical account as homework reading, then discuss the issues in class and, following the discussion, assign exercises to be done in small groups in class. Teachers may use the whole module or, alternatively, only parts of it, as they see fit. Finally, the module may be useful to students in revision and preparation for practical inquiry-oriented examinations, as well as for paper and pencil tests which require inquiry skills, such as the unseen research in the biology matriculation examination in Israel.

Vee diagrams

Vee diagrams were originally developed "to help students and instructors clarify the nature and purpose of laboratory work in science" (Novak & Gowin, 1984, p.55). Their use has been extended to other areas, including analysis of research reports. The Vee diagram has a V shape. At the lower apex of the V the *event* under consideration (e.g. phenomenon, experiment) is recorded and inside the V the *focus question* is written. The right side of the V is allocated to methodology (records of observations and measurements, transformation into tables or graphs and conclusions), whereas the left side is allocated to *concepts, principles* and *theories.* The Vee can be used for content analysis of laboratory manuals, for analysis of results of an investigation as well as for planning investigations. It is expected to help students match theory and inquiry skills and, thereby, enhance the meaningfulness of hands-on activities. For more details see Novak & Gowin, 1984 (pp.55-75; 114-118).

White's procedure

White (1988, pp.189-191) puts forward three suggestions which should enhance the meaningfulness of the school laboratory:

(a)   Have students create their own explanation of the purpose of the experiment.

(b)   At the end of the experiment students should list all propositional knowledge they used, or thought of, in the experiment.

(c)   Use more common materials and real every day life problems.

The learning cycle

"The learning cycle is a method of instruction that consists of three phases called exploration, term introduction and concept applications. Use of the learning cycle provides the opportunity for students to reveal alternative beliefs and to argue and test them thus.... develop more adequate conceptions and thinking patterns" (Lawson et al 1989, p.89). The examples provided by Lawson et al (1989) demonstrate the teaching of concepts underlying inquiry skills such as controlled experiment (p.93) inference (p.97), hypothesis (p.99) and prediction (p.101).

Inquiry process tests

Inquiry process tests are defined as tasks which require students to apply their inquiry skills in solving novel problems. Two kinds of such tests have been routinely used in the last 20 years as parts of the biology matriculation examination offered to Israeli students upon completion of their high school studies. These are, an inquiry laboratory test which requires the student to design and actually carry out an investigation in a period of $2^1/2$ hours (Tamir,1974), and an analysis of unseen research report which is included as one of four sections in the paper and pencil test (Tamir,1985). In both tests students are required to apply high level cognitive reasoning and demonstrate in-depth understanding of the procedures of scientific research.

Analysis of students' answers to inquiry process tests

Typical answers given by high school students to inquiry process tests have been collected and used to design diagnostic exercises. Students can either complete them individually as homework, or, even better, solve and discuss the various items in small groups. In both alternatives, following the first step, the items are discussed by the whole class under the teacher's supervision (for more details see Tamir & Nussinovitz, 1980 and Appendix 1, Task 1.2).

TEACHER EDUCATION

The best way to incorporate the instructional approaches described above in teacher education is to actually involve prospective or practicing teachers in the various activities, first as students and later on as teachers. While this suggestion may apply to all the approaches, certain comments based on the author's personal experience regarding each approach may be in order.

Invitations to inquiry

The author devotes a whole semester in the biology method course to invitations to inquiry. Use is made of the loop films and slide sequences produced by the BSCS in the U.S. (40 films and 20 slide sequences have been produced).

In the first session the author teaches the student teachers (the number of student teachers is between 25 and 30). In the second session the author teaches another invitation to inquiry to high school students who come to the video studio at the university. Both lessons are videotaped and analysed right after the lesson (each session lasts 3 periods). During these two weeks the prospective teachers organise themselves in groups of three. Each group selects a topic and prepares a lesson based on the teacher's guide which accompanies each invitation to inquiry. Every week a different team teaches a different class of high school students. While the planning of the lesson is carried out by the team, the actual teaching is divided so that the first individual begins, the second continues and the third ends the lesson. Each lesson is videotaped and analysed by the whole group. The videotapes are also available for further viewing by the prospective teachers. Following this extensive experience the student teachers become quite familiar with inquiry skills as well as with difficulties that high school students have, and in particular, with preconceptions and misconceptions that high school students possess regarding inquiry skills and their underlying concepts (see also Tamir, 1990).

The module "Basic concepts of scientific research"

At the Hebrew University we offer a special workshop which meets 10 times for 3 hours and deals with teaching in the laboratory. The module serves as a text in this workshop so that the prospective teachers actually study and become familiar with it. No further use is made of the module during the teacher education period, but it is hoped that when the prospective teachers begin to practice, they will make adequate use of the module. In the trials it was found that with the aid of the teacher guide practicing teachers were able to teach the module successfully with no further help.

Vee diagrams, White's procedures, the learning cycle

The relevant references cited in relation to each of these approaches claim that they are very effective. White's procedures are simple and straightforward. The use of Vee diagrams and the learning cycle will probably benefit from direct experiences involving the prospective and inservice teachers. Both Novak & Gowin (1984) and Lawson et al (1989) offer useful suggestions for teachers which apply to teacher educators as well.

Inquiry process tests

Prospective teachers are expected to study student assessment but often this study includes only the traditional multiple choice and essay tests with little or no attention given to alternative tests. The author has been using the biology matriculation examination as a vehicle to discuss inquiry process tests with prospective teachers. At least one assignment during the biology method course involves innovative testing. For example, the prospective teachers may be asked to score papers of students' answers to practical laboratory tests. The scoring key is based on the Practical Tests Assessment Inventory (Tamir et al 1982) which is purposefully designed to reveal misconceptions such as confusing hypothesis, problem and assumption (See Appendix 2).

Exercises based on students' answers

One session of the biology method course is devoted to modeling the use of these exercises. The student teachers work in small groups and following that, the decisions of the groups are discussed by the whole group.

Summing up

The major premise of this article is that meaningful active inquiry is based on thorough understanding of the concepts underlying inquiry skills, and that students should be provided with opportunities in which explicit instruction of these concepts takes place. In order to educate science teachers who are capable of employing the suggested instructional approaches, teacher educators should try some of the ideas presented in this article. Further research is needed to find out the effectiveness of these ideas and suggestions.

REFERENCES

APU (1984). *Science in school at age 15, Report No.2.* London, Department of Education and Science.

Friedler, Y. & Tamir, P. (1984). Teaching and learning in highschool laboratory classes in Israel. *Research in Science Education,* 15, 89-96.

Friedler, Y. & Tamir, P. (1986). Teaching basic concepts of scientific research to highschool students. *Journal of Biological Education,* 20, 263-270.

Lawson, A.E., Abraham, M.R. & Renner, J.W. (1989). A theory of instruction, NARST Monograph Number One.

Moriera, M.A. (1980). A non traditional approach to the evaluation of the laboratory instruction in general physics courses. *European Journal of Science Education,* 2, 441-448.

Novak, J.D. & Gowin, D.B. (1984). *Learning how to learn.* Cambridge, Cambridge University press.

Schwab, J.J. (1963). *Biology teachers' handbook.* New York, Wiley.

Tamir, P. (1974). An inquiry oriented laboratory examination. *Journal of Educational Measurement,* 11, 25-33.

Tamir, P. (1985). The Israeli "Bagrut" in biology revisited. *Journal of Research in Science Teaching,* 22, 31-40.

Tamir, P. (1990). Teaching for meaningful active inquiry. *International Journal of Science Education,* to be published.

Tamir, P. & Lunetta, V.N. (1978). An analysis of laboratory activities in the BSCS Yellow Version. *The American Biology Teacher,* 40, 353-357.

Tamir, P. & Nussinovitz, R. (1980). *Analysis of students' answers in inquiry practical laboratory tests.* Jerusalem, Israel Science Teaching Centre (in Hebrew).

Tamir, P. & Nussinovitz, R. & Friedler, Y. (1982). The design and use of a Practical Tests Assessment Inventory. *Journal of Biological Education,* 16, 42-50.

Tasker, R. (1981). Children's views and classroom experiences. *Australian Science Teachers Journal,* 27 (3), 33-37.

Tobin, K. & Fraser, B.J. (1990). What does it mean to be an exemplary science teacher? *Journal of Research in Science Teaching,* 27, 3-26.

White, R.T. (1988). *Learning science.* Oxford, Basel Blackwell.

APPENDIX 1

A Sample of Students' tasks

Identifying and formulating problems

Task 1.1.

In the Olympic Games in Moscow the coach of the British swimming team demanded that the water temperature in the pool be kept constant at $24^{O}C$, since any temperature change greater than $2^{O}C$ may affect the swimmer's performance it was decided to carry out an experiment to test the coach's claim.   Which of the following problems should be studied?

(a)   Does the water temperature affect the swimming speed?

(b)   Can the water temperature be kept constant?

(c)   In what temperature will the swimming be fastest?

Task 1.2

A student is presented with an apparatus which has been designed to measure the rate of exhaling carbon dioxide.   After becoming familiar with the way the apparatus works, the student is asked: "Formulate a problem related to human respiration which can be studied by the use of this apparatus."   Following are the answers given by different students to the above question.   Read each answer and indicate:

1.   Is the problem defined and formulated properly? — Explain.

2.   Is there a reasonable relationship between the suggested problem and the variable which can be measured by the given apparatus? — Explain.

        (a)   How much CO_2 will a person exhale following an intense physical activity?

(b)   What kind of gas is exhaled from human lungs?

(c)   A person engaged in intense physical activity exhales and inhales much faster than under normal activity. The amount of CO_2 exhaled will increase with increased activity up to a certain limit.

(d)   We know that the concentration of CO_2 in the blood determines the rate of human respiration. The more CO_2 exhaled the more oxygen is needed urgently. For example, after running, the CO_2 level in the blood rifes and we need more oxygen. In the apparatus, the more NaOH is added in order to change the colour of the indicator the more CO_2 is being exhaled.

Formulating hypotheses

Task 2.2

A researcher wanted to study the problem: "is there any relationship between the light intensity and the rate of growth in plants?" Formulate at least two hypotheses which may direct this study.

Task 2.3

Beri-Beri is a disease characterised by fatigue, muscle weakness, lack of movement coordination, heart malfunction and, eventually, death. The disease is common among people who eat white rice as their main diet. A Japanese physician found that people who ate rice with the skin were less inclined to suffer from the disease. People who ate, in addition to rice, meat, fish, and uncooked vegetables did not suffer at all. Formulate at least two hypotheses which may be offered by the Japanese doctor as possible explanations for the cause of the Beri-Beri.

Testing hypotheses by designing experiments

Task 5.3

The student is presented with two test-tubes each containing pea seeds and indicator solution. In one test-tube the seeds are dry and in the other they are germinating. These instructions follow: This apparatus can be used to study the problem: "What is the relationship between the state of the pea seeds and their rate of respiration?"

1. Formulate a hypothesis which relates to the problem just stated and which can be tested by the apparatus before you.

2. Design an experiment to test your hypothesis. In your design indicate:

    (a) the dependent and independent variables;
    (b) the constant variables;
    (c) the control;
    (d) the treatments;
    (e) how will you measure the dependent variable
    (f) any other relevant comments.

APPENDIX 2

The scales used for scoring formulating problems and hypotheses are presented below:

Formulating problems

Formulating hypotheses

Relevant problem presented in the form of a question	6
Relevant problem not presented as a question	5
Relevant problem followed by a hypothesis	4
Hypothesis instead of a problem	3
Non relevant, unfocused question	2
No problem presented	1
No answer	0

Adequate, presented as "if... then..."	7a
Adequate, stated well but not as "if... then..."	7b
Adequate but too cumbersome, inaccurate	6
Adequate but includes substantive error	5
Inadequate/irrelevant hypothesis	4
Problem instead of hypothesis	3
Assumption instead of hypothesis	2
No hypothesis is presented	1
No answer	0

PREPARATION OF SCIENCE AND MATHEMATICS TEACHERS FOR THE TWENTY-FIRST CENTURY[1]

Sarah B. Berenson
North Carolina State University, Raleigh, North Carolina

Ann C. Howe,
University of Maryland, College Park, Maryland

Introduction

The National Council of Teachers of Mathematics has proposed new *Standards* that provide mathematics educators with visions to revitalise and restructure school mathematics. In relation to mathematics teacher preparation, the working draft of the *Professional Standards for Teaching Mathematics* (1989) contains the following statement that could be generalised to any discipline, including science education.

> ....if teachers are to change the way they teach they need to learn significant mathematics (science) in situations in which good teaching is modeled. The Collegiate community is beginning to examine aspects of the college undergraduate curriculum and, perhaps even more important, the models of instruction used in collegiate classrooms. Technology and its use in doing, teaching, and learning mathematics (science) is the responsibility of the mathematics (scientific) community as well as the mathematics (science) education community. Teachers need to learn in technology-rich environments if they are to teach using technology (National Council of Teachers of Mathematics, 1989, p.151).

These ideas are the underpinning of a National Science Foundation (NSF) grant, *Preparation of Mathematics and Science Teachers for the Twenty-First Century* at North Carolina State University (Berenson, Howe, & Stiff, 1988). The project teams scientists and science educators, and mathematicians and mathematics educators to work collaboratively to change 13 undergraduate courses in the science and mathematics education curriculum. Physics, chemistry, mathematics, statistics, science methods, and mathematics methods courses are being taught using technology and active learning strategies. The project proposed to address the misconception among undergraduates and faculty that *Telling is teaching* and *listening is learning*. The assumption of this project was that if our undergraduates who are preparing to become science and mathematics teachers of grades 6-12 are immersed in a learning environment that required them to use technology and active learning, then they will use technology and active learning strategies when they become teachers.

Models of Change

The NSF project faculty are involved in making changes to the courses they teach. Educational change has often been attempted using a *top-down* or *outside-in* model of change. That is, an outside person (administrator or consultant) instructs the inside people (faculty) how to change. Goodlad (1975) and Berman and McLaughlin (1978) advocated that the teacher is the true educational change agent. The research of Sirotnik and Clark (1988), and Lightfoot (1983) identified the power of decisions that a teacher holds once the classroom door is closed. These findings suggest that an *inside-out* model of change may be most effective. Therefore, our belief was that the faculty have valuable perceptions and knowledge as to how to implement instructional changes in their courses. We consider the faculty to be the change agents for this NSF project, and the outside people — view their roles in the collaborative process as that of providing resources and moral support for the faculty throughout the change process. Kilb and Berenson (1990) stated several principles for successful change from their work with high school teachers, and these principles have been transferred to this project. They are: (1) faculty can become change, (2) an inside-out model of change is most appropriate for lasting change, (3) outside people must believe in the inside people and should not force their ideas on the group, (4) change takes place over five to ten years, (5) groups of five to seven professionals work best for change projects, (6) change agents need assistance and support to become innovators, (7) activities during the change process need to be carefully structured so that the inside people experience success, and (8) successful experiences with students and colleagues provide the best reinforcement for faculty.

Change at the University

The change model shown in Figure 1 has three phases: (1) knowledge-building, (2) vision-making, and (3) risk-taking. Faculty are **building their knowledge base** concerning appropriate computer and calculating tools that can be used in their science or mathematics courses, and they have learned to use these new tools. They are also **building their knowledge** about instructional alternatives to the lecture method of teaching. Faculty are **making their visions** by identifying how these technological tools can be used in their classes for demonstrations, laboratories, assignments, and assessments. These visions are extended by the faculty's involvement in the development of curriculum materials for their pilot classes. The faculty has also **taken risks** with their students by implementing changes to their Fall 1989 classes. This cyclical change process will continue over the next four years as faculty learn more about technological tools for instruction and active learning strategies. By being involved in the evaluation of these course changes, they will begin focusing on what and how their students learn science and mathematics. Their curriculum materials will be revised and extended over time.

FIGURE 1 — Model of change : An inside-out approach for improving the science and mathematics education undergraduate curriculum

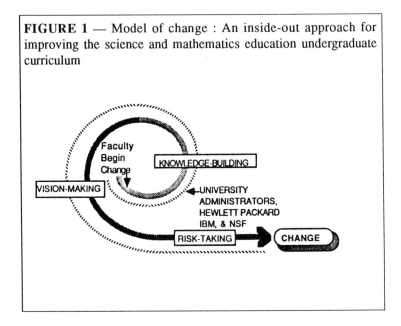

EVALUATION OF YEAR ONE PLOT

Base-Line Data

Before this NSF project began in 1989, it was necessary to examine the faculty's practices and attitudes toward using technological tools for undergraduate science and mathematics instruction. Any differences between NSF project faculty and their colleagues' practices and attitudes toward technological tools also needed to be examined. The project faculty and a random sample of non-project faculty were sent a survey to provide information about their teaching methods, instructional uses of computers and calculators, and attitudes toward using computers. The response rate to the survey was 85%.

The analysis of the data indicated, with only one exception, that the project faculty were not different from their colleagues in the instructional uses of technology and active learning strategies. Both groups of faculty used lecture more than any other teaching method, and seldom used questioning or discussion with their undergraduates.

Inquiry and guided practice were used most infrequently, but there were significant differences for this strategy between the project and non-project faculty. Both groups seldom used computers for instruction nor did they use or give assignments that required their students to use computer tools such as spread sheets, symbolic manipulators, or plotters. Conversely, the combined faculty's attitudes about using computers for instruction were positive. Approximately one-quarter of the combined faculty frequently permitted students to use scientific calculators for tests and assignments, but only three professors required their students to use graphic or symbolic calculators.

Year One Faculty Surveys

A modified survey was distributed to both groups of faculty who provided the base-line data in Spring 1990. The NSF project faculty (n=19) was sent the survey and a cover letter. The random sample of non-project faculty (n=72) used in the base-line data collection and who were still at the university, were also sent the survey and a cover letter. Return envelopes were numbered to identify faculty, but names were checked off and envelopes were thrown away when the surveys were returned. Follow-up calls were made as needed after three weeks to remind faculty to return the survey. The response rate to the survey was 81%.

Means, standard deviations, and t-values were calculated for the project and non-project faculty groups of the Year 1, Part 1 (instructional Methods) of the survey using *Statistical Package for Social Science* (SPSS-X). The base-line data and Year 1 data of the NSF project faculty were examined for among-group differences. Rank sums, corrected for ties, were calculated for each item on Parts 2-5 of the survey and then chi-square statistics were obtained to determine if the two faculty groups differed in their use of instructional technologies. Similar analysis was also used to determine differences among the NSF project faculty's and non-project faculty's base-line data and Year 1 data. Data collected on Part 6 (faculties' attitudes concerning computers and calculators) of the survey were analysed using rank sums of the two faculty groups for each of the 15 items, and chi-square statistics were used to determine between-group differences for Year 1. Means of both groups were compared for total attitude (Year 1) using the t-test statistic. Also, this analysis was used to determine among-group differences of total attitude before and after one year of the project.

Instructional methods

The t-test analysis of Part 1 (Year 1) indicated that the NSF project faculty used less lecture and more discussion, inquiry, and cooperative learning strategies than the non-project faculty. Table 1 presents the means of the percent of class time devoted to each method, the standard deviations, and t-values for each of the five instructional strategies. When the base-line data and year 1 data were compared for the project faculty, changes were noted in the use of lecture and inquiry strategies, but they were not statistically significant. Before the project began, the NSF project faculty average use of lecture was 56% and, after one year, had decreased to 44%. Consequently, there was an increase in the use of inquiry strategies from a mean of 13% to a mean of 19%.

TABLE 1 — Means, standard deviations, and t-values of five teaching strategies used by project and non-project faculty after one year of the NSF project

Teaching Strategies Faculty Group	Number	Mean (% of class time)	Standard deviation	t Value
Lecture				
NSF Project	17	44.4	21.7	-3.27*
Non-Project	56	65.1	26.3	
Discussion				
NSF Project	17	15.9	9.4	1.83*
Non-Project	56	10.9	10.9	
Question/Answer				
NSF Project	17	16.1	9.6	1.03
Non-Project	56	13.2	11.2	
Inquiry & Guided Practice				
NSF Project	17	19.2	24.1	1.86*
Non-Project	56	7.7	14.1	
Cooperative Learning				
NSF Project	17	5.6	5.8	1.75*
Non-Project	56	2.7	6.3	

*p<.05

Instructional Uses of Technology

Table 2 presents the mean ranks and chi-square statistics for each item of Parts 2-5 of the survey for both faculty groups. Before the project began most NSF project faculty and the non-project faculty did not use technology tools for instruction, nor did they respond differently from one another on Parts 2-5 of the survey.

After one year, differences between the two faculty groups were evident on several items. The NSF project faculty used computers or calculators and microcomputer-based labs for class demonstrations more than their colleagues. Also, they used simulations for demonstrations more frequently and required their students to engage in drill and practice for assignments more than the non-project faculty. Significantly higher use of symbolic calculators by the project faculty was noted after the first year of the project. The comparison of the base-line data and Year 1 data found no significant differences among either group of faculty, nor were they expected after only one year of this three year project.

Faculty Attitudes

No differences were found in the analysis of the base-line data between the NSF project faculty and the non-project faculty before the project began. After one year of the project, the NSF project faculty had significantly better attitudes concerning the instructional uses of computers and calculators than their colleagues. The mean attitude score of the project faculty was 61.14 (sd=8.44), and the non-project faculty mean was 50.06 (sd-9.08). The t-value of these two means was 4.25 (p<.05). The statistics of individual attitude items, presented in Table 3, indicated that the NSF project faculty had more positive attitudes on nine of the 15 items after one year.

Since the base-line survey did not contain the last five calculator items, only the means of the first ten items were compared to determine among-group differences. The NSF project faculty's mean before the project began was 37.05 (sd=6.54) and after one year was 40.93 (sd=6.34). A t-test (t-value = -1.81) indicated that their perceptions about computers were significantly different after participating in the project for one year. However, the non-project faculty's perceptions did not change after one year (x_1=34.72;x_2=33.84).

TABLE 2 — Mean ranks and chi-squares of NSF project faculty and non-project faculty instructional use of technology after one year of the NSF project.

Instructional Use	Mean Rank		
	NSF Project Faculty	Non-Project Faculty	Chi-Square*
Part 2. Extent of Technology Use			
1. Use computers/calculators to demonstrate	47.00	33.96	5.28**
2. Student assignments require comps/calcs	33.47	38.07	.65
3. Require computers for class tests	38.26	36.62	.35
4. Require calculators for class tests	36.18	37.25	.04
5. Use a computer teaching lab.	44.11	35.38	2.82
6. Would use comp. tchg. lab. if available	36.32	37.21	.03
7. Use MBL for demonstrations‡	48.11	34.09	6.03**
Part 3. Software Used for Demonstration			
1. Word Processor	37.47	36.86	.02
2. Spread Sheet	37.56	36.83	.03
3. Data Base	37.59	36.82	.04
4. Symbolic Manipulator	40.29	36.00	2.05
5. Plotter	37.82	36.75	.09
6. Graphics Generator	37.06	36.98	.00
7. Simulations	44.21	34.81	3.90**
8. Laser Discs‡	39.38	36.28	.95
9. Video Clips‡	41.12	35.75	1.88
10. MBL‡	42.47	35.34	2.82
Part 4. Student Use for Assignments			
1. Word Processor	40.85	35.83	1.15
2. Spread Sheet	35.38	37.49	.33
3. Data Base	39.32	36.29	.90
4. Symbolic Manipulator	40.59	35.91	2.79
5. Plotter	39.26	36.31	.61
6. Graphics Generator	36.06	37.29	.19
7. Simulation	42.03	35.47	2.51
8. Tutorial	41.35	35.68	2.25
9. Drill & Practice	42.71	35.27	4.49**
10. APPLE MBL‡	39.82	36.14	3.32
11. IBM MBL‡	37.15	36.96	.01
Part 5. Kinds of Calculators Used			
1. Arithmetic	33.94	37.93	.63
2. Scientific	34.21	37.85	.42
3. Graphics	41.17	35.57	3.71
4. Business	38.85	36.44	.88
5. Symbolic	41.09	35.76	4.29**
6. Fraction	36.53	37.14	.06

‡ Items added to 1990 survey.
* Chi-Square statistic corrected for ties.
** $p < .05$

TABLE 3 — Mean ranks and chi-square statistics of NSF project faculty and non-project faculty attitudes after one year.

Attitude Items	Mean Rank		
	NSF Project Faculty	Non-Project Faculty	Chi-Square*
1. Computers will change the way my subject is taught	47.35	33.86	5.84**
2. Computers cause students to ask more questions	49.56	32.04	10.14**
3. I don't use computers because they are inaccessible	39.03	33.88	.81
4. Computers increase student motivation	47.88	33.12	6.88**
5. Computers do tasks that can't be done on overhead or chalkboard	45.74	34.35	4.44**
6. There is not enough time for computers & cover syllabus	45.16	32.64	5.03**
7. Computers increase students' ability to visualize	42.78	34.71	1.99
8. Programs free students to explore concepts	49.91	31.62	11.01**
9. Students learn more when I demonstrate with computers	47.16	31.33	9.93**
10. My administration supports instructional uses of computers	40.91	35.14	1.08
11. Calculators free students to focus on concepts‡	42.13	34.22	1.97
12. Students should not use calculators for tests‡	39.79	35.48	.68
13. Calculators increase class time for other tasks‡	44.88	33.91	3.81
14. Students may become overdependent on calculators‡	44.32	33.38	3.87**
15. Students require instructions on the use of calculators‡	51.44	31.88	11.89**

‡ Items added to 1990 survey.
* Chi-Square statistic corrected for ties.
** $p < .05$.

Year One Faculty Interviews

Individual interviews with the 12 faculty who have actively participated in the first pilot of physics 1 and 2, introductory chemistry, calculus 1 and 2, mathematics of finance, and introductory statistics have been completed. Results indicated that all have changed at least 20% of their courses by introducing technology and active learning strategies. The calculus courses and mathematics of finance have been completely revised. Most faculty expressed that the project had provided them with a focus for improving instruction, and that they had carried these new ideas over into other courses they teach. They also stated that they had increased their knowledge about teaching and technology and were more motivated to teach. In addition, some felt that the project had increased avenues of research, collegiality, and opportunities to develop curriculum materials, report at professional meetings, and to participate in other proposals.

Uses of technological instructional tools in the Fall 1989 pilots included: computer simulations, computer graphics, computer tutorials, microcomputer based laboratories, the Newlett Packard 28S and 19B calculators, laser disc, and videos. Active learning strategies included both in class and out-of class assignments requiring cooperative learning groups, class discussions, probing questioning, student-generated problem solving, and inquiry/guided practice.

Physics 1 and 2

Three professors each taught a pilot course of physics 1, and one continued to pilot changes in physics 2. Each used computer simulations, microcomputer-based laboratories, and video segments for class demonstrations. All had their students work in pairs on assignments in the physics courseware lab for two hours each week. They also provided their students with guided instruction sheets for these lab assignments. One of these professors was sceptical about the time taken for class discussion, and is concerned that students need class time to view problems worked by the professor. The other two professors encouraged students to discuss their concepts by eliciting students' concepts in group discussion, and then asking probing questions to have students consider their misconceptions. Both of these professors are comfortable with teaching less content to improve student understanding of physics concepts. Also, each of the three professors plan to incorporate laser disc demonstrations in Fall 1990.

Introductory chemistry

One professor taught a pilot course in Fall 1989, and continued the pilot with another class this Spring using computer simulations and the video disc for class demonstrations. Outside of class, this professor had students working in the chemistry computer laboratory using simulations and tutorials. Before the project, this chemistry professor had only lectured, but now has incorporated class discussions using problem-posing with his students. Next year, this professor is considering using cooperative learning groups, both in and out of class and has located another laser disc to use for class demonstrations. Also, we anticipate that IBM will provide this professor with the new Personal Science Lab (PSL) analog device for collecting the representing pH data.

Calculus 1 and 2

Two mathematicians and one mathematics educator piloted the HP 28S, a graphing and symbolic manipulating calculator in two calculus 1 courses in the Fall pilot. The mathematics educator demonstrated several calculus concepts using the IBM *Mathematics Exploration Toolkit*. Hewlett Packard contributed 10 calculators and the University purchased 20 more, that were loaned to pairs of calculus students for the semester. Because they had to share, calculus students were forced to work together, both in and out of class. One group project was assigned in the Fall pilot. Both mathematicians requested that they continue their pilots with their Fall students in calculus 2 for Spring semester. As one of these professors stated, *Once you use this calculator, there is no going back!* This professor also shared his insights about the value of the group projects in helping students learn together. He noted that these group projects became the basis for study groups among the college freshmen and that students were improving their ability to communicate mathematically with one another. The Spring pilot is requiring 10 group projects.   These professors will continue with a Fall 1990 pilot of calculus 3.

Mathematics of finance

One mathematician and one mathematics educator revised mathematics of finance using the Hewlett Packard 19B symbolic and graphics calculator that were loaned to each student for the semester. The course focused on using the HP 19B to solve problems, centering class discussions on which formula to use and which quantities were associated with the variables in that formula. Calculating time was greatly reduced, increasing the number of problems that could be solved during class.   All assignments and tests for this course required students to use the calculator. Cooperative learning was used frequently, both in and out of class. The students were encouraged to bring real-world problems to class for discussion and solution.   After the pilot, the mathematician commented:- *This makes me not want to teach the old way. Each day I come out of class uplifted — we have fun!   Now I want my students to be able to think — not spit back.*   This pilot project also continued in the spring and the faculty foresees that the course can be expanded to include new topics for which there has never been enough time for with paper/pencil calculations.

Statistics

Two statisticians and one mathematics educator teamed to teach the Fall pilot using the computer as a demonstration tool. Simulations and software that graphed data were used for these demonstrations.   The statistician who had taught this class before had never used class discussion and began to use discussion, guided inquiry, and cooperative learning groups in class.   Since these methods were new, this professor reflected that, *Things go better when I don't just lecture.*   She also noted that next year she needs some additional strategies to assure that more students have an opportunity to join in discussions, rather than the few dominant or target students in the class.   Plans for next year include using the statistics computer teaching lab that was recently established for more in class problem solving.

Year One Student Case Study

The mathematics of finance pilot was selected for a first year case study since so many changes were made to this course. Two-thirds of this class were juniors preparing to become mathematics teachers in grades 6-12. Final grade was used to compare the pilot mathematics of finance courses with a traditional mathematics of finance course taught by the same professor. The pilot class used the HP 19B calculator and the other class used a standard scientific calculator. Final grade distributions for these two classes are noted in Table 4 and shows that the pilot class achieved at a significantly higher level than the control class.

Qualitative data were obtained from the pilot students before and after taking the course through the use of surveys and interviews. Before the course, few students thought that using the calculator would make the class easier, but at the end of the courses many students observed that it did make learning easier for them. Also, most students thought that the calculator would eliminate tedious arithmetic and be less boring, but after the course, fewer students perceived the calculator in this matter.

After the course, many students felt positive about using the HP 19B calculator to teach and learn mathematics. Benefits mentioned by the students included (a) tedious arithmetic was eliminated, (b) time allocated to focus on the meaning of problems, (c) problems were easier, and (d) class was more interesting. Some students who rated their mathematics ability as below average, expressed that they did not have to worry about remembering arithmetic algorithms or making careless mistakes, and therefore were able to concentrate on strategies for problem solving and were more motivated to understand the relationships needed to solve the problems.

Conversely, some students felt that the calculator prevented them from learning the skills required for solving problems. One student expressed ambivalence about using the calculator because it seemed to him that anyone could learn to solve problems using this calculator, and it took away the advantage he normally had over other students in his mathematics classes.

While some students had been allowed to use calculators in previous math courses, none had ever been taught to use calculators or other tools as a part of the course content. Several students realised from this experience the importance of teaching students how to use appropriate tools rather than simply be allowed to have access to them in class. They considered this course to be a valuable experience that would affect the way they teach mathematics.

TABLE 4 — Pilot and control mathematics of finance final grade distributions by percent : Fall, 1989

	% of Students Achieving Final Grade				
Classes	A	B	C	D	F
HP 19B Symbolic Graphing Calculator Pilot Class	46	25	23	3	3
Scientific Calculator Control Class	23	13	15	18	31

DISCUSSION

The preliminary results of this NSF project after one year indicate that the faculty is beginning the change process to consider the instructional uses of technology and alternatives to the lecture method of teaching science and mathematics. They are engaged in building their knowledge about technological tools for instruction and different methods of teaching that involve their undergraduates in active learning. Preliminary visions are being made and risks are being taken by the faculty to change the way they teach. These visions will be modified, as the faculty learn more over the next few years. Larger risks will be taken with students and their colleagues, as faculty gain in confidence and receive reinforcement for their efforts to change.

The change model used for this project is an inside-out approach that teams scientists with science educators, statisticians with mathematics educators, and mathematicians with mathematics educators. The principal investigators for this project, view their role as supporting the faculty by providing resources to assist the faculty in the change process. We recognise that lasting innovations take place over five to ten years (Russell, 1948; Peters & Waterman, 1984) and that the faculty's perceptions of teaching and learning will be different each year that they are actively involved in the project. At the end of the first year, faculty perceived the effects of the project to be positive, especially in relation to their teaching.

Because of this project undergraduates who are preparing to become mathematics and science teachers are learning science and mathematics in technological environments. Also, they can no longer remain passive, listening to lectures — they must participate, question, answer, and communicate with one another and their professors. Some students are actively questioning the beliefs they have held about the value of paper and pencil calculations. We consider this to be beneficial to these undergraduates to help them rethink how students learn and how good teachers teach. If these undergraduates are to be prepared to teach in the twenty-first century, their undergraduate experiences should provide them with models of good teaching and learning.

REFERENCES

Berenson, S.B., Howe, A.C., & Stiff, L.V. (1988)
Preparation of mathematics and science teachers for the twenty-first century at North Carolina State University. A proposal to the National Science Foundation. Raleigh, NC : Center for Research in Mathematics and Science Education.

Berman, P. & McLaughlin, M.W. (1978)
Federal programs supporting education change. Vol.VIII : *Implementing and sustaining innovations.* Santa Monica, CA : Rand.

Goodlad, J.I. (1975)
The dynamics of educational change. New York : McGraw-Hill.

Kolb, J.R. & Berenson, S.B. (1990)
Improving leadership skills among high school mathematics teachers with collaborative research. A final report to the National Science Foundation. Raleigh, NC : Center for Research in Mathematics and Science Education.

National Council of Teachers of Mathematics (1989)
Professional standards for teaching mathematics. A working draft. Reston, VA : National Council of Teachers of Mathematics.

Peters, T.J. & Waterman, R.H. (1984)
In search of excellence. New York : Warner Books.

Russell, B. (1948)
Authority and the individual. New York : Simon and Schuster.

Sirotnik, K.A. and Clark, R.W. (1988)
School-Centered decision making renewal. *Phi Delta Kappan,* 69 (9), 660-664.

CHANGING LEARNER'S CONSTRUCTS IN ELEMENTARY SCHOOL SCIENCE TEACHER EDUCATION

Dr. Charly Ryan
King Alfred's College, Winchester, U.K.

Ana Maria Onorbe de Torre and Jose Maria Sanchez Jimenez
Escuela Universitaria de E.G.B. Guadalajara,
University of Alcala de Henares, Spain

1.   Introduction

This paper presents an analysis of progress to date in developing an elementary school science course within two initial teacher education courses.   The development is being carried out jointly in two institutions, one in England and one in Spain, with roughly equivalent intakes to teacher education of about 170 students per year, and on the edge of the commuter belt for their respective metropoli.

Considerable work has been done on learner's constructs in a wide variety of areas of science (e.g. Osborne and Freyberg 1985, Giordan and de Vecchi 1987, Champagne et al 1985).   Analysis of this work shows that the constructs that learners bring to the classroom prior to instruction can be difficult to change, with, for example, graduate physicists using pre-Newtonian arguments to explain physical phenomena, or using speed, velocity and acceleration interchangeably, as if they had had little formal science education.   If it is the case that formal schooling can have only a moderate impact on learners' views of major science concepts, then we can expect that when students enter teacher education they will bring with them a number of constructs that are not those accepted by scientists.   If the science that the teacher teaches is different from the accepted view used by scientists, we can hardly expect this to provide a sound basis for pupils to learn scientists' science. In order to provide a rational basis for action, we have started by investigating a number of concepts held by intending teachers (Ryan et al 1989, Ryan 1990), and to explore differences between the two countries. This is part of a larger research effort, with four main areas which aim to establish:

—   a base line of typical students' knowledge and understanding of science concepts and processes;

—   strategies to challenge and change the students' interpretation of that knowledge;

—   strategies for students to use in the classroom;

—   strategies for students to evaluate their own science teaching in the classroom.

Each of these four areas will now be discussed in turn.

2.   Student teachers' knowledge and understanding of science concepts and processes

We have investigated a number of concepts which are basic to an understanding of chemistry, namely:

(i)   conservation of matter during a variety of physical and chemical changes,
(ii)   states of matter,
(iii)   purity

2.1   Conservation of matter

With conservation of matter, student teachers' responses were not readily predictable from their formal educational qualifications (Ryan et al 1989). However, while some have discussed the low impact of formal education on students' science concepts (Clough et al 1987), there was a clear trend for the science understanding of student teachers to be related to the amount and type of formal science education that they had received. As might be expected, students tended to give answers that were more scientifically acceptable for physical rather than for chemical change. A half of the Spanish students conserved mass during combustion and this did not depend on whether they were students studying science or not, whereas only a quarter of British students did. Exploration of this national difference requires further work.

2.11   States of matter

This work has so far been carried out only with British students.   This showed that while the majority of students were using the categories in a scientifically acceptable way, largely based on the bulk properties of the materials, there were some exceptions, for example 9% of the students did not classify powders as solids. However, the transition to a scientifically acceptable classification of powders as solids was relatively easy to produce.

What the work did show was that very few students used a particulate theory to help in their classification, and that the classification of the states of matter into solid, liquid and gas applies readily only to chemically pure compounds.   This relationship between the state of matter and the concept of *pure* led to work on student's concepts of *pure*.

2.111   Student teachers' concepts of pure

There was an expectation that cultural differences might show up more clearly with *pure* than in the other work we have carried out.   In earlier work with British students (Ryan 1990), the most usual criterion for pure was *natural* and it was expected that *natural* be more obviously culturally defined.   In order to make the materials more appropriate for the two countries, the items were adapted from the earlier work and they are listed in the first column of Table 1.   As with, the earlier work, the student teachers in this sample are not producing a classification that a chemist might do, using a chemical definition of pure, such as made of a single element or compound.   What is also striking is that the rank order of materials is similar for the scientists and the non-scientists in both countries.   The explanation for the ranking of purity in Table 1 is largely explained by the reasons given for the criteria for pure, Table II, where the majority favour the criterion *natural*. Analysis of the pure and not pure groups shows that aluminium foil and clear glass are seen as natural by about a third of the students, that potatoes with soil on them, are purer than washed potatoes, and that manufacture or manipulation generally makes materials less pure. It is well established that the context in which a problem is set can affect the response (Clough et al 1987). It may be that the important aspect of the context here is the everyday nature of the materials used. Everyday materials were chosen as they are recommended for use with young learners, and so they were used as a role model for intending elementary school teachers. However, it may be that the everyday nature of the materials may have elicited an everyday construct, rather than a scientific construct. If this is the case there are major implications for teacher education and for pupils learning science. These implications will be drawn from a more detailed analysis of the data, using a larger sample.

Having established that initial teacher education students do have constructs which are not those used by scientists, in the next section the implications for teacher education are discussed.

3. Changing students' science concepts

Needham (1987) gives a strategy that has been widely used for changing learners' constructs. This involves the learner going through the following stages:

> orientation
> elicitation
> restructuring of ideas
> application of ideas
> review of learning.

These steps are made explicit to the students as they are presented to them. It is hoped that making explicit the structure of learning will act as a metacognitive strategy and so make the learning more effective (Anderson, 1989). This explication also acts as an appropriate role model for students when they act as teachers. The sorting activities associated with elucidating students concepts of states of matter and of purity provide a sound way into the first two stages of this procedure, i.e. orientation and elicitation. Students are asked to carry out two apparently simple sorting activities, the first being to sort a collection of everyday materials according to their perceived states, as solid, liquid or gas. This activity shows the difficulty of applying these terms to many everyday materials, and for the need to apply them to pure materials. The second activity is to resort the materials into pure and not pure materials and to give their criteria for the sorting. Their criteria can then be compared first with the criteria of other students, secondly the application of the criteria to the materials by other students, and thirdly with the use in science of scientists' criteria. In these activities the students have moved from implicit to explicit criteria, and have been through the process of explaining them to their peers. These two practical sorting activities have the advantage that they can be used with pupils of different ages by appropriate choice of materials, to match their everyday life.

Students can often remember that they have carried out many separations in their compulsory education but can rarely recall being told that the materials at the end of the separations were purer than at the start of the operation. It may be that students may need only to carry out thought experiments rather than carry them out again practically, though one must not forget that for some students there is a considerable positive affective dimension to carrying out such practical activities.

Work on the restructuring of these ideas, the next stage in the overall learning process, is stimulated by these sorting activities. Preliminary analysis of videotape of discussions during and after the sorting activities show that the activities act as an appropriate stimulus for the exchange and clarification of ideas, some of which conflict with their personal view. According to the body of work on attribution theory, these are the two key factors in eliciting attributions, i.e. causing learners to explain observations: unexpected (versus expected) events, and non-attainment (versus attainment) of a goal (Hewstone, 1988).

The next stages of the restructuring of ideas, namely the construction and evaluation of ideas and points of view used by science, and the final two stages, application and review of learning, are still being developed. Strategies, such as keeping journals, are being evaluated as a way to monitor development and responses of individual students. Again, making this strategy explicit to students will act as a further metacognitive strategy.

The work we have carried out has developed in parallel to the work of others, such as that with primary school teachers in England (Kruger & Summers 1988, 1989). We are also in a position to draw on the considerable work of other groups in the next step in the project, the development of strategies for students to use in the classroom.

4.   Strategies for students to use in the classroom

Development work in Britain (SPACE Project, 1990) and in New Zealand (Biddulph and Osborne, 1984) shows that with serving primary school teachers the approach advocated by Needham (1987) and described in Section 2 above can produce sound results. The proposal here is that students will adopt the same scheme for their teaching as was used by the tutors in structuring the student teachers' learning, namely orientation, elicitation, application, and review. As yet, only pilot programmes have been tried which indicate that with pupils between the ages of seven and eleven the approach is viable with initial education students. Student teachers are impressed by the energy and enthusiasm that pupils put into such an apparently mundane task as sorting materials into solids, liquids and gasses. This energy and enthusiasm shown by the pupils provides motivation for the students to persist with the innovation. The approach being developed for use in the next phase of analysis of this section of the work will involve the students in a more systematic action research approach to their science teaching, requiring them to reflect on their classroom practice. This is described in the next section.

5.   Strategies for students to evaluate their science teaching in the classroom

It is proposed that students will draw on the range of strategies available for their analysis of their science teaching in the classroom. This will include data gathering in the classroom using techniques such as audio and video recording, paired observation and triangulation. The aim is for students to be able to answer the following questions based on classroom data:

What did the pupils actually do?
What were they learning?
How worthwhile was it?
What did I do?
What did I learn?
What do I intend to do now? (Ashton, 1980).

What comes out from this exercise as most powerful for student teachers is the realisation that they do not teach as they think they do, i.e. their practice does not match their stated philosophy. This is a problem not simply for intending teachers but also for serving teachers. Thus the curriculum that the teacher plans and perceives is not necessarily that received or perceived by the pupils (Ingram and Worrall, 1990). It is expected that students will use the same learning cycle to learn appropriate strategies for their teaching as was used in the students' own science learning and which they attempt to use in their classrooms. In this way it is hoped that they see that teaching and learning approaches can be used in school and in college. This is also a way to show that school and college are linked.

Thus the orientation and elicitation phase could be approached by their analysis of a standard text on primary science teaching (Harlen, 1985). As a result of such an analysis, students produce lists of guidelines such as:

Children's observations should lead to dialogue with pupils and with the teacher.

Children's interest must be stimulated by the activities that the teacher chooses.

Science is the search *for* rather than the answer *to* how and why.

Children do their own investigation. Both teachers and pupils are learning and investigating together.

While this might be considered as a statement of the students' intended philosophy, when one comes to look for the accepted way of teaching, there is a wide divergence of opinion on how science ought to be taught.

The stage of comparison with accepted theory is much more problematic than comparing students' science with scientists' science. There is an implication in much of the work in this area that the comparable stage in science teaching, comparison with science's view is a simple matter of stating the one view. However, there is often more than one science theory that can be applied to the interpretation of phenomena. For instance, the analysis of the dispersal of a smell around a room can be used as evidence of the particulate nature of matter (Children's Learning in Science Project, 1987), if one is actually interested in the speed with which the smell pervades the room it is probably more appropriate to use a theory of fluid flow, which usually assumes that matter is continuous. This problem of which accepted theory to choose becomes even more difficult in the complex case of choosing between theories of teaching. However, if we look at the teaching and learning from the pupils' point of view the choice becomes easier. Pupils can only take the teacher's theory of teaching in the way that they perceive their teacher's actions. What is important from the learners' point of view is what the teacher allows them to do as learners, rather than what the teacher said was the intended pupil behaviours. For the pupils the action speaks louder than the word. Thus, for them, the theory they attribute to their teacher's actions is much more important than the theory that their teacher produced by the analysis of the text outlined above. The theory that the pupils attribute to their teacher is closer to that which an observer might attribute to their teacher's actions. It is only when the student teacher is able to compare their theory in action with their espoused theory that they will be able to take steps to reduce the gap between these two theories and so ensure that their teaching becomes more effective in conveying their view of the scientific phenomena that they are teaching.

6.   Conclusion

The programme described above is an ambitious and long term undertaking within initial teacher education.   We also intend that the outcomes of this research will feed into and strengthen our work with serving teachers, which in its turn can feed back into initial teacher education.   It is only through attempts at such ambitious programmes that we will be able to move to a more rational basis for teacher education, based not only within a sound theoretical framework but also within classroom practice.   Such a synthesis of theory and practice will also go some way to reducing the gap between theory and practice perceived by student teachers. In addition, one particular advantage of the work reported here is that we are in a position to make comments on the cultural context of the students and to reflect on structural constraints on teachers' teaching and, most importantly, pupils' learning.

TABLE I — Student Teachers classification of pure

Item	BrSc No.	BrNS No.	SpSc No.	SpNS No.	BrSc %	BrNS %	SpSc %	SpNS %
Sea Salt	12	31	16	12	63	89	100	100
Sugar, brown	10	35	9	12	53	100	56	100
Natural Sponge	9	21	16	12	47	60	100	100
Water	8	18	8	0	42	51	50	0
Potato, dirty	7	27	5	11	37	77	31	92
Stoppered flask	6	27	0	5	32	77	0	42
Potato, washed	5	27	7	3	26	77	44	25
Aluminium foil	4	19	7	0	21	54	44	0
Table Salt	3	19	7	0	16	54	44	0
Sugar, white	2	18	—	—	11	51	—	—
Milk	1	6	6	1	5	17	38	8
Aerosol	0	0	0	0	0	0	0	0
Copper coin	0	15	7	0	0	43	44	0
Coca cola	0	0	0	2	0	0	0	17
Elastoplast	0	9	0	0	0	26	0	0
Epsom salt	0	17	8	2	0	49	50	17
Glass marble, clear	0	9	0	9	0	26	0	75
Glass marble, coloured	0	9	12	1	0	26	75	8
Lemon juice	0	9	1	7	0	26	6	58
Plastic sponge	0	3	1	0	0	9	6	0
Polythene bag	0	12	2	0	0	34	13	0
Potato, cooked	0	18	0	2	0	51	0	17
Potato puree	0	15	0	1	0	43	0	8
Sweet	0	0	0	0	0	0	0	0
Toffee	0	0	0	0	0	0	0	0
Wire nail	0	13	5	0	0	37	31	0

BrSc   British Science students sample size 19
BrNS   British Non-science students sample size 35
SpSc   Spanish science students sample size 16
SpNS   Spanish Non-science students sample size 12

TABLE II — Student Teachers' criteria of pure

Item	BrSc No.	BrNS No.	SpSc No.	SpNS No.	BrSc %	BrNS %	SpSc %	SpNS %
Natural	9	15	7	12	47	42	44	100
Cannot be reduced further	4	0	0	0	21	0	0	0
Described by its name	2	0	3	0	11	0	19	0
One phase	0	12	0	0	0	33	0	0
One substance	0	0	5	0	0	0	31	0
Element	4	0	0	0	21	0	0	0
No response	0	9	1	0	0	25	6	0

BrSc   British Science students sample size 19
BrNS   British Non-science students sample size 35
SpSc   Spanish science students sample size 16
SpNS   Spanish Non-science students sample size 12

405

REFERENCES

Ashton, P., Hunt, P., Jones, S. and Watson, G. (1980)
An Approach to Evaluation, Milton Keynes, U.K. Open University Press.

Anderson Linda, M. (1989)
Learners and Learning, in Maynard C. Reynolds, *Knowledge Base for Beginning Teachers,* Oxford, Pergamon Press.

Biddulph, Fred & Osborne, Roger (1984)
Making Sense of Our World : an interactive approach, Hamilton New Zealand, University of Waikato.

Champagne, A.B., Gunstone, R.F. and Klopfer, L.E. (1985)
Effecting Change in Cognitive Structures Among Physics Students, in L.H.T. West & A.L. Pines (Eds), *Cognitive Structure and Conceptual Change,* Orlando Academic Press.

Children's Learning in Science Project (1987)
Approaches to teaching the particulate theory of matter, Leeds, University of Leeds.

Clough, E.E., Driver, R. and Wood-Robinson, C. (1987)
How do children's scientific ideas change over time? *School Science Review,* 69, (247) pp.255-267.

Giordan, A. and de Vecchi, G. (1987)
Les Origines du Savoir : des conceptions des apprenants aux concepts scientifiques, Lausanne Delachoix & Niestle.

Harlen, W. (1985)
Primary Science : Taking the Plunge, London, Heinemann.

Hewstone, Miles and Antaki, Charles, (1988)
Attribution Theory and Social Explanations in Miles Hewstone, Wolfgang Stroebe, Jean-Paul Codol and Geoffrey M. Stephenson (Eds), *Introduction to Social Psychology,* pp.111-141, Blackwell, Oxford.

Ingram, J. and Worrall, N. (1990)
Varieties of curricular experiences : backmarkers and frontrunners in the primary classroom, *British Journal of Educational Psychology,* 60, pp.50-62.

Kruger, K. and Summers, M. (1988)
Primary school teachers' understanding of science concepts, *Journal of Education for Teaching,* 14, pp.259-265.

Needham, R. (1987)
Teaching Strategies for Developing Understanding in Science, Leeds, University of Leeds.

Osborne, R. and Freyberg, P. (1985)
Learning in Science : the implications of Children's Science, London, Heinemann.

Ryan, C. (1990)
Student teachers' concepts of purity and of states of matter, *Research in Science and Technological Education,* 18, forthcoming November.

Ryan, C. , Sanchez Jimenez, J.M. and Onorbe, A.M. (1989)
Scientific ideas held by intending primary teachers in Britain and Spain, *European Journal of Teacher Education,* 12, (3) pp.49-61.

SPACE Project (1990)
e.g. Russell, Terry & Watt, Dorothy, *Evaporation and Condensation,* Liverpool, Liverpool University Press.

TEACHER EDUCATION IN THE 1990s:
TOWARDS A NEW COHERENCE

Lillian Greenwood
Institute of Informations,
University of Ulster, Jordanstown, Northern Ireland

Leslie Caul
Stranmillis College, Belfast, Northern Ireland

Introduction

There is a certain attractiveness in the idea that children through their capacity to control a machine, in this instance a computer, would liberate themselves from the constraints of normal classroom - based learning. While recognising a clearly optimistic note in the power of programming both as an aid *in* learning, (the making explicit implicit thought processes) and *to* learning, (freeing the individual from the constraints of teacher-led and group oriented learning) the computer clearly offers a new flexibility and power to educators. Four years ago we evaluated a simple problem-solving environment using BOB, a simple language in schools. The influence of Papert et al (1980) and LOGO is apparent in our work as we sought to unravel the complexities of using computers as an integral part of classroom life (see Greenwood and Caul 1989a and 1989b). In essence BOB showed the following.

Bob in the classroom

The use of BOB in the classroom (see Greenwood and Caul 1989a and 1989b) indicated how important teacher commitment was in encouraging and motivating children. This is in contradiction to Papert's thesis but finds support in many empirical studies of LOGO in schools (see De Corte and Verschaffel 1987 for an account of assessment of LOGO). However, as Papert suggests classroom management, the availability of machines and motivated users are appropriate measures of success. Nevertheless, where a teacher was knowledgeable and a skilful programmer able children benefitted from using the package.

Where the program (BOB) was successful the abler children were able to break down problems, write procedures and debug programs. However, less able children found the program difficult and abstract.

In evaluating BOB we were unable to break into the child's thinking. We needed an idea of how a child arrived at a conclusion. This is our version of what De Corte and Verschaffel (1987) called the "metacognitive." The importance of how children process thought is highlighted in the Education Reform Act (1988) and the Education Reform Order (1989). In Northern Ireland as in the rest of the United Kingdom IT and the use of computers becomes an integral aspect of the curriculum.

IT as a cross curricular theme

IT is a cross curricular theme, one of six that theoretically weave the lattices of the new "common curriculum" in Northern Ireland. While the IT Working Group and its parent partner NICC make statements for IT, the computer environment is to the child a new system with properties to be learnt. Unfortunately for the teacher there is a scarcity of contemporary evidence on child-computer interaction (see Lewis et al 1990).

A gap exists in the educational literature on the theoretical issues involved in introducing IT into schools. Ostensibly, there is no systematic analysis available to illuminate how a learner moves through the mastery curve in managing computer systems (Driver 1989). However Papert and Weir (1978) have written accounts of children moving from regarding computers as toys to using them as "information prosthesis." The accounts described LOGO, Papert's problem solving language as the vehicle of discovery.

Would a theory of computer competence, however, be qualitatively different from existing accounts of learning? How, for example, would learning in a computer environment differ from that of the normal curriculum? And, indeed, how would IT contribute to a child's mastery of the tasks of the "common curriculum."

The attempt to achieve IT attainment targets (NICC 1989) may indicate that many well rehearsed explanations of learning adequately account for those situations where the computer is used to display or compute a mechanical exercise. Presentation and storage of data fit neatly into the kinds of theory that account for learning performance within the classroom. Theories of writing, for example Graves (1984), account for both pen and ink work as well as word processing. However, this theory of learning becomes inadequate when claims are made for the computer as a tutor for thinking. Where the computer is used in this way stronger claims for an alternative approach to learning can be made because the learning environment can be sensitive to different degrees of skill manifested by a user. Papert et al (1980) make claims for skill transfer from one domain to another (see De Corte and Verschaffel 1987 for a critical account of Papert's claims). Nevertheless, if Papert formalisation of cognitive development is correct, LOGO and other microworlds have the potential to enhance the thinking of children in school. However LOGO provides, as yet, little evidence to suggest that programming computers produces cognitive enhancements that are general in their applicability (Pea and Kurtland 1984).

In a previous study Greenwood (1989) suggested that although IT has potential as a learning vehicle it is difficult to integrate into classroom life. For example, at a simple level when should a computer be used? Are problems and applications planned before they are computed? Should children be encouraged to think on the screen? Where do programming languages fit into the curriculum?

While NICC categorically define IT to contain 5 strands; i.e. Presentation, Data Storage and Retrieval, Modeling and Simulation, Communication and Social Issues, IT must be considered by teachers, not only as activities that have an educational outcome, but also in terms of the theoretical issues that are at the core of understanding and using computers. There can be three non exclusive patterns of use in computing:

1.   Where a package is used within the limitations set by its author. Here a user can operate a number of patterns which have been set by developers.

2.   Where a user may program a computer to achieve a goal.

3.   Where two users wish to communicate using an "on line" system.

It is within these activities that IT should be located if "IT" is to become one of the foundations of the curriculum.

IT in the core of the common curriculum

From September 1990 all teachers will have to include aspects of IT in their work. The new attainment targets set by NICC have finally heralded the movement of IT into the mainstream of education. Among the advantages brought to the curriculum by the new IT may include opportunities for children to work co-operatively, to discuss and share ideas and for outcomes to be the product of teamwork. As long as such work remains outside the mainstream of assessment pupils have nothing to lose and a great deal to gain from IT (Brine,1983; Hawkins 1983). However, the establishment of a series of attainment targets related to specific performance in IT is open to question.

What will happen when work is serious and grades depend on it and children compete for grades? (Olson 1988).

Concern about the statutory nature of the "Common Curriculum" suggest that its requirement and especially those in IT for reasons given above should be examined in some detail.

In mathematics it is envisaged that pupils will make "wide use of computers and computer-control devices such as the floor turtle" (Hibbett et al 1989). The Working Group on the Mathematics Curriculum argued that school leavers should be at ease with computer equipment, familiar with more common forms of software, and therefore able to adapt to "the specific needs of the workplace"

(Hibbett et al 1989). Generally speaking the use of computers occurs in two areas. Firstly, there is a reliance on the use of LOGO in the generation of shape and design in mathematics (Key Stage 2 years - p.5-7). Secondly, also at Key Stage 2 use is made of computers to store and process information and to interpret a variety of graphic representation.

The Working Party considering the Science Curriculum makes an interesting distinction when it argues

> It is not possible to include them (IT strands i.e. communication et al) within the existing attainment target on IT and microelectronics in a way that produces a coherent target with clearly defined progression levels. (McGarvey et al 1989).

Attainment Target 3 : IT in Science states that:

> Pupils should be able to use IT appropriately and effectively to communicate and handle information in a variety of forms and for a variety of scientific purposes. (NICC p.38, 1989).

The Working Group on the English Curriculum (NICC 1989) adopted a different style of presentation from that presented in Mathematics and Science. While recognising the social impact of new IT, Pettigrew et al (1989) are not all that specific about its value save to recognise word processing as a valuable aid in writing and drafting written work. The group argued that IT could never be central to the work in English and remained conservative in its interpretation of how English should be taught. However, there are important areas of knowledge that English teachers could address. For example data interpretation and communication are as integral to English as they are to the rest of the curriculum.

Children's learning and IT

IT poses a range of problems for teachers in evaluating its potential in schools. In particular, there is no specific theory of CCI (Child Computer Interaction). Part of this deficiency comes from a lack of imagination. Certainly it is difficult to conceive a need for new theoretical principles when schools use slow computers and inefficient software.

Yet concern must be posed in terms of IT that will attain a more sophisticated level of application. Such systems may require the use of new concepts of intentionality and meaning in understanding children's use of them. Such uses may not lend themselves to any of the, as yet, new post-Piagetian conceptualisations of learning (see Driver and Scanlon, 1989).

While as yet incomplete, cognitive sciences seem to offer a means of decoding CCI. Firstly as Scaife (1989) argues they offer techniques for producing situations that can be directly investigated in terms of IT and learning. And, secondly, cognitive science offers a range of concepts that can be used to model those learning processes and a vocabulary for communicating the nature of a child's understanding of IT itself.

IT offers an exciting prospect for educational purposes, the computer and hypermedia in particular. The use of microworld can remove some of the strictures on children's thinking and reduce to some extent limitations on self-discovery. As in this account of BOB the learning experience can be structured to build on a small stock of primitives to a fuller representation of the cognitive domain. In theory there can be a sensitive mapping of the child's mental model and the contingencies contained in the program (see Greenwood, 1989). As described above children can work at their own speed, build up procedures from simple rules and enhance their reasoning capacity.

However, how are we to model such learning? The use of a programming language can make precise our understanding in a variety of learning situations. For example, BOB enabled the authors to compare the thinking of children of different ages and ability. Previous studies of IT have seen the computer as a variable in the learning situation in the same way as psychological theory defined its constituent parts. However, a more imaginative and creative approach could begin to conceptualise the computer in a novel and sensitive way. BOB has been illustrative of an approach that was conscious to both the psychological issues and the process of modeling solutions. Yet BOB was unable to marry successfully both concerns in a convincing manner.

The future of IT in education depends upon the interaction between children's developmental skills and the design of modeling systems. The next phase of our work will explore and elaborate an extension of the basic theoretical issues of learning. While BOB enabled an articulation to be grounded in classroom practice, further research needs to reflect more sensitively ideas from computer systems and from human learning theory. Such an analysis should address the characterisation of a learning system and the internalisation of its properties. Thus educational theory may influence computer science and not, as has been the case the reverse.

Research in an IT environment

The advent of the WIMP operating systems together with the demands of IT attainment targets in the U.K. have reconstructed research needs. First, the metacognition of IT applications have to be coded. This involves a search for a child's understanding of IT. Second, the construction of learning concepts should be encoded as an aid to understanding how children think using a computer. Then will a child's solution/program be indicative of true thought.

To these ends we have written a problem solving package that operates on the APPLE series using hypercard. The package invites users to address a short series of classical problems (you will recognise Towers of Hanoi) and records the metacognitive processes at work. This we propose as a cross cultural study of thinking across nations in Europe.

[Those interested in participating in the study can contact the authors, Leslie Caul at Stranmillis College, Belfast: DBAA 3100 @ QUEENS — BELFAST Centre VAXI or Lillian Greenwood at the University of Ulster at Jordanstown : CBK923 @ UK AC ULSTER UJVAX.]

415

REFERENCES

Caul, L. and Greenwood, L. (1989)
Thinking About Thinking: An evaluation of BOB, a computer package designed to introduce children to problem solving. 14th Annual Conference of ATEE, 1989. Sweden.

Driver, R. and Scanlon, E. (1989)
Conceptual Change in Science. *Journal of Computer Assisted Learning.* Vol.5, No.3, Blackwell Scientific Publications.

De Corte, E. and Verschaffel, L. (1987)
LOGO: A Vehicle for Thinking. Occasional Paper. Centre for Instructional Psychology. Leuven: Katholieke Universiteit.

DENI (1989)
The Way Forward. Bangor, Co. Down.

Graves (1984)
Children and Writing. Oxford: Heinemann.

Greenwood, L. (1989)
Unpublished M.Sc. Dissertation. University of Ulster at Jordanstown.

Greenwood, L. and Caul, L. (1989a)
Across the Corridor and Up the Stairs. *Micromath. A Journal of the Association of teachers of Mathematics.* Vol.5 No.2. Oxford: Basil Blackwell Ltd.

Greenwood, L. and Caul, L. (1989b)
Problem solving through programming: theoretical perspectives of BOB, a computer package designed to help children with problem solving in the classroom. *ESAI,* Dublin. Vol.9.

Hawkridge, D. (1990)
Who Needs Computers in Schools and Why? *Computer Education,* Vol.15, No.1-3. Great Britain. Pergamon Press plc.

Hibbett (1989)
>Report of the Mathematic Working Party. NICC, Belfast.

McGarvey (1989)
>Report of the Science Working Party. NICC, Belfast.

NICC (1989)
>Cross-Curriculum Themes: Consultation Report: Northern Ireland Curriculum Council, Belfast.

Papert, S. (1972)
>Teaching children to be mathematic versus teaching about mathematics. *International Journal of Mathematics, Education, Science and Technology.* Vol.3 pp.249-262.

Papert, S. and Weir, S. (1978)
>*Information prosthetics for the handicapped,* MIT Artificial Intelligence Memo 496.

Papert, S. (1980)
>*Mindstorms: Children, computers and powerful ideas.* New York: Basic Books.

Pea, R. and Kurtland, M. (1984)
>On the cognitive effects of learning computer programming. *New Ideas on Psychology.* 2, pp.137-168.

Pettigrew (1989)
>*Report of English Working Group.* NICC, Belfast.

Piaget, J. (1955)
>*The Language and Thought of the Child.* New York: World.

Scaife, M. (1989)
>Education, information technology and cognitive science. *Journal of Computer Assisted Learning.* Vol.5 No.2. Oxford: Blackwell Scientific Publications.

NEED FOR NEW INFORMATION TECHNOLOGY IN THE TEACHING OF PHYSICS AND CHEMISTRY IN PORTUGAL

A. Cachapuz, I. Malaquias, I.P. Martins,
Marília F. Thomaz and N. Vasconcelos

University of Aveiro, Portugal

Many of the western industrialised nations are facing severe problems with their economies, authority relations between institutions, and values. Commentators and critics analysing this crisis have spent a good deal of time focusing on the family and especially on the school. The crisis in schools and teaching, they admit, is complicated and widespread, but one step towards a solution may be the rapid introduction of personal computers into schools. It was argued this will give the students new skills, skills that are necessary in international competition for markets and jobs. It will also make the tasks of teaching more interesting and creative (Apple, 1989).

The growth of information technology (IT)* in schools is not a slow movement. In one recent year, a fifty-six per cent increase was reported in the use of computers in schools in the United States. Also France, Canada, England, Australia, and many other countries have recognised their importance. Nowadays, it is nearly impossible to find a subject that is not being "computerised," though mathematics and science remain the home base for a large portion of the use of computers in schools (Apple, 1987).

---

* Information technology (IT) may be defined as the technology associated with the handling of information : its storage, processing and transmission in a variety of forms by electronic means, and its use in controlling the operation of machines and other devices (D.E.S., 1989, p.1). Computers are at the core of IT.

It is important for teachers to recognise that although IT, and computers in particular, is only one of a range of sources of information, it is one with particular qualities, namely, the speed of retrieval, the vastness of some data bases and the facility to provide continuously updated material (D.E.S. 1989). Moreover information technology skills need to be regarded as enabling, in the same way that speaking, listening, reckoning, reading and writing are fundamental to all school subjects (Sparkes, 1989). Pupils should be allowed to enter data obtained from their own experiments into prepared programmes. This may then be manipulated to obtain results (for example, a least squares plot) and to print out the results for inclusion in the final report. Likewise, they should be encouraged to use word processors to produce their project reports.

Over the next twenty years, almost everyone will need to acquire the practical skills of operating information retrieval systems and the cognitive skills of accessing and interpreting information presented by electronic means (Sparkes, 1989). IT is here to stay and will become increasingly used throughout further and higher education.

Some advantages of the use of computers in the learning process may be pointed out:

(i) Learners enjoy using computers

In our society, the computer has very high positive motivational value. Although the computer is not always pictured favourably, for most learners, particularly most young ones, it is presented as an exciting new device. So students are "prepared" for computers, even eager to have contact with them. In the field of learning these motivational issues cannot be neglected. Although we cannot know what the evolution of the computer will be, for the moment, it generates very strong positive interest in both classrooms and informal learning situations (Bork, 1985).

(ii) Individualisation

The time required for learning may differ from student to student. A central problem in any educative system is how to reach the individual student effectively. With good material available, computers can allow individualisation responsive to student needs.

(iii) Learning faster

Student time is an important issue, and anything that can increase efficiency, such as the computer, is important.

(iv) Visualisation

Computers have an increasing capability to provide interactive visual information, such as drawing graphics.

(v) Simulation

Computers are excellent for simulating the real world, particularly in science. There are programmes for investigating wave motion, molecular motion and particle motion in the absence of friction. Chemists have access to programmes that model industrial processes, such as the Haber Process. Biologists can carry out variations of Mendel's experiments and Physicists can run their own "Chernobyl" nuclear accidents, with less damaging consequences to the environment and themselves. Computer simulation can be very important in the process of building and testing concepts and representations of natural phenomena. They can extend the natural world, not in direct observable concepts but in unobservable and ideal situations, for example, a frictionless world. Simulations can extend the range of manipulable objects, real or "imagined."

Though we don't as yet have a full picture of how students learn in computer simulated environments, a properly designed simulation can introduce a new dimension in science teaching if it allows the student to test his/her naive ideas about the world and confront them with reality. Computer simulations can be based on an established model or on an alternative model, assumed by some students. That is, we can simulate alternative realities.

The situation in Portugal

In Portugal there is a lack of knowledge concerning the

extent of the use of new information technology in the teaching of science, particularly in Physics and Chemistry.

The goal of this preliminary study is to identify present trends about the use of new information technology by Physics and Chemistry teachers in middle (8th and 9th grades) and secondary (10th to 12th grades) schools in Portugal*, in comparison with more traditional forms of teaching resources.

Hopefully, identified trends might be the starting point for recommendations in the training of Physics and Chemistry teachers. To make useful recommendations some independent variables were selected, namely, the sex of the teacher (is the use of IT mostly done by men?), teaching experience (do the younger teachers use IT more extensively?), academic background (which academic qualifications are more related with the use of IT?) and professional qualifications (are professionally trained teachers more able to use IT?).

For example, concerning the variable, sex, several studies suggest that females are far less likely to use computers than males, and that this tendency holds at all age levels (Durndell et al 1987).

DESIGN

The study presented is part of a larger project developed since 1986 (Cachapuz et al, 1989) involving a documental analysis of curriculum material (official programmes and textbooks) and two surveys, one addressed to teachers (N=725) and one to students (N=9000, analysis in progress).

In this study only aspects directly concerning the use of IT by teachers are explored. Teachers were asked to appraise the level (frequency of use) of each of nine teaching aids (computer, "diaporama,"[†] video materials, opaque projector, slides, overhead projector, experimental work, blackboard and work sheets) which are

* Since 1985, a national project, the MINERVA PROJECT, has been developed in order to introduce new information technology, particularly computers, in the schools, from pre-primary to secondary level. At present, nearly 40% of middle and secondary schools are already involved.

[†] "Diaporama" : slides, text and sound.

included in their teaching. The questionnaire used to gather background information concerning the teaching of Physics and Chemistry in Portugal was administered during February 1987 to 725 teachers (37% of the corresponding total population) of which a representative sample of 521 respondents was selected for final analysis.

RESULTS

Table 1 shows the percentage of teachers who use each of these teaching aids.

TABLE 1 — Teachers' use of different teaching aids

Teaching aids	Teachers' use (%)
Computer	19.5
"Diaporama"	29.5
Video materials	45.0
Opaque projector	42.0
Slides	57.5
Overhead projector	86.0
Experimental work	98.0
Blackboard	99.0
Work sheets	99.5

Overall results (Table 1) show that only a minority of Physics and Chemistry teachers use new information technology in their teaching: 19.5% computer assisted teaching; 29.5% "diaporama"; 45% video materials. As expected most of the teachers use more traditional teaching aids: experimental work (98.0%), blackboard (99.0%) and worksheets (99.5%).

Teacher's sex

The sample was formed by 19.5% of men and 80.5% of women.

FIGURE 1 — Teachers' use of IT (%) vs sex

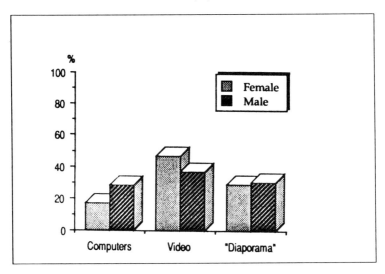

The results (Figure 1) suggest substantial differences in the case of the use of video materials and computers. The latter were mostly used by men ($X^2 = 6.03$, $a < 0.02$). Summers (1990) shows that male students, at the start of a one year secondary postgraduate teacher training course, had greater knowledge of computers, were more favourably disposed to computers and were more confident than females. This probably reflects a differential perception of social roles which were reinforced throughout the educational system. It is known that in primary schools boys and girls handle IT equipment with similar confidence. However, during the late primary years and adolescence, the interest boys have in technical artifacts is frequently reinforced, whereas that of girls often lacks encouragement (D.E.S. 1989).

TABLE 2 — Teachers' use of IT (%) vs years of teaching experience

Professional experience (years) New IT	<1	1-5	6-10	11-15	16-20	<20
Computers	24.5	25.2	12.7	21.6	12.7	18.5
Video	32.1	36.5	46.3	46.4	50.0	56.6
"Diaporama"	38.5	19.8	27.8	28.1	30.4	24.7

Teaching experience

The results (Table 2) show that as teachers' experience increases, the use of video materials also increases. On the contrary, younger teachers with less years in the profession ($\leq$ 5 years) are those who use the computer more extensively ($x^2 = 4.42$, $a < 0.05$). This result suggests that recent university pre-service courses should do more preparation in this area. It also suggests the need to organise adequate inservice courses for older teachers.

FIGURE 2 — Teachers' use of IT (%) vs academic background

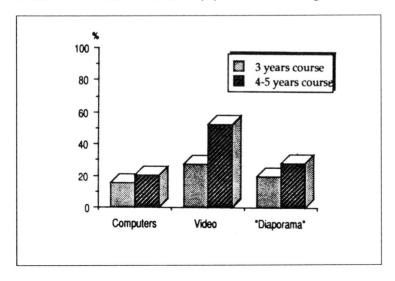

Academic background

Figure 2 suggests that longer academic courses tend to increase the use of IT, namely in the case of video materials (x^2 = 20.36, a < 0.001). Teachers with a university degree in Physics tend to make more use of computer assisted teaching than teachers with a Chemistry or Physics/Chemistry degree (x^2 = 3.35, a < 0.10).

TABLE 3 — Teachers' use of IT (%) vs professional background

New IT \ Professional experience (years)	Teacher training degree	No teacher training degree
Computers	19.6	20.1
Video	53.5	27.9
"Diaporama"	31.1	27.3

Professional qualification

Generally, teachers with a training degree tend to make extensive use of IT (Table 3).

In the case of computers no improvement was detected, probably because a substantial proportion of teachers with a training degree are the older ones, i.e., those for whom professional programmes had no component in this area at the time. In support of that, teachers with no training degree, but involved in recent training programmes, make more use of the computer in their classes (31.1%) than those not involved in those programmes (15.6%).

CONCLUSIONS

The main conclusion of this study is the need to improve, in Portugal, specific training programmes for Physics and Chemistry teachers with a focus on the use of IT. Despite the results of this study suggesting that recent teacher training programmes are moving in the right direction, some recommendations must be made:

1.   It is necessary to promote inservice teacher training programmes with special attention to the use of computers in the teaching of Physics and Chemistry.

2.   These programmes should be mostly directed to teachers

(i)   without a university degree in Physics,
(ii)   with more than five years of teaching experience,
(iii)   so that a more balanced pattern of male/female users emerge.

The implementation of these courses raises some problems. The area of instructional computing is so recent and evolving so rapidly that it is difficult to keep abreast of it.   Software is still emerging.   Hardware is changing rapidly.   All of these conditions make the task of trying to teach teachers and potential teachers about instructional computing very difficult.   Perhaps the best approach in the training of teachers is to develop in them the ability to select teaching strategies and media in relation to their objectives and students.   Sometimes, the best answer will be the computer, but sometimes it will not.   Educators need to look at what they know about teaching and learning, about curriculum and students, and take all factors into account in deciding when to use a computer and when not.   The issue of deciding what computers can do well is an important one (Langhorne et al 1989).

It is important for teachers learning about computers to understand that computers, like any component of modern technology, are neither inherently good nor inherently evil in learning applications (Bork, 1985).   Possible negative consequences of new technology in education include the de-skilling and de-powering of teachers, and also the creation of inequality which is brought about by the high costs of this particular technology as it applies to education in the limitation of access to new technology.   The cost of computers is still comparatively high.   So, the addition of computer curricula most often means that money must be drained from one area and given to another (Apple, 1987).

Clearly, not all content and not all objectives are best met by having students interact with information technology. Decision making based on understanding of content, understanding of learning processes, and understanding of students can guide educators to use technology to its best advantage and opt for other strategies as appropriate. The success of innovation is dependent on sound decision making, on looking at the potential applications of innovation, studying current status, comparing needs and capabilities, and selecting where that innovation fits best. So it is with computers. It clearly has specific capabilities (Langhorne et al 1989).

REFERENCES

APPLE, M.W. (1987)
"Mandating Computers : The Impact of the New Technology on the Labour Process, Students and Teachers." In Walker, S. and Barton, L. (Eds), *Changing Policies, Changing Teachers — New Directions for Schooling?* Milton Keynes : Open University Press, pp.75-95.

APPLE, M.W. (1989)
"Teaching and Technology : The Hidden Effects of Computers on Teachers and Students." In Weis, L. et al (Eds), *Crisis in Teaching — Perspectives on Current Reforms,* Albany : State University of New York Press, pp.227-251.

Bork, A. (1985)
Personal Computers for Education. New York : Harper & Row, Publishers, Chapter 7.

Cachapuz, A., Malaquias, I., Martins, I.P., Thomaz, M.F. and Vasconcelos, N. (1989)
Towards innovation in pre-service and inservice training of Physics and Chemistry Teachers in Portugal. Paper presented at the ATEE 14th Annual Conference, Kristianstad, Sweden.

D.E.S. (1989)
Information Technology from 5 to 16, Curriculum Matters 15. London : Her Majesty's Stationery Office.

Durndell, A., Macleod, H. and Siann, G. (1987)
"A survey of attitudes to, knowledge about and experience of computers." *Computers and Education,* 11, pp.165-175.

Langhorne, M.J. Donham, J.O., Gross, J.F. and Rehmke, D. (1989)
Teaching with Computers—A New Menu for the '90s. London : Kogan Page.

Sparkes, B. (1989)
"Information technology in science education." *SSR, 71* (254), pp.25-31.

Summers, M. (1990)
"Starting Teacher Training — New PGCE students and computers." *British Educational Research Journal, 16* (1)

THE SECONDARY SCHOOL DIRECTIVE COUNCIL'S SOCIALISATION PROCESS : COMPONENTS AND PATTERNS OF ORGANISATIONAL MATURITY

Maria de Fatima Chorão Sanches

Department of Education — Faculty of Sciences
University of Lisbon

Theoretical perspective

Argyris (1957) suggests that the nature of the value system of an organisation is likely to determine individual behaviour and create different opportunities for personal and professional growth within the work context.   In the process of becoming mature, people develop along a continuum defined by seven dimensions:

1.   passivity vs. activity,
2.   dependence vs. independence,
3.   behaving in a few ways vs. capability of behaving in many ways,
4.   erratic shallow interests vs. deeper and stronger interests,
5.   short time perspective vs. future time perspective,
6.   subordinate perspective vs. equal or superordinate position,
7.   lack of awareness of self vs awareness and control over self.

Building on this theory and borrowing from Mclelland's (1953) achievement motivation theory, Hersey and Blanchard (1982) integrated the maturity concept in the area of leadership.   In their model of situational leadership, the style that the leader might use is viewed as a function of the maturity level of the group or people that the leader is trying to influence.   In Blanchard's conceptualisation, the focus is on the follower's maturity as a diagnostic tool, viewed as necessary for the leader to adjust his or her leadership style to the environmental contingencies.

Applied to the organisational field, maturity is dichotomised in job and psychological maturity. Job maturity encompasses knowledge, ability and experience whereas psychological maturity consists of willingness or motivation to perform a task. High maturity individuals are characterised by a high sense of work responsibility, little need for direction, support and external incentives. Yet, high maturity people seek information needed for improving or maintaining of performance level. Moderate maturity people need a higher level of communication, support, clarification and explanation of the issues.

Purpose of the study

In the present study, the concept of organisational maturity was conceptualised as a fundamental component of the socialisation process that a teacher undergoes while becoming a Secondary School Directive Council (DC) member. Specifically, organisational maturity was defined in terms of (a) Argyris's maturity categories, (b) DC member's motivations, and (c) self-efficacy (Bandura, 1986) to perform the DC functions. Accordingly, the process of becoming and being a DC member was explored under the following assumptions:

1.   Organisational maturity is an outcome generating from a combination of experience, motivation and self-efficacy to perform school governance functions.

2.   A sense of independence and organisational efficacy outcome (Bandura, 1984) would represent a higher degree of maturity.

3.   The larger the DC's experience, the greater the likelihood of the greater sense of maturity.

The literature on organisational socialisation has predominantly focused on the newcomer. The organisational member who initiates a different role within the same organisation

(Van Maanen and Schein, 1979) has also been considered. DCs are elected among the school faculty to take a new role — school governance — while remaining in the teaching function. As DC members, teacher approach the new role without receiving previous education or formal training in administration matters, being then required to adjust perceptions regarding the social reality that the new role implies. Given the specificity of this organisational situation, it appears relevant to study organisational maturity as part of the DC members' socialisation process.

Being the continuation of a previous research on the nature of school governance self-efficacy and motivation and their relationship (Sanches, 1988), the present study purported to identify (a) the socialisation structures that were viewed as significant regarding the subjects' passage from teacher to DC member, and (b) possible patterns of variation along the maturity continuum.

Data collection and analysis

Secondary School DC members were the target population in the study. The Directive Council is composed of faculty members, students, and staff representatives. Only the faculty members were included in the study. From a national sample of secondary schools, sixty DC members were selected according to their extreme opposite levels of organisational self-efficacy.

The qualitative data came from indepth interviews conducted in the schools over two periods of four hours each. Data was tape recorded and transcripts submitted to content analysis. Higher levels of data integration and abstraction were systematically pursued. The subjects were asked to report incidents or episodes about school governance practices in order to identify (a) the organisational structures that had impact on the DC members' socialisation, and (b) the meaning they attributed to the performance of the new role.

Results

A first assumption of the study concerned the existence of a centralised school system as a socialisation context that was common to all the Directive Council members. Yet differences in the ways the Directive Council members would act regarding the culture of orientation imposed by the centralisation context were expected. Initiated at the electoral process, a certain sequence was traced in the socialisation cycle throughout the differential lengths of the subjects' school governance experience. Organisational patterns concerning the impact of the central hierarchical structures were revealed. Two organisational groups were identified, characterised, and labeled as innovators and keepers of the school status quo.

1 — COMPONENTS OF THE ORGANISATIONAL MATURITY PROCESS

The cognitive context of the Directive Council Socialisation

Establishing the person's centrality in the organisation, defining a social space and time (Van Maanen 1990), creating an interpretive order regarding what is unfamiliar or complex within the organisation are essential steps in the socialisation of a newcomer. Representations of the new role are determined by the way the individual processes the information about the organisation, and the diverse nature of the sources of information itself. Motivations and sense of organisational efficacy (Sanches, 1988) constitute cognitive factors that combine themselves in the construction of the social mapping of both the new activities and the organisational environment. Moreover, they influence the decision to become and remain in the school governance position. To this extent, they may be considered as components of the psychological context of the school governance socialisation.

The present study indicates that organisational maturity is linked to these cognitive elements of socialisation. The development of the Directive Council members' governance maturity was in part determined by the nature of the teachers' motivations to accept Directive Council membership. Among other types of motivations, the desire to learn about the "hidden school" and to "know how a school looks like from inside" (Sanches, 1988) expressed an interest in school as organisation. In this sense, school governance motivation constituted a prior element of the social map which makes the landscape of the school organisational life both intelligible and meaningful.

School Governance — a new teacher role

Attributed to teachers by legislation, the exercise of school governance was viewed as a democratic process in which, by rotation, all certified teachers should participate. Beyond the plurality of motivations that were centred on school (Sanches, 1988), the decision to become a DC member without formal preparation was based on the personal capacity of "running the risk." Despite the pervasive affirmation that no one would qualify better than the teachers to perform the DC functions, a question was then raised: should all teachers take such a risk? Moreover, should school governance be considered as a new teacher's role? Reflection on this issue led a subject to think in the following terms: *I do not know if the rest of the teachers should risk it.... Before they come and prove themselves one does not know whether or not they are good (31, 2, M, A, SU).*

The data showed that the most frequent position among the subjects was that the teachers should be given the opportunity to "risk it" and "prove" themselves. Viewed from this angle, being able to take the risk and prove themselves represented part of the psychological component of the socialisation process of those teachers who decided to become school governors. Yet, implicitly, a dilemma arose in some subjects taught. A dilemma in terms of a potential opposition between the requirement of a specific leadership school governance profile on the one hand, and, on the other hand, a high value attributed to a school governance model because it is elective, representative of all school sectors, and participatory.

The Directive Council collegiality as a maturity setting

Three Directive Council structural features appeared to have created a specific leadership atmosphere: being generated through an electoral process, composed by a corpus of teachers, and characterised by a team approach to both task organisation and decision-making. Occurring in such an environment, the passage from novice to expert was indeed permeated by a pedagogical process that took place inside the collegial structure of the Directive Council. Presidential leadership practices, defined as the dominance of the Directive Council president in decision-making, were also found in some schools. However, when collegiality prevailed, a socialisation context was created that facilitated the novice member's organisational growth. Such a group approach to the DC novice's socialisation was illustrated by a DC president while describing how the electoral process had been organised in her school:

> When I started, three colleagues remained from the former DC team. It is very important that (school governance) continuity exists, otherwise it is a complication. Then, a problem was raised: who stays? And I said, I myself, again? I am not going because actually four new teachers were going to enter as when this DC started. One has to give lots of assistance. These last two years were much better because everybody was able to manage here by themselves. Initiating a team, all new again... not that! But someone has to go on! (016, 2, P, E, UR)

The collegial structure of the Directive Council team appeared then to be a significant context for the development of the novices to occur. As a subject reported, the presence of an "expert" in the DC team was viewed as a crucial condition for some teachers to become a DC team member. *"I told them (The other colleagues) that I would accept only if some of the actual DC members accepted. I would never risk to go with five colleagues without a previous administering experience" (108, 2, E, M, SU).*

Experiential learning and school governance practical knowledge

Socialisation in the school governance role was dominated by a learning-teaching process which became a source of enrichment of both personal interests and DC work meaningfulness. A DC president in a rural school stated his personal effort to becoming acquainted with the school legislation by saying

> How many times haven't I studied! I have my notes. But the school policies seem like a forest... In this way, I ended up learning about what I never had a great interest in before, that is the school law. (043, 1, P, E, RU).

A beginner DC, at the first year of her mandate, referred to her initial stage of experiential and continuing learning about school governance: *I recognise that I need to improve and learn more. I am at an initial stage of learning.* A more experienced subject documented a similar situation: *I have been lucky in the sense that I have acquired experience on my own throughout these years.* Revealing a somewhat different level of socialisation other subjects pointed out:

> Now I have acquired some experience. We learn
> at our own cost. With mistakes, with more trials
> and errors but always learning.

Another DC subject, in the second mandate, evaluated the progress he had made since the first year of experience as follows: *In fact, it is just after two years that one knows where to search for things, which law to apply, and that one becomes fully inside the school matters (47, 1, P, E, UR).*

School governance —
Temporary vision versus unlimited time vision

According to the law, the teachers remain in the Directive Council functions for a two years mandate if they are elected by the school faculty or, for a year only, if the DC is designated by the Ministry of Education. These school governance time frames influenced the DCs perspectives regarding school governance in ways that distinguished the keepers of the school status quo from the innovators.

Performing temporary functions appeared to lead the keepers of the school status quo to a restrictive attitude toward change. This group of subjects tended to present a short mandate as the basis for limiting their leadership role to keeping the school fiat going. External contingencies seemed to preclude them not only from using a longer range planning approach. Indeed, they appeared to feel a greater difficulty in dealing with environmental uncertainty and contingency. Taking initiatives that could exceed the legal time of the mandate appeared tied to a sense of futility. Furthermore, they tended to reveal a sense of negative organisational self-efficacy.

Even when changes were recognised as necessary, situational factors constituted established forces that were not worth the effort to face. As a DC member reflected: *and then we started thinking, is it worth while to introduce changes if we are going to leave this position?* A negative sense of efficacy in regard to innovation was revealed by some respondents:

> The situation I found when I became a DC member was like that and it has remained as it was before. There is no alternative to make changes (021, 1, P, A, UR).

> But changing all this! Only if all staff members were fired. We cannot modify certain aspects because we have not personnel enough, and that would interfere with so many things (31, 2, P, E, UR).

> It is not worth to make big changes because next year I am going to leave this position and another person will come and might disagree with my way, so, why should I be introducing changes? Running the risk of facing all these people in a big battle and, in the end..... if I win.... everything would come back to the previous situation (022, 2, P, E, UR).

II — THE IMPACT OF THE SCHOOL GOVERNANCE MACRO CONTEXT ON THE DIRECTIVE COUNCIL SOCIALISATION

Contextual structures of socialisation were both internal and exogenous to school: internal when referring to the impact of school faculty on the DCs role identification, and external when they concerned the impact of the hierarchical and formal nature of the interaction between school Directive Council and central instances. The data revealed that the DC members' maturity growth also occurred in reference to the macro-context represented by the Ministerial offices.

The organisational difficulties that a novice had to face were not expected to be overcome in the context of the school-ministry interaction, however. The initial dependence of the beginner DCs on the Ministerial Offices was not viewed as unsurmountable. It was assessed as a source of administrative inefficiency, however:

> It is superable but it is not efficient because you see in the first years those who have no experience at all, either they are wise enough by preparing themselves, actualising themselves, never taking risks, and if so, they are constantly asking the ministerial department's advice for what it is necessary to be done, asking this and that, or due to the huge bureaucratic machine, which the ministry really is, before we will hear from them and get the information... As a result, things run slowly, they are not solved as fast as they should be (11, 1, M, E, UR).

The limits imposed by the formal and vertical system were more evident in the keepers of the status quo than in the innovators. Although acknowledging constraints, the latter were prone to report independence in acting and initiating change. On the other hand, despite acting in a centralised school governance context, they had found the freedom to experiment, modernise, and expand the school frontier to community.

Sense of organisational powerlessness

Negative effects of the centralisation system regarded a slow problem-solving process, particularly in rural areas:

> Because there are certain aspects which surpass us. (....) and when the solution for the problem arrives, there is no need for the solution anymore because the appropriate timing is gone (29, 1, P, E, RU).

As a consequence, a sense of exclusion and isolation was associated with a sense of dependence on the Ministerial offices. A subject clearly stated a sense of futility while saying *we feel a bit powerless,* or as another subject put it, *they determine.... that is it.... they legislate and nobody explains anything.*

III — EFFECTS OF THE SCHOOL GOVERNANCE
EXPERIENCE ON TEACHERS

The assessment of their school governance practices and the meaning that the DC members attributed to the DC work were also objects of analysis and they are described below.

Self-actualisation and professional development

Feelings of personal enrichment were stated by some respondents, to the extent the school governance experience worked as a means to discover new self-efficacies and other dimensions of professional growth.

> The previous school governance experience was enriching, and it developed in me the taste for this. I discovered in me what, to a certain extent, I ignored, that is to say, my organisational capacity. (11, 1, P, E, UR).

> There were aspects which enriched myself, such as acquiring new knowledge, contacting people, having the need to deal with several matters, taking initiatives. As far as it concerns me, personally, I think I got the most out of it. (3, 1, E, M, RU).

The passage through the DC position constituted a way of changing the teachers' attitudes toward school, and enlarging their sense of professional responsibilities. Some DC members reported that the school governance experience would help them to become better teachers. Others portrayed former DC members as the most willing teachers to participate and have a greater activity in promoting school activities beyond teaching. Moreover, those teachers adopted a more collaborative attitude regarding the Directive Council itself. As a DC member noted, the teachers with school governance experience had changed their "way of being" in school, and they were the ones who contributed the most to achieve the educational mission set for the school.

> My perspective about school has changed a lot
> since I am here as a DC member, even as a teacher.
> Here, we develop a greater awareness of the
> existing student-teacher problems, for example.
> ...And, in the future, I am sure that, because of my
> experience here, I have the obligation to
> collaborate in a different way with the DC, what I
> would not feel if I had not become acquainted with
> the problems that do exist in this school (4, 1, M,
> E, RU).

Organisational self-efficacy assessment

A sense of organisational efficacy regarded specific areas of
school governance but it was also expressed in global terms.
Positive feelings of self-efficacy were intertwined with feelings of
work satisfaction. While evaluating her DC experience a DC
president said:

> In the beginning, I thought it would be more
> difficult than it actually is. I even thought I could
> not do it. ...My argument to refuse was that,
> between being a good teacher and a bad DC
> president, I preferred to be a good teacher. But,
> after all, I think that everything is running well.
> Yes I can say so. No doubt about it, I consider
> myself satisfied with the work I have accomplished
> (36, 2, P, A, SU).

Feelings of negative efficacy and isolation either from
ministerial instances or from faculty appeared usually associated with
dependence, inoperative problem solving, and in conjunction with
arguments that had to do with a low school budget and lack of school
autonomy, as it is illustrated below:

> Those problems I could not solve them due to
> Ministerial inefficiency. (...) I could not do that
> because we do not have material capacity... I have
> no budget... nobody has money, I am tired of
> asking, I keep asking, always asking (23, 1, P, E, UR)

The innovators differed from the improvisers regarding organisational self-efficacy. Feelings of negative efficacy outcome were more likely to emerge in the keepers of the school fiat than in the maximisers. Innovators tried to maximise resources. More modest accomplishments were reported by the improvisers who tended to use satisfying strategies predominantly. As a president said, the goals they had pursued were not completely achieved: *we have introduced some changes but not very dramatic. In fact, the big problems remain the same, they are still to be solved.* Viewed from a personal cost-benefit perspective, the DC experience tended to be more rewarding for those who had attained a greater organisational maturity. For these, the costs of involvement were minimised by exercising a leadership style composed of a greater sense of efficacy and organisational freedom to solve school problems.

In contrast to innovators, improviser DCs did not appear to be enthusiastic about their work accomplishments. A subject illustrates this position while saying that *this work of school governance is not gratifying; we get few fruits at the end of the academic year* (32, 1, P, E, UR). Feelings of much more to be done remained along with dissatisfaction concerning the results of their effort.

School governance retention factors

Retention in the school governance as an organisational outcome emerged from the interaction among the following main socialisation components: the desire to transmit the school governance practical knowledge, a sense of professional responsibility for ensuring school governance continuity, and a concern with school effectiveness.

> I have passed from one to the other (DC mandate), from the first to the second, because there was another college who had already passed, and also to have the opportunity to make use of my experience with those who come for the first time (25, 1, M, E, RU).

He was the only one who knew something about
school governance matters. so he felt compelled to
stay and help the others (06, 2, UR).

While integrating the novice in the DC structure, school
governance collegiality appeared to help both reduce the initial
organisational uncertainty of the novice members, and ensure a
certain margin of success along the socialisation cycle. On the one
hand, working as a team permitted the transmission of the
accumulated personal experience and practical knowledge about
school as an organisation. On the other hand, in contrast with the
ministry as a socialisation referent, the nature of the DC internal
context worked as a source of constant support and feedback. As a
consequence, the DCs organisational self-efficacy was either
developed or reaffirmed. A novice DC illustrates this double
socialisation perspective in the following way: *My DC colleagues
have been helping me in everything; there has been a true
camaraderie among all of us* (025, 2, M, E, RU). When
respondents reported both the organisational need for the personal
willingness to remain as a DC member, the socialisation process was
evaluated positively. A longer mandate was suggested on account of
personal, interpersonal, and work accomplishments. These
characteristics were typical of the innovators' group.

The interaction of personal and structural factors determined
the differential nature of the DC socialisation process and appeared
to be associated with the subjects' decision to remain or leave the DC
position. In this regard, collegiality and presidentialism represented
antithetical leadership practices.

Negative school governance experiences tended to be
associated with presidentialism in decision-making. A presidential
school governance leadership tended to be less frequently associated
to team cohesiveness than collegiality. On the contrary,
cohesiveness, made up of common school governance goals and
horizontality of interpersonal interaction among all DC members,
constituted powerful retention motives as is illustrated below.

As far as this DC team is concerned, we can work
together; this makes me feel sorry to leave the DC,

and it is something that might lead me to
continue... the expectations we had, the things we
are committed to, and which we have not finished
yet (12, 2, M, A, SU).

In some schools, the DCs put their efforts together around a
common school "theme" (Van Maanen, 1990). Indeed, a sense of
ownership regarding a pedagogical school project, conceptualised
and carried out in common, as well as the need to preserve its
continuation and spirit also led to school governance retention. As a
DC member in a suburban area of Lisbon said:

If we come to the conclusion that what we have
done might be lost, and if we see that there are no
guarantees that our work will be continued as we
would like to, I think it deserves our commitment
to remain as DC members (17, 2, M, E, SU).

In sum, collegiality practices, team cohesiveness, personal
and team commitment, and DC membership retention were main
school governance socialisation effects on teachers.

The meaning of the DC work

In congruence with the findings pertaining to the complex
nature of school governance motivation (Sanches, 1988), the
socialisation effects were dichotomised in two broad categories.
One regards the self and the other the school. At a personal level,
self-learning experience appeared as a major reward. Although the
worth of the DC experience was emphasised by all of the subjects,
they were nevertheless divided regarding the level of work
accomplishments. Evaluating school governance work in global
terms, a DC member said that *administering the school opens up a
whole world which we ignore when we teach classes only... that is
restrictive indeed.* In this view, school governance experience is
presented from a job perspective enrichment. It is something that
completes the professional life of the teacher. In sum, school
governance comes embedded in the professional career of teachers.

IV — PATTERNS OF ORGANISATIONAL MATURITY—THE INNOVATORS AND THE KEEPERS OF THE SCHOOL STATUS QUO

1. The Innovators

The analysis of data suggested that high maturity subjects tended to be defined by the following categories:

1. Sense of independence from the Ministerial directives.

2. Attitude of assertiveness in relation to some Ministerial policies.

3. A large vision concerning the school frontier.

4. A sense of future perspective concerning school planning.

5. A longer school governance experience.

6. Personal satisfaction regarding the outcomes of their work.

7. Feelings of recognition from the school actors.

8. A sense of organisational self-efficacy and accomplishment.

9. A positive attitude toward pedagogical innovation.

2. The Keepers of the School Status Quo

The moderate organisational maturity group was characterised by the following features:

1. A sense of dependence on the ministry support.

2. Need for clarification, particularly when taking initiatives that were not anticipated.

3. Passivity in relation to Ministerial policies, even when they disagree with them.

4.   A sense of conformity regarding the school administering status quo.

5.   A sense of powerlessness regarding school administration.

6.   A sense of uncertainty regarding the planning of school activities.

7.   Emphasis on bureaucratic rather than on pedagogical areas of school administration.

8.   A tendency to improvising as an administering problem-solving strategy.

9.   A tendency to maintaining the school organisational fiat.

Conclusion

Conceived as a democratic process, the entry in the DC position is understood as a right and a rotative process that should be opened to all teachers. The conditions of entry to a given occupation are crucial in the socialisation of its members. Secondary school teachers do not transfer into the new role a technical school governance expertise, in the sense that a prior formal education in school administration matters has not been provided or required till the present. As a result, initiation in the school DC role may be equated to a "sink-or-swim" (Lortie, 1975) approach. Yet, given the historical origin of features of the present school governance model (Sanches, 1987), one may say that the school governance socialisation process may be understood as a *continuous rather than a discontinuous framework* (Lortie, 1975, p.65).

Not all occupations influence novices to the same degree. Some organisations regulate the neophyte's experience in ways that are conducive to producing profound changes and to inculcating specific organisational cultures. When socialisation structures are strict, the novice's *culture orientation* tends to prevail and influence the novice's attitudes and organisational behaviour, as Lortie (1975) suggests.

Socialisation signified indeed a turning point in the novice's perceptions of self, school, and the new role itself. While looking at how successful the DCs perceived their role identification, data showed that initial feelings of inadequacy or doubts concerning self-efficacy tended to be reduced after a period of practical learning. The DC members who were less overwhelmed by bureaucratic requirements might have conceptualised school governance as a pedagogical role, although different from teaching. In fact, as one subject expressed it, *we fight everyday for making pedagogy to have priority over bureaucracy.* In this sense, for the innovators — those who attained a higher level of organisational maturity — the passage from the teaching to school governance role was not perceived as a dramatic change.

In conclusion, some points are to be emphasised in the socialisation cycle:

(a)   the relevance of the experiential and practical learning-teaching process within the collegial structure of the DC team;

(b)   the DC members' retention in the position as outcome of an enlarged sense of professionalism, collegiality, organisational cohesiveness and solidarity among the DC team members;

(c)   the development and enhancement of the DC's organisational self-efficacy along the process of socialisation, and the maturity growth in a continuum characterised by feelings of a greater independence, broadened vision of the school frontier and school ownership.

REFERENCES

Argyris, C. (1957)
  Personality and Organisation. New York: Harper & Row, Publishers

Argyris, C. and D. Schon (1978)
  Organisational Learning : A theory of action perspective. Reading, Mass: Addison-Wesley.

Bendura, A. (1986)
  Social foundation of thought and action : A social cognitive theory. Englewood Cliffs, NJ. Prentice Hall.

Hersey, P. and Blanchard, K. (1982)
  Management of organisational behavior : Utilizing human resources. Prentice-Hall, INC, Englewood Cliffs, New Jersey 07632.

Lortie, C.D. (1975)
  Schoolteacher : A sociological study. The University of Chicago Press.

Mclelland, D.C. et al (1953)
  The achievement motive. New York : Appleton-Century-Crofts.

Sanches, M.F.C. (1988)
  Teachers' school governance motivations : The role of organisational self-efficacy. In Jordana, R. (Ed). *Procedings of the 13th ATEE Conference,* II, pp209-228.

Van Maanen, J. (1990)
  Experiencing organisation : Notes on the meaning of careers and socialisation. In Van Maanen, J. (Ed) (c19977). *Organisational careers. Some new perspectives.* London; New York : John Wiley, UMI.

Van Maanen, J. and E.H. Schein (1977)
  Improving the quality of work life : Career development. In J.R. Hackman and J.L. Suttle (Ed). *Improving life at work.* Santa Monica, California : Goodyear.

VISIONS OF INSERVICE TRAINING

Kauko Hämäläinen
Armi Mikkola

Helsinki University, Finland

During the past two decades vocational further education in different sectors has increased rapidly. In Finland, for example, employers use about one per cent of the overall labour costs for the inservice training of their personnel. According to the estimates by the Ministry of Education the figure will be doubled in the next five years.

The quantitative growth of further education has been accepted as a self-evident fact, and no questions about the contents and quality of further education have been raised. In discussions concerning developments in vocational life, we can often hear arguments that this trend increases the amount of free-time, causes both unemployment and shortage of labour at the same time and divides the population into an educated elite and an ill-fated group of drop-outs from the labour market. Questions about the foundations of these arguments — what is really behind these changes and how can we control them — are left unpondered. We might well ask whether the users and planners of further education really know what we are doing, why and how and for whose benefit we are acting, i.e. what is the real function of further education?

The general debate about the future of adult education is marked by superficiality and lack of vision. As no one takes pains to analyse the state of the matter, new visions cannot be created. What everybody seems to have forgotten is that the future tasks of adult education cannot be fully understood without a deeper analysis of the changes going on in vocational life and in our social activities, what lies behind these changes and what are the alternatives for development. In other words, we must anticipate the future.

So far adult education, and especially vocational further education for adults, has been marked by constant development of new administrative and organisational models and laying emphasis on quantitative and financial problems. Evaluations about the need for further education often only list the wishes of the target group involved (cf. e.g. Oldroyd & Hall 1988). These things are also important, but they easily leave aside the future and basic values behind adult education.

1. Basic values behind further education

The basic values behind vocational further education are not a popular topic for discussion, be it due to lack of interest or ability. Tuomisto (1988) suggests that the reason might be an apparent freedom of values and taking things for granted. It seems that the planners as well as the target group of inservice training think that since the training is related to their work and gives them better professional qualifications, it is objective and has no values attached to it. It seems that the same kind of illusion that plagues the development of technology is at work here. Technical development is conceived as something driven by a "secret force," without taking into account that technical research and the application of new technical inventions if anything is based on values. In further education this means that the values for inservice training have been assimilated from outside, without questioning the sensibility and consequences of these values. The planners of inservice education usually don't stop to think about for whom, and what kind of education they are planning. Indeed, for whose benefit are they acting: the society's, the employer's, the people in inservice training, or when talking about schools; the students' benefit, or are they perhaps just looking after their own interests, or the interests of the organisation they work for?

Another reason for the lack of debate on values might be that education is only seen as a medium for achieving some concrete skill. Perhaps, factors like this lie behind the criticism that further education is incoherent, fragmentary and inconsistent with the aims of organisations.

Even though never mentioned in general debate, there certainly are basic values that affect vocational inservice training. If we take into consideration, for example, the definitions of the values governing further education by Finnish committees on adult education, we will notice that the greatest emphasis is laid on development needs that concern labour policy and the productivity of society and industry. Cultural, ethical and moral values, the values that affect peoples' private lives and social interactions, are left to lurk in the background. The same phenomenon can be seen in the inservice training within companies and organisations, as well as in the curricula of the institutions offering further education.

The demand for education follows this same trend. The most popular courses offered by the institutes of further education are those providing skills that can be instantly applied to every day work. On the other hand, extensive, interdisciplinary courses providing general education and knowledge on social changes are not thronged with students.

The question to be raised here is whether this point of view that lays stress on productivity and concrete needs of business and industry, as well as on international competitiveness, is in balance with other areas of human life? It might also be wise to consider the kind of future scenarios that these sets of values offer and where they might lead to.

People working in further education — teachers, researchers, planning officers, administrative personnel — are all influenced by values, whether consciously or unconsciously. All educational decision-making involves values, especially in setting the aims and choosing the content, and in the recruitment of personnel. When planning inservice training, what has to be determined is what are the qualities that people need for coping with the future tasks as employees, as citizens and as family members. It is a question of anticipating future society: what skills will be needed then and how we would like to influence that society today. (Hirsjärvi, S-Remes, P. 1986)

2. Basis for planning inservice training

The need for education may be considered from various points of view. The most common points of view are the following:

1. Needs and development plans of the employees.
2. Needs of organisations.
3. New information available.
4. Visions of future society and working conditions.

Part of the inservice training available is provided by outside organisations and establishments. In this case, the aim is usually to acquire new information from one's own professional field. Courses of this type enhancing professional competence in a concrete way seem to be the most popular.

Training of individual employees as well as groups working together is a necessary, but not an adequate prerequisite for the development of an organisation. From the point of view of an organisation, the training of different individuals and groups must be coherent and support the aims of the whole organisation.

The continuous increase of information, both quantitative and qualitative, in all fields of science — during the last few decades for example, in medicine, technology and the natural sciences — must be taken as one of the starting points for further education planning.

Comparing different visions and alternatives for the future, i.e. anticipating the future, is still a strange area for further education. Our connections with futurology are few and the use of research results in this area non-existent. Still, the future is present, without our noticing it. All the people involved in the planning of further education are in a constant flow of decisions and actions, shaped by unconscious visions of the future.

2.1 Employees' needs

The most common way to study the prevailing educational

needs is a survey among the people participating in training and schooling programmes. In Finland hundreds of such surveys have been conducted within different professions. These surveys help to find out things held in esteem and thus motivating them in their training.

The appraisals done by the employees are generally very conservative. People are only able to desire for things they already know. You cannot wish for something you know nothing about. The employees' wishes are usually very general in nature, like: more information on management skills, human relations or occupational psychology.

A model example of such a survey is Yrjönsuuri's research (1990) which studied teachers' conceptions of the adequacy of their schooling. According to the survey teachers felt they were well qualified to teach the subjects of their field. They also felt their teaching skills were good. However, they judged their abilities in social interaction poor. This may well be the reality, but the result may also have been influenced by the fact that teachers are simply not aware of the vast amount of new information available, for example in the fields of biology and physics; information that could raise the level of teaching considerably.

The teachers' satisfaction with their own teaching abilities may be a consequence of their lack of current knowledge. If they were familiar with the latest teaching methods, development of different cognitive functions, teaching gifted children, or with the use of computers in the classroom, they would probably have less reason for satisfaction. Defects in the command of one's own subject, as well as teaching methods do not necessarily reveal themselves in everyday work. Teaching can certainly be carried out relying on experience and time-honoured methods.

However, the discrepancy that instantly reveals itself, is in ability to interact. If the teacher has problems with the students, or easily runs into conflicts with his or her colleagues, problems may occur daily. No wonder if they are given special emphasis in the surveys on educational needs.

Another good example can be found from the medical profession. When doctors are asked what kind of new information they need most, they can name nothing that they haven't already heard of, in order to be able to judge it as important. A doctor cannot want more information on the use of laser in diagnosing cirrhosis of the liver, until he has heard of it.

2.2. Inservice training and organisation development

The principles that govern the running of an organisation should also be applied to inservice training. This means that one of the starting points for inservice training is that it should support the profitable activities of the organisation (see e.g. Helsilä, 1985).

Inservice training must be seen as part of all the activities of the organisation. The management may define the central goals of development and provide training and other activities for the personnel so that the goals can be achieved (see Robinson & Robinson, 1989). Often in large business organisations training that involves general management has been concentrated under the top management (Peltomäki, 1988). This way, a unity in the management system, corporate culture, and certain ways of thinking and acting common to the whole company can be pursued. It is becoming more and more common that the training units within companies operate under the direct control of the top management, who take an active role in the development of inservice training and see to it that adequate resources are allocated for it. This is how an educational organisation should also work.

An organisation-specific training strategy would create an ideal situation for using training as a medium to enhance productivity and the quality of work and the well-being of the personnel. The training strategy should be closely linked to other development projects within the company. In this way inservice training can be expected to increase the human resources available (Vaherva, 1985).

The most common way to set about improving working conditions is the appraisal of the present state of the organisation according to a certain set of criteria. A diagnosis of the organisation helps to pinpoint the factors that need changing to ensure that the aims of the organisation can be achieved. What may need improving are the knowledge and skills of the personnel in certain areas, common attitudes, abilities to interact, or human relations in general, clarifying goals and management practices. Defects in these areas could act as the starting point for the development of inservice training and also lead to other development projects.

As far as schools are concerned, typical starting points for the development of further education have been different kinds of school-specific surveys. For example, projects based on the OD-method and the effective school-movement are founded on a problem-oriented evaluation of present activities. Generally they lack any visions of the future. Once the area of development has been chosen, the available research material on the subject and experiences in other organisations should be studied and applied to one's own organisation. The issues that best promote the efficiency of the organisation should be chosen for further development. In sum, the choice should be based on the aims and future visions of the organisation.

The advantage of development based on the needs of the employees is that once the personnel evaluate their own activities, they usually commit themselves to the cause. Motivation is certainly stronger when a person can analyse his or her own work and participate in the evaluation and choice of the development areas.

The weaknesses are similar to those of the evaluation of personal needs. The personnel are usually only able to appraise the present situation on the basis of their previous knowledge about the organisation and the pressure for change that it is under. The personnel are unable to focus their attention on new information concerning the organisation. That is why organisational diagnoses should include, or be preceded by training that sheds light on new information and experiences from other organisations. In this way, new aims for the organisation can be set and the present activities evaluated in the light of the new objectives.

When evaluating the present activities of the organisation, it would also be wise to reflect future visions. This would ensure that the development would not only be confined to daily routine, but would bring new dimensions to work.

2.3 Visions of future as a starting point

In recent years a number of projects on the future of school have been launched all over the world. Seminars under the name "School 2000" seem to be especially popular. One of the major projects is probably School Year 2020 by Imtec, which has participants from more than ten countries. The problem with these projects is that more often they concentrate on criticising the present instead of offering alternatives for the future.

The following questions could set the guidelines for the future of further education and could well be presented jointly by the people working in further education and futurologists:

—   What kind of an idea do we have of our chances to predict and influence the future?

—   What is the course of future development? What changes are needed and what kind of factors affect the future?

—   What is our conception of the objectives of education now and in the future, and what is our conception of the human being?

—   How do we evaluate the future of education in comparison with, for example, work and free-time?

—   What is our conception of teaching in the future?
(see e.g. [Hirsjärvi, S-Remes, 1986]).

If the planners and teachers in further education looked for the answers to these questions in collaboration with future-oriented research, I believe that they would find clear and well-founded visions. This means that people in further education — planning officers, teachers, financiers and students — all have to be ready and willing to consider the values governing further education and to develop new methods of thinking.

The duty of educational planners is to encourage educands in inservice training to ponder the goals and future challenges of their organisation. So in the beginning of a long-term training period, appraisals based on visions of the future may serve as the basis for further training in the future. However, we must bear in mind that imaging a new reality may prove difficult, at least in the beginning. As attempts to renew some set ways of school planning, for example, to renew student evaluation, imaging new alternatives is accepted only up to a certain point.

The real difficulty is met when one should try to image oneself a larger entity, such as an institute of education, totally different from the present reality. What also may cause trouble is differentiating two kinds of visions of the future: visions about what is considered possible, and visions of what is considered desirable. A thorough perception of the future requires total detachment from present realities — an ability that should be encouraged in education. However, the most important is to try to live and act according to the challenges set by visions of the future. Thus, the visions must be conceived as challenges (Hirsjärvi, 1985).

The following factors should be taken into consideration when planning and carrying out training of directors of educational institutes and laying out development plans for schools: eventual changes in the status of the family, social problems, changes in youth culture, demographic developments, changes in the labour market, increasing international contacts and changes in values in general (see Hämäläinen & Mikkola, 1989).

Visions of the future can be looked at from many angles. I will give some examples of possible trends that may affect the school of the future. Examples can be used as a basis for discussing the future scenarios of further education. One trend may be the increasing social problems. Alongside with economic growth and higher living standards, unemployment will accompany shortage of labour, financial problems, crime, alcohol and drug abuse will stay on their present level or will increase. These factors together with inequality, alienation and isolation will put the school of the future in a situation more difficult and challenging than ever (see Antikainen, 1989).

Another trend is the changing status of the family. The family as an institution is losing its privilege of socialisation. Financial problems, questions of time (e.g. working overtime, business trips, parent's studies) and the loosening of family ties (families with one parent, increasing amount of co-educators outside the family) have their effect on the home. There are parents who haven't developed any models for values or roles, and thus cannot pass these to their children. In cases like this the only education a child receives is schooling (Mäki-Kulmala, 1989). Probably in the future schools are expected to show a stronger educative spirit and to get a firmer hold of the students, i.e. schools are expected to take greater responsibility of socialising the young.

The third trend is the growing importance of different youth groups, the youth cultures. As the young have increasingly more purchasing and consuming power the importance of entertainment and cultural industry in the socialisation of the young has grown tremendously. Material things may act as substitutes for social relations, and be the building material and indicator of one's identity. On the one hand, the new generation is more independent of the pressures of home, school and other authorities, and can freely build up its identity. On the other hand, the lack of housing and prolonged studies may also cause young people to be dependent on their parents for a longer time.

The attitudes of the young towards work and professional careers are changing. The intrinsic value of work and the models of career and success held in high esteem by the preceding generations have lost ground for the freedom of self-expression and leisure. If the value of work and belief in education lose their importance in the future — for which unemployment and polarisation of the labour market seem to lay foundations — the motivation and demand for education amongst the young may be marked by vast changes difficult to control (Maljojoki, 1987).

The models of thought and behaviour adopted from the youth cultures are in conflict with the expectations and institutional mechanisms of the school. For example, the language instruction at school still teaches usage of language that has very little in common with the students' conception of the world (Stafseng, 1989). Of course the youth cultures should not dictate the development of the educational system, however it would be wise to consider how school could cope with the problems characteristic to the youth cultures and important to the young (Jokinen, 1987). Will the school of the future be plagued by a clash of different cultures, or will these cultures just drift further apart? In any case, the school of the future will operate in an increasingly controversial and complex situation.

The fourth possible trend has to do with demographic developments. The internationalisation and integration going on right now in trade, industry and culture will probably have dramatic effects on migration. The importance of local, national, and international identity will change. The school must also turn into a multicultural institution (Antikainen, 1989).

The fifth trend is connected to the working life. The internationalisation of economy and business, changes in the structure of companies and the development of large corporations are the reality of tomorrow. Changes in working conditions and the use of computers have different effects on different professions. The service sector of the industries will grow stronger. How these and other changes affect education is hard to predict.

The fast changes in working life will mean that youth education will no longer correspond to the direct needs of the labour market. Adult education will increasingly meet the needs of the labour market with the help of periodical training (training-work-training-work). Hence, using the future career as a means of motivating the young works no more. On the other hand, for the unemployed, training or rather the lack of it will mean more and more often an implement of selection between employment and unemployment (Antikainen, 1989).

The trends I presented are complex but clearly show that the primary duty of the school in the future will be to create facilities that help the students to cope with everyday life and the life-long education. Access to the labour market can no longer be used as a motive and this will put the schools in a difficult situation. The structure and contents of both general and vocational education will change radically.

The skills needed for controlling one's own life alone, and especially mobility from one job to another, require wide basic education supported by further education. Both basic and further education should act as the forerunners of change, and not only react to changes already taking place. They should encourage the discovery of life-preserving ideas, creativity and innovation, and also, when necessary, suppress old, out-dated ideas.

3. Development trends for inservice training

The following will give an outline of what the future of inservice training could, or should be. After an examination of the relationship between research, training and work, a list of future scenarios for further education will be presented.

The common conception about training is that knowledge and information acquired through research is mediated to the students, who then apply them to their work. In many fields this model of thought has become out-dated. In rapidly developing fields the problem is how to keep up with new information (Schön, 1983). The distance with up-to-date information grows in two dimensions. The amount of knowledge to be applied in one's work increases all the time, and constant education is necessary in order to keep up with the flow. Also the level of knowledge and skills required in today's professions is getting higher. Work and the society set new demands on us constantly. This applies to all professions and jobs from cleaners to computer experts.

One of the most difficult problems within education is the connection between new information, theory and practice, which often greatly differ from each other. Research follows its own logic and so does practice. If practice is solely based on experience and individual methods, professional competence and basic general knowledge about one's own work are left undeveloped. This phenomenon is familiar both in basic and further education.

According to Schön (1983) these problems may be

understood with the help of the ideology of education described above. Development based on the application of knowledge and solving problems encountered in one's work with the knowledge gained in inservice training are not valid methods anymore. Basically, work means defining problems and defining your role in the process of how they came about and how they can be solved. It is not enough to acquire new information and to be able to solve problems; what is important is to perceive and define them. This is particularly difficult in cases when the working community is used to functioning in a certain way considered self-evident.

Thus, ready-made formulae in problem solving are not enough; work should become more and more like research. For perceiving, determining and solving problems, and drawing conclusions from them is what research is all about. Like research, also work demands increasingly the ability to perceive and conceptualise problems, to set them into frameworks and to study them in the light of theory (cf. Kolb, 1984).

According to Schön and Kolb educational planning requires a whole new outlook on the relationship of work and training, and on the learning abilities of people at work. For any changes to take place in working conditions, peoples' attitudes and beliefs about their own work must change. The aim must be an attitude marked by self-initiative and willingness to tackle problems. This can be achieved by developing an independent, professionally conscious mind which is also open to growth. Considering the resolutions and consequences of professional problems and attempting to understand one's own actions should be included in vocational inservice training. An example of this can be found in Engeström's (1988) report on developing the functions of a health centre.

Hence, training can no longer be restricted to satisfying the demand for education just by coming up with effective ways to mediate information. Neither can training adopt its goals, contents and methods directly from outside its own field (see Hämäläinen & Mikkola, 1989). It is not enough that training is composed of different kinds of "packages" of information, or modules of subjects and topics picked out by the planners: it should also consist of learning to analyse one's own work, applying new information and finally evaluating one's work in the light of it.

We cannot simply assume that the best solutions have already been found and are now passed on in inservice training. This is true in all fields of human activity, for example in management skills, corporate culture, or in the application of technical innovations. However, when teaching simple, basic facts, the old method of information emitted in only one direction does work.

When developing action and methods of work in a working community, training should be based on learning through work. Practical training alone does not suffice, theory should also be included in inservice training. Mediating should create conceptual systems which help the employee to understand different phenomena in his work. Instead of leading to adopting knowledge, training should facilitate adopting it into use. As the availability and amount of information increase and new information gets rapidly out-dated simultaneously, inservice training should focus on teaching general concepts and structures of information (Hämäläinen & Mikkola, 1989). However, to enable any practical changes the instructional contents should be connected with the real problems of everyday work. This can be achieved by drawing the examples used in teaching from the employee's own work.

The pattern of thought I described requires that inservice training not only teaches new knowledge and gives instruments for problematic situations, it should especially focus on the ability to perceive problems and to find a way to apply the acquired information in the problem-solving situation. The people participating in inservice training should concentrate on the analysis of the development needs in their work by making use of the new information and by applying this information to problematic situations. Also, the development analysis should be founded on visions of the future.

When considering the relationship between work and inservice training, the following factors should be considered:

— Inservice training should be closely related to work. The content of the training should cover the field and relevant problems in the work of the employee. The content of teaching should be future-oriented, i.e. lay the basis for the kinds of working methods that the employee and his company will be adopting in the future.

— Inservice training, both individual and training in groups, will take place in alternating periods. Already when signing a contract of employment the employer and the employee will agree upon the right for training and different training programmes.

— Practical experience and theoretical frameworks can be brought together by reflecting upon personal experiences of indifferent situations at work. The problem-oriented approach draws upon the experiences, feelings and thoughts of the personnel as a source, and as a receiver of information.

— More and more, inservice training will take place in groups, including in this way the whole personnel and the problems of the working community.

— The organisation and methods of inservice training will change and become more diverse.

— Inservice training will be relevant to the employees' work and take place in the company itself, not in a separate institution.

The integration of work and training requires employees' active participation in the planning, carrying out and evaluation of their training. In addition, changes are needed in the following areas of training:

— Theory will become more important in inservice training. The significance of theories and central conceptions will increase, as the perception of problems related to one's work require the ability of conceptualisation and seeing matters in the theoretical frameworks. The problem in inservice training is how to combine theory with practice.

— Teaching resources in inservice training will change their nature and focus. Teaching will be accompanied by diverse consultative methods, which is especially necessary when the training deals with the whole working community. This sets new challenges for the teachers who will function as groups of experts instead of lecturing individually. The working methods in the training will become more student-centered.

— Inservice training will cover longer periods of time. The people giving inservice training will be responsible for longer processes which include other services besides training.

Since stricter requirements will be set on the competence of the teachers, special attention has to be paid to teacher training.

The costs of inservice training will go up, as the training may require the presence of several experts at the same time and since various functions are related to the training (consulting and research, information and material services). Closer relationship between inservice training and working life and the rise in training costs will accentuate the problem of inequality in education, if the availability of inservice training for an individual employee depends on the employer and on the nature of contract between the employer and employee.

The institutions offering inservice training will become more numerous and diverse. As far as the clients of inservice are concerned, a risk in the future may be that training will be offered haphazardly and that new ideas and methods will be applied without thorough theoretical understanding of the foundations and consequences of these methods.

Considering visions of the future and making use of them requires great professional competence of the planners of inservice training. The fastest way to change and improvement is the inservice training of the planners of inservice training. It is the duty of the people in this field to keep up with the changes in this world

462

and to apply this knowledge into education, and at the same time give the people they are dealing with the tools to cope with and react to change by improving their ability to perceive and solve problems. If the institutes of further education are to meet the challenges they are faced with, they need to turn into institutes of the future. Both contextually and in their functions, the institutes of further education should act as the forerunners of change and set an example to other educational organisations.

463

REFERENCES

Antikainen, A. (1989)
Millaista tulevaisuutta varten kasvatamme? Kasvatus 1/1989.

Clarke, J. et al (1982)
Subcultures, Cultures and Class : A Theoretical Overview.
Hall, S. & Jefferson, T. (ed) Resistance through Rituals.
Essex : The Anchor Press Ltd.

Engeström, Y. (1988)
Reviiriorganisaatiosta kokonaispalveluun.
Rakennushallitus. Raportti 4, 1988.

Harman, W. (1976)
An incomplete guide to the future. San Francisco : San
Francisco Book Co.

Helsilä, M. (1985)
Tuloskeskeisyyttä henkilöstöhallintoon.

Hirsjärvi, S. & Remes, P. (1986)
Voidaanko tulevaisuuteen vaikuttaa? Koulutus ja
tietoyhteiskunta — tutkimuksen osaraportti. Jyväskylän
yliopisto. Kasvatustieteiden cutkimuslaitoksen
julkaisusarja A. Tutkimuksia 1.

Hämäläinen, K. and Kansanen, P. (1987)
*Tutkimuksen asema opettajien perus — ja
täydennyskoulutuksessa.* Kasvatus 5/1987.

Hämäläinen, K. and Mikkola, A. (1989)
Fortbildningens visioner — var finns de? Konferens om
det finsk-svenska samarbetet i lärarfortbildning. Uppsala,
22. — 24.11.1989.

Jokinen, K. (1987)
Nuorisokulttuurit ja koulutus. Esitelmä kolmansilla
valtakunnallisilla koulutustutkimuksen päivillä
Jyväskylässä, 21. — 23.10.1987.

464

Kivinen, O. and Rinne R. (1989)
Korkean tason koulutus remonttiin. Kommentti
Opetusministeriön 16.1.1989 päivättyyn muistioon
Koulutuksen kehittäminen. Opetusministeriö.

Kolb, D. (1984)
Experimental Learning. Englewood Cliffs : Prentice-Hall.

Larsen-Freeman, D. (1986)
Techniques and principles in language teaching. Oxford : OUP.

Maljojoki, P. (1987)
*Yhteiskuntakehitys ja nuorten koulutuksen kysyntä —
kuljemmeko koulutusoptimismistä koulutuspessimismiin?*
Kasvatus 2/1987.

Mäki-Kulmala, A. (1989)
Alussa oli kasvatus — kasvatus on vasta alussa.
Nourisotutkimus 1/1989.

Oldroyd, D. and Hall, V. (1988)
Managing professional development and inset. A
handbook for schools and colleges. Bristol : NDC SMT.

Peltomäki, A. (1988)
Tuloksellinen koulutus. Aavarantasarja 9. Turku.

Robinson & Robinson (1989)
Training for impact. London : Jossey-Bass.

Schön, D.A. (1983)
The reflective practitioner. New York : Basic Books.

Stafseng, O. (1989)
Youth culture and language socialisation. Working Papers,
No.241. Institute of Sociology. University of Oslo.

Tuomisto, J. (1988)
Aikuiskoulutuksen arvolähtökohtien tarkastelua.
Aikuiskasvatus 1/1988.

EDUCATION OF MENTALLY RETARDED PUPILS IN THE COMPREHENSIVE SCHOOL IN SWEDEN

Inge Carlström and Lena-Pia Hagman

Kristianstad University College, Kristianstad, Sweden

1. BACKGROUND AND AIMS OF THE PROJECT

The Swedish National Board of Education gave us the commission to describe and analyse the school situation for mentally retarded children and adolescents who are educated within the comprehensive school system. Integration of this kind is occurring all over Sweden and seems to get more and more common. However, as one of our preliminary studies showed, this aim also means that many questions have to be solved (Carlström & Lindholm, 1986).

With this in mind the aims of the project have been formulated as follows:

- to describe how the education of mentally retarded pupils is/could be carried out within the comprehensive school;

- to throw light upon "critical factors" connected to this educational situation, that is factors which may have positive or negative effects on the pupils.

The project consists of two studies differing from each other in character. In this summary they will be referred to as Study A and Study B, respectively. (Carlström & Hagman, 1989a, b).

The research questions of the two studies have been defined more narrowly as follows.

Study A

- How can the school situation be described during one year for a group of mentally retarded pupils who get their education in the comprehensive school?

- What attitudes to the education of these pupils characterise the school staff at the schools in question?

Study B

- What experiences and attitudes to the education of mentally retarded pupils do the following three groups have?

  — Chief administrators of the County Councils responsible for the education of mentally retarded children and adolescents.

  — Administrators of the County School Boards ("länsskolnämnd") responsible for educational matters of the same kind.

  — Head masters in the comprehensive school.

The plan for the whole project — Study A and B — is shown below.

Year 1

Three counties were selected to participate in the project, namely the counties of Jönköping, Kopparberg, and Jämtland. Interviews with chief administrators showed that in these counties —

  — there was an interest in participating in the project;

  — there were schools suitable for our studies;

  — the integration strivings had reached a point suitable for the project;

—   the relations between the school authorities were without greater problems;

—   there was willingness to support the project by appointing a "field leader" for the practical project work.

During the first year we visited each county a couple of times to select schools and pupils.   The final selections were guided by three criteria, namely:

1.   The education of mentally retarded pupils should be established, that has been going on for some years.

2.   The school management as well as the teachers should be positive to participation in the project.

3.   For practical reasons the schools should not be scattered too much geographically.   (To make the field leader's work easier — some of the counties are quite large).

Year 2

This year was the data collection year.

Study A

These data aimed at describing the practical school situation for the retarded children and was collected mainly by the field leader. Observations were also made by us as project leaders when we visited the schools.   Different methods were used to get as deep and diversified knowledge as possible.

Study B

Data was collected by questionnaires to:

—   chief administrators responsible for the education of mentally retarded children and adolescents at all the County Councils in Sweden.

468

—   Administrators with the same kind of responsibility at all the County School Boards in Sweden.

—   Head masters in some comprehensive schools in the three selected counties (see above).

Year 3

Treatment of data and final documentation.

2. STUDY A AND B : MORE DETAILED DESCRIPTION OF THE DESIGN

2.1 Study A — The field study

21 pupils were selected for this study (see Table 1 below).

TABLE 1.   Survey of the pupils of Study A

School Level		Boys	Girls	Total
First Level	(grades 1-3)	2	5	7
Second Level	(grades 4-6)	5	2	7
Third Level	(grades 7-9)	4	3	7
TOTAL		11	10	21

As can be seen above, the pupils are evenly distributed among the three grade levels. The sex distribution is even as well. Since we are interested in the group of pupils as a whole, the minor differences between the sexes within each grade level are considered to be of minor importance.

The data collection methods used by the field leader were as follows:

•   Pupil records from the school (summarising information

from conferences and meetings concerning the pupil, from psychological investigations concerning him/her and so on).

• School development programmes for the pupils (defining goals for his/her development in the school situation, pedagogical and methodological methods to reach these goals, evaluation of the outcomes and so on. Such developmental programmes were not used in all our schools (although recommended in the Swedish Curriculum Plan). In some cases we therefore gave practical suggestions concerning the design and use of such a programme.

• "Diary" records according to a simple outline.

• Interviews with the members of the school staff who had profound experiences of the pupil in question (class teacher, special teacher, psychologist, headmaster and so on).

• Observations by the field leader when he/she visited the schools. These observations were made in a rather informal manner and mainly focused critical aspects of pupil change from one visit to another.

2.2 Study B — The survey study

The target group of the survey study is shown below:

TABLE 2. The Survey Study Group

Group	Number	Dropout	Total
1. Chief administrators responsible for the education of mentally retarded children and adolescents at all the County Councils in Sweden.	30	7	23
2. Administrators with the same kind of responsibility at all the County School Boards in Sweden.	24	5	19
3. Headmasters in Comprehensive Schools in the three Counties under study.	33	—	33
TOTAL	**87**	**12**	**75**

The dropout rate for groups 1 and 2 are 23 and 21%, respectively. The reason for this was in most cases said to be lack of time for a questionnaire of this rather elaborate kind.

In general, the persons who did answer it gave exhaustive answers. However, we have to be somewhat careful when generalising the results to the whole country. We also want to point out again the rather "visionary" aspects of the questionnaire. We did not ask for field descriptions of the situation right now, but about attitudes and suggestions for the future. The questions concerned pedagogical and methodological matters, organisation and resources, inservice training of the teachers and relations between parents and school.

The data collected are mostly of a qualitative kind. The data of study A were categorised and condensed into "case studies" for each pupil according to the following themes:

—   *Background*

—   *The situation during the autumn term*
     socially/emotionally
     academically

—   *The situation during the spring term*
     same aspects as above

—   *Critical factors of the pupil's environment*
     organisation/administration
      resources
     pedagogical/methodological factors
     inservice training
     home-school relationship

3. RESULTS

This chapter will give a summary of the most evident results from study A and B. We also discuss some practical suggestions for the future concerning the education of mentally retarded children in the Swedish comprehensive school.

3.1 Emotional and social aspects

Puberty can make these pupils more insecure of themselves. This often happens to normally gifted children as well which we all know. In the case of mentally retarded children, however, their feelings of insufficiency may to a greater degree be linked to the growing insight that they are different, that they "do not belong." This interpretation is supported by some of the teachers as well. But there are also a few examples of positive development, i.e. signs of growing openness and self security.

The teachers often complain of weak powers of endurance in the pupils as well as of concentration difficulties. The tenseness that may be shown is mostly ascribed to their working on "top level" most of the time. According to the teachers there is a great risk that the pupils get used to the feeling of "not understanding" the work they do or what is said in the classroom.

On the social side no mobbing in the deeper meaning of the term is reported, although teasing and nagging are admitted in some cases. The general impression is that the retarded pupils are accepted, not much more. They are not rejected, but they are not welcomed into the fellow circle either.

The boys in our group seem to have a somewhat easier social situation than the girls because of their interest in sports which they share with their normally gifted class-mates. As is well known, girls of the corresponding ages favour friendship with just one or perhaps two "best friends." These contacts are mostly verbal in nature, why it is easy to see the inferiority of retarded girls in this respect.

The staff at the schools seem to be very well aware of the social problems of their mentally retarded pupils. The trend is that they give priority to social matters before academic ones.

Generally speaking, one gets the picture of some social and emotional positive development over the school year although it is a slow one. For example, there are some teachers who tell that their retarded pupils have become more ready to initiate contacts with their class mates and that they are met with a growing acceptance as well.

3.2. Academic achievement

Not surprisingly, the pupils find the theoretical subjects most difficult, especially Swedish, English and maths. The social sciences may get increasingly difficult as well. Time concepts and mathematical concepts are also hard to understand for many pupils.

The pupils generally get most of their training in Swedish, English and maths by the special teacher, alone or in a small group. Some of them do not take enough responsibility for their school work. They do not arrive in time for lessons, forget their books or to do their homework and so on. Family cooperation and support is badly needed also in this respect, teachers say.

The pupils are often described as rather quiet in the classroom. Many of them seem to do their work rather mechanically. How much do they really understand? The teachers ask. How much is just adaptation to class norms?

In the written "development programmes" abstract aims like responsibility, active listening, better concentration, and less carelessness are as common as the more academic goals like being able to read and write acceptably. Teachers also very often stress that they have to build on the pupil's strong sides and not confine their work to the weak ones.

Although the development over the year is irregular and consisting of many ups and downs, the overall direction seems to be weakly positive. "The development is positive in relation to the pupil's level" is a frequent expression from the school staff.

3.3 Which pedagogical conditions should be fulfilled?

According to correspondent groups the most important qualifications of the school staff are:

— positive attitudes to integration and willingness to work for it

— competence

— motivation.

A very common view is that the retarded pupil's total situation has to be considered. It is necessary to know the emotional and social qualities of the pupil and not only the cognitive ones. It is important that many views from the different perspectives of the school staff influence a developmental programme. In that way you get a more exhaustive and detailed picture of the retarded pupils' needs and possibilities.

When thinking along these lines, it stands clear that a pupil's total situation (home-school-leisure time) means varying kinds of influence as well. Therefore, communication and cooperation between these sectors of the pupil's life should be something to strive for as is pointed out in our data.

We now turn to the more practical pedagogical and methodological views expressed in the data material.

Here we find many demands for more varied working forms in the classroom. Since the teaching should work against segregation of the retarded pupils, it should not be confined to traditional teacher dominated lessons (lectures, teacher question — pupil answer). A narrow teacher strategy like that is hardly compatible with the individualisation strivings which many representatives of our groups find so necessary. Instead, pupil activating and flexible working methods are suggested. Group work is widely used and the experiences concerning the retarded pupils generally seem positive. (Some teachers point out, however, that you have to plan the group composition extra carefully in these cases).

Laborative practical work is proposed, mostly in the natural sciences though. In our opinion, however, laborative working methods could be used in the social sciences as well. Like some people in our studies say — active working methods benefit all pupils.

Generally, there seems to be strivings to keep the retarded pupil as much as possible in the classroom with his/her classmates. Still, we know from our observations and visits that some pupils spend the greater part of their school week alone with the special teacher. Naturally, it is difficult to talk about "integration" in its deeper social meaning if the pupil only sporadically meets any classmates to socialise with. So, it is important to balance the time in class with the time separated from class in a conscious way.

Drama and role playing are suggested as alternative working methods in the classroom, since they stimulate sides of the pupil other than the cognitive ones. There is evidence from some teachers that drama helps to make retarded pupils more spontaneous and sure of themselves.

The importance of adapting the teaching methods as well as the concrete teaching material to the level of the pupil is frequently stressed. Some teachers construct their own material, some use material from the lower grades.

The possibility of adapted studies in a wider meaning is shown as well. For example, some pupils in our study exchanged English for lessons in Swedish or maths.

Teachers who have a mentally retarded pupil in their class often point out that this needs extra planning. Therefore, extra resources are demanded.

Finally, it is emphasised that teachers who work with retarded pupils must have positive attitudes to their work, i.e. to integration. Patience, love and tolerance are other examples of frequently named teacher qualities. Not less important is, of course, a positive school management.

3.4 Organisation and administration

Up till now, the comprehensive school and the schools for

mentally retarded pupils have belonged to different administrative authorities in Sweden. The local commune has the responsibility for the ordinary comprehensive schools while the special schools for mentally retarded pupils answer to the county council.

The official ambition is, however, that the communal authorities take over the responsibility for the education of the mentally retarded pupils as well. This striving is in line with the general decentralisation trends in Sweden. A governmental commission is working on this issue at present.

The results of both our studies generally indicate an accepting or even positive attitude to a common communal authority for both school systems. Still, many questions are raised. What will a communal management mean to the teachers in the special schools and what will it mean to the kind of specialised competence they have? How will the school situation change for the retarded children? Many of the respondents also point out that the reform must not be hurried on too fast.

The respondents in the survey study also suggested some *integration models* for the education of retarded children and adolescents.

First — and this is very important — they often stress that there is not just one model suitable for all pupils. We do agree on that. Instead, there has to be flexibility and even fantasy some times.

With this in mind we can distinguish at least the following models ranked according to frequency of suggestions:

1. One mentally retarded pupil in an ordinary class in the comprehensive school (what we generally call individual integration).

2. A group (perhaps 3-4) of retarded children are integrated in an ordinary school class ("group integration").

3. A group of retarded children and slow learners are taught together in some subjects, perhaps Swedish and maths. On

these occasions they are separated from their ordinary classes and (often) taught by a special teacher. This model may be especially suitable for grades 7-9.

4.   Retarded pupils belong to a special class located at a comprehensive school ("local integration").

When discussing the future role of the special schools, respondents point out the importance of using the staff competence there in wise ways, even though the communal authorities take over the responsibility for this school system.

3.5 Resources

Some administrative resources for the education of the integrated pupils are suggested. A suitable class must be chosen with reference to the composition of children as well as the number of children. A relatively common recommendation is 15-20 pupils. Other respondents mean, however, that the actual number of children is much less important than the class structure itself.

Generally speaking, it is considered important that the school where a pupil is integrated can collaborate with and learn from special schools for mentally retarded children. The following conclusions can be drawn regarding the kinds of consultative resources that are suggested.

Teachers at the special school should advise their colleagues at the comprehensive school on methodological questions and educational material. They should also be of help in the work with developmental programmes for the integrated pupils.

The practice that a teacher from the special school visits the comprehensive school — perhaps a couple of times every week — generally gets positive comments. It is pointed out, however, that this assistance must be used in a flexible way. There seems to be a risk that the "7 hours a week assistance," from the special school, which an integrated child automatically is entitled to in Sweden, sometimes could be used in a more effective way.

The pupil assistant is another educational resource in the comprehensive school. The assistant is regarded as a great help. According to some respondents, however, there may be a risk that the bond between the assistant and the integrated pupil grows too strong. It is also seen as advisable that the teacher now and then exchanges his/her teaching tasks with those of the assistant or the special teacher. In this way it will be easier for the teacher to get a good opinion of the integrated pupil's total situation in the class.

For the time being most pupil assistants are untrained for their task. Consequently, it is often pointed out that they should get satisfactory training. Qualification as a pre-school teacher is one suggestion.

The assistant's task is to give pedagogical stimulation and support to the integrated child in the everyday school situation but also to be an informant of the child's needs and wants, for example in the work with developmental programmes. As we noted above, the assistant could be of great help regarding the other pupils in the class as well. Some examples are also given that the assistant spend some leisure time with the pupil, to take him/her to the cinema and so on.

Very often the retarded children need some other special training like speech training and physical training. Sometimes this kind of support can be given by the special teacher, in other cases other specialists are needed.

Time resources are also discussed in both our studies. A general view is that more time is needed for the class teacher (as well as the special teacher) to plan the work with the integrated pupil, to carry through and evaluate developmental programmes and so on.

Finally, the girls and boys in the class as a whole make a very important resource as regards the integrated pupil. As a few in our studies point out, everyone in the class has a responsibility to create a positive atmosphere there.

3.6 Inservice training

Questions about inservice training in special education and

integration raised a lot of interest in our studies.

The following subjects are suggested for inservice training:

- knowledge about different kinds of handicap;

- developmental psychology (for example perceptual and motor development, identity development);

- personality psychology;

- learning difficulties in reading, writing and mathematics;

- developmental work in school (how to start a developmental project);

- methods in special education (for example how to make developmental programmes for pupils);

- flexible ways of working in the class (for example training in laborative working methods).

There is a demand for introductory courses (minimum 2 days) for teachers who are going to have integrated pupils in their class in the year to come. Moreover, short recurring courses for teachers and headmasters are needed as well. Some respondents in our studies have the opinion that the whole school staff must be better informed than the case is today, since all of them share a responsibility for the pupils in their school.

The inservice training should preferably be given by consultative personnel — teachers — from the schools for mentally retarded children.

Finally — but not less important — is the demand for more satisfactory training in special education within the ordinary teacher training programmes at the Teacher Colleges.

3.7 Relations between parents and school

School staff as well as parents strongly emphasise the need of early information and discussions concerning the integrated child. What are the child's possibilities, problems? How can the school help and support?

Frequent contacts between parents and school are necessary and should be taken continuously during the school years. Natural contact persons in comprehensive school are the child's class teacher or special teacher, but sometimes other persons may be suitable. A "contact plan" is suggested.

"When the retarded children in our study started comprehensive school, the relations between parents and school often seemed to be rather bad." Most often this could be ascribed to insufficient information from the school in question. In all the cases we studied, however, the relations gradually had become much better.

Parents wanted the school staff to give straightforward and honest information — even if it could be painful. They meant that adequate information about their child's school situation strongly contributed to make the whole family more secure.

Some respondents wished for a better cooperation between the parents of integrated children as well. By sharing experiences their parent role could be made easier and the actions for the good of their children made more efficient.

Teachers sometimes expressed the view that some parents had very unrealistic expectations of their retarded child. This means, among other things, that purely verbal school information may not be enough in all cases. Parents should, therefore, participate in more concrete ways in their child's school situation to get a better understanding of what is happening.

Respondents consequently point out the value of parent participation in making developmental programmes, conferences and meetings. Help with the homework as well as a generally supporting attitude to school are positive factors too. Perhaps parents and school could collaborate somewhat more regarding the child's leisure time activities as well?

The attitudes of the school staff to the parents appeared generally positive. Most of them seemed to agree with the following teacher remark: "Parents should be considered a great resource in the integration work."

REFERENCES

Carlström, I. & Lindholm, L-P.
Problem vid undervisning av utvecklingsstörda elever i grundskolan. Ett utredningsuppdrag för Skolöverstyrelsen. Forum för pedagogisk orientering och debatt, Nr. 21. Kristianstad: Högskolan, 1986.

Carlström, I. & Hagman, L-.P.
Undervisning av utvecklingsstörda elever i grundskolan. Redovisning av fälterfarenheter. Pedagogisk metodisk utveckling, Nr.112. Kristianstad: Högskolan, 1989a.

Carlström, I. & Hagman, L-P.
Undervisning av utvecklingsstörda elever i grundskolan. Synpunkter från särskolchefer, ansvariga på länsskolnämnder samt rektorer i grundskolan. Pedagogisk metodisk utveckling, Nr.109. Kristianstad: Högskolan, 1989b.

Carlström, I. & Hagman, L-P.
Education of mentally retarded pupils in the Comprehensive School in Sweden. A summary of a research project. Pedagogisk metodisk Utveckling, Nr.116. Kristianstad: Högskolan, 1990.

THE EUROPEAN DIMENSION IN THE EDUCATION
AND TRAINING OF FOREIGN LANGUAGE TEACHERS

Gerard M. Willems

Centre for International Education, Netherlands

"Moving forward to the twenty-first century with a pedagogy largely fashioned in the nineteenth is, at best, open to question. What is called for is not simply pedagogy but multi-cultural pedagogy" (Bell, 1990)

"A Burmese student struggling with French confided that: "Pour moi, le mot *'je'* manque de précision" .... For him, French was a clumsy instrument for the expression of social relationships .... "(Riley, 1989).

"....as each individual must be able to look at another culture, another way of thinking and working, so we begin the process of redefinition of how we look at the rest of the world..." (David Coyne in his key-note lecture at ATEE's 1990 Conference in Limerick).

."...rationality is a cultural variable. ...we must beware of cross-cultural value judgements: who are we to say that we are more civilised than the Romans?" (Riley, 1984).

1. Introduction

Foreign language teaching in the Netherlands is in trouble (Willems, 1987; van Els 1990). Forces are being mobilised to tackle the problems. During a national language congress in the Spring of

1990 organised by, amongst others, the brand-new Foundation for the Advancement of Foreign Language Teaching (a clear sign of how serious matters are!), the Minister for Education was officially handed a rather disquieting survey of foreign language teaching in the Netherlands entitled: *Horizon Taal.* It is critical of the quality, efficiency, purposefulness and spread of foreign language teaching. The Minister's reaction was clear: foreign language teaching must be improved. This should preferably not be achieved by raising the number of teaching hours as finances will not be forthcoming, but by raising its effectiveness and efficiency.

Also the unification of Europe at grassroots level is facing problems which, perhaps, are even bigger than those at the top. The latter will eventually be overcome, if only because of economic necessity. However, work towards a solution of the problems at the basis of the European Community has hardly started yet. Only recently does the bottom-up process of establishing empathy with Europe and a sense of European citizenship in our youth through education, seem to have become a serious issue in Brussels. Ignorance among the young of other ways of living and other forms of social interaction in the various national and speech communities of Europe is a marvellous breeding ground for ethnocentrism and mutual stereotyping. Such stereotypes may have a long-lasting influence on a naïve and undeveloped mind if education does not provide an antidote. If we want a European sense of belonging to develop, and at the moment one has to look high and low to find a trace of one, education will have to take on the responsibility for promulgating, even promoting "European-ness."

This paper attempts to create a link between these two problems. A shift in emphasis in foreign language teaching from form-oriented to more communication-oriented work should make teaching more efficient and effective, and also, at the same time, offer the chance of introducing a European dimension into language teaching. This means that language teachers, more responsibly and knowledgeably than was the case in the past, will give shape to a kind of intercultural language education in which the unique ways of communicating in the various European communities are highlighted. If done in the right way, this could stimulate in our youth an awareness of their own culture and respect for the culture of other speech communities and nations with which, before long, we will form a political and monetary union. Below, an attempt will be made to elucidate this idea. This can best be done by first looking at a few problems.

II. Definition of the problems

1.   In order to develop into the United States of Europe it is of the utmost importance for Europe that its inhabitants speak several, but at least two, of its languages. This mastery will have to be mainly oral (receptive and productive), however important written command may be in commerce and industry. In the context of the development of what has come to be called "la citoyenneté Européenne" in Brussels, oral command of one or more foreign languages is of supreme importance. That this view is shared in policy-making circles in Brussels becomes apparent when we look at programmes like ERASMUS and LINGUA, which are meant to offer tomorrow's European intelligentsia a chance to learn foreign languages and become acquainted with other ways of looking at life.

        In spite of much lip-service paid to the importance of the development of oral proficiency in foreign language teaching, this aspect of linguistic skill has never had any real priority in the foreign language classes in the Netherlands and other European countries for a number of reasons, which will not be dealt with here. Reading skills still form the nucleus of the national examination of linguistic skills. The testing of oral communicative skills (which are usually interpreted as meaning: speaking skills) is left to the schools themselves. Somehow the emphasis in language teaching policy will have to be shifted. This will not prove easy.

2.   Even if the tradition in foreign language teaching could be influenced to such an extent that oral communicative skills would become the focus of learning, it would prove impossible to prepare the learners, in the time allowed (4-6 years), for all the situations in which they may

be called upon to function in the foreign language later. Therefore, we shall have to help and stimulate them to make as efficient and effective use as they can of what language command they have acquired in school. In other words we shall have to help them develop their strategic competence in order to compensate for shortcomings in their language proficiency and to stimulate their ability to negotiate meaning appropriately. Too little attention is paid to this aspect of language command at present.

3.   One of the most frustrating consequences of an inadequate command of a language is the fact that one cannot play the desired role in communicating with speakers of that language. In order to be able to do this one must dispose of a set of interactional routines. During exchanges of staff and pupils between schools, which are strongly stimulated at present, learners may find themselves staying in families abroad. Pupils will subsequently need to be able to function discursively on a different level from the one they naturally use in their peer-group. Classroom teaching, generally speaking, does not pay sufficient attention to the discourse routines they are then in need of (Faerch et al, 1984). If these routines are sufficiently automatised, they may not only enable the speaker to play the desired role in the interaction, they also give him* time to activate his (socio) linguistic competence. Moreover, as research suggests, they also play a stimulating role in the language acquisition process (Hatch, 1983).

4.   The European 'spirit' is hardly evident in large sections of the population of the European states. A lot of stereotyping of each other's cultures is at the basis of a lot of jokes that are bandied about, and the emotions engendered by international football championships could hardly be considered a sound basis for generating new feelings of European solidarity. Personal and socio-cultural filters prevent us from seeing the other culture in its true perspective. These filters consist of criteria which we have developed ourselves or which have been instilled in us by the socio-cultural group to which we belong. They find

their origin in unpleasant personal experiences or in historical events that have determined the present political or economic situation. They cause us to find certain things normal or good and others strange or even wrong. These attributive concepts are handed on to our own cultural surroundings as characteristic of the other culture. The problem is that the other culture is not given a fair deal as incompleteness in the information is accepted. Thus, the image we have, or get, of the other culture is warped. We then proceed to generalise on the basis of such partial and incomplete information to our heart's content. Feelings of solidarity with the other culture become difficult if not impossible.

Foreign language teaching can contribute to counteracting such undesirable trends, which are so frustrating for European unification. Of central importance here is the development of a sensitivity in the learner for the otherness of the other culture through an emphasis on the different ways in which the other speech community generally reacts to life and "does things with words" (differences in discourse regulation and speech-act realisation). An important aspect of this sensitivisation is the development of the above-mentioned strategic competence (and a meta-communicative awareness of this competence) during the learning process. This competence helps the learner to learn to negotiate meaning and to help himself when his (socio) linguistic competence is inadequate or lets him down. The meaning that is negotiated in international discourse is full of cultural pitfalls, and misunderstandings are lying in ambush. A sensitivity to possibilities and possible problems coupled with a linguistic capability to negotiate meaning are of great importance for successful intercultural communication. An insight into the way in which foreign language discourse is regulated guides the learner into the quintessence of the otherness of the other culture. Superficial stereotyping on the basis of practical knowledge may thus be discouraged. The learner may be induced to put his own culture in perspective instead of considering it the absolute norm by which everything else has to be judged. The problem is, of course, that in our curricula hardly any attention is paid to aspects of communicative competence like this. Oral discourse, at best, comes at the bottom of the list of proficiency requirements, and consciousness-raising concerning discourse phenomena seems out of the question.

5. 	At present, it is only geography and history teachers and, exceptionally, economics teachers who, in the course of their training, are brought into contact with Europe's unification process in some of its facets. In view of the importance of foreign language teaching for the success of this process, language teachers, too, will have to be given a thorough introduction to "Europe." They need this in order to cooperate with their geography and history colleagues in school projects. For the time being, however, such introductions do not yet feature very largely in language teacher education curricula in the Netherlands nor elsewhere in Europe.

III. Implications for language teacher education

1. 	In the light of the above-mentioned problem areas we will have to devote explicit attention in pre and inservice language teacher education, to discourse phenomena and speech-act realisation. Both of these reveal how people use their meaning potential in their particular culture-specific way. Also, as suggested above, concentrating on the formulaic nature of speech-acts and discourse regulation is an effective way of setting about language teaching. In writing the foreign language teacher education curriculum it is just as indispensable to pay careful attention to the regulation of oral interaction as to the morpho-syntactic properties of the foreign language. If we wish to introduce the European context into language teaching this regulation, with its socio cultural and meta-cognitive basis, can no longer be ignored. Raising the learner's consciousness of the "grammar" of oral interaction must no longer be left to chance as has been done for so long in the past.

To be sure, the acquisition of pragmatic and discoursal skills in the foreign language was, and still is, guaranteed here and there in teacher education by offering the student an extended stay in the target language country. The chances of being allowed such a stay, however, are slim for the individual student, even today in the age of programmes like ERASMUS and LINGUA. Such a stay, however, is of the greatest importance for the language teacher to help him develop an insight into the regulation of foreign language discourse and give him an opportunity of becoming skilled in its manipulation. Policy makers in Brussels seem to underscore such a statement with their LINGUA programme. However, the length of the LINGUA stay abroad (3-6 months) appears a major obstacle for most teacher education institutes, as their profession-oriented programmes cannot easily accommodate such a long absence of the student (Bruce, 1990). Shorter (too short?) stays of just one month are now being considered. Therefore, a raising of the student's awareness of discourse and speech-act conventions and formulas is necessary. No less so for those students who are lucky enough to be allowed a lengthy stay abroad. For they may pick up an easy fluency in the foreign language during such a stay (invaluable in itself as this may be!), but it seems naive to expect them to go in for sufficient reflection on pragmatic and discourse differences between mother-tongue and foreign language. This is as unwarranted as expecting foreign language learners in a natural acquisition situation, and without a basic grounding in grammar, to develop a conscious knowledge of the foreign language's morpho-syntactical regulation. The study of morphology and syntax is, and has been, since time immemorial considered a matter of course in language teacher education curricula. By the same token a study of speech-act realisation and discourse regulation** should be made a compulsory component of the student teacher's curriculum.

2.   In the preceding section discourse regulation and speech-act realisation were taken together. It may be useful to deal with speech-act realisation separately here. A

foreign language teacher needs an insight into "how things are done with words" in the foreign (and contrastively his own) language. He needs an insight into the distinction between direct and indirect, conventional and unconventional speech-acts if he is to heighten his awareness of how language "works" in human interaction. This awareness forms the basis of his evergrowing realisation of how the other speech-community often looks at reality differently, and of how members of that community deal with one another differently, in other words of how that community has a different cultural perspective from his own. When using indirect and unconventional speech-acts, for example, we appeal to knowledge we share with our interlocutor. We take it for granted that he will understand our implications, and that he shares our discourse rules.

Teachers who have developed a respectful insight into the otherness of such conventions in the foreign language are satisfactorily equipped to immunise their students against the tendency to stereotype other speech-communities or nations on this point. They can show how relative such conventions, including mother-tongue conventions, are and that what seems funny or strange or even weird, is nothing but another way of dealing with reality, intrinsically neither better nor worse than what is customary in the mother-tongue. Study of discourse conventions and a comparison of speech-act realisations in both the mother-tongue and the foreign language should therefore become an issue in language teacher education curricula and should be appropriately introduced into the classroom.

3.   Furthermore, study of the use of compensatory strategies (CpS) in foreign language communication will have to be made part and parcel of language teacher education. The more incomplete our oral command of the foreign language, the more we shall have to revert to a skill of compensating for shortcomings in our competence. In order to be able to do that efficiently and effectively we

need the necessary phrases and vocabulary, practice in using them appropriately and again, of course, awareness. The student teacher not only needs to become adroit in availing himself of all sorts of CpS, he also needs to be stimulated to think about the phenomenon itself and experience the use of CpS for communicative as well as learning purposes.

As foreign language learners we shall never become native speakers (NSs) of that language. This can never be the purpose of foreign language teaching. Therefore, in our communicating with speakers of the foreign language there will be a more complicated process of negotiation of meaning than is the case in our mother-tongue. Beside a command of vocabulary and morpho-syntactic phenomena we need for this negotiating process a knowledge of language formulas (speech-act realisations and discourse regulatory formulas) and a skill in using them appropriately on the basis of our socio-cultural and meta-communicative awareness. The complexity of the process naturally entails misunderstandings. It is, therefore, not at all a wild thought to introduce exo-linguistic discourse into the input material that we confront learners with. This discourse contains misunderstandings that may typically arise between non-NSs (NNSs) and NSs, and between speakers of various European languages via a lingua franca. The inevitable use of all sorts of CpS (for vocabulary, but also for discourse regulation and speech-act realisation) in this sort of communication may serve as examples of an intercultural negotiating process and will reveal the importance of CpS. It will also bring foreign language use nearer to the learner's experience and could therefore be more motivating.

4.   Europe and its unification should not be made into a separate school subject. It needs to be integrated into topics dealt with in relevant school subjects. Foreign languages, on the basis of the above reasoning, as carriers of a cultural load, should be among those subjects. Cooperation between all subjects concerned in school projects should be one of the ways in which Europe is given

a place in the curriculum. Obviously, in this context language teachers need to be able to communicate with their colleagues in the other subjects. Therefore they should be given a basic introduction into Europe's history and its present state of affairs.

IV. How are these requirements to be realised in the curriculum?

1.   For the analysis of discourse by the student, an inventory of discussion topics will have to be made and in order for him to study speech-act realisations a list of examples of unconventional indirect realisations in context is needed.

     Points of interest for discourse analysis will certainly have to include opening and closing routines and turn-giving, turn-keeping and turn-taking conventions, cohesion and coherence conventions, routinised "chunks" of discourse and the use of the so-called "gambits" (Coulmas, 1986; Kasper, 1986; Edmondson, 1986; Nattinger & De Carrico, 1989).

     Equipped with such inventories the student will have to learn to make analyses of NS and NNS discourse produced on the basis of the same communicative tasks. In making these analyses the student should distinguish as much as possible between discourse conventions and speech-acts (at times they may overlap). Discovering differences and similarities between NS and NNS discourse and its regulation will no doubt be an invaluable preparation for the student teacher for the intercultural language classroom later, as well as for his own observation potential if he is allowed a lengthy stay in the target language country during his training. He will experience the cultural embedding of a language at first hand and see how cultural differences manifest themselves in language use.

2.   Learning to use CpS in the mother tongue takes place largely unconsciously. We pick up this component of our communicative competence more or less automatically.

As a rule we do not reflect on our use of CpS. It is therefore striking that in institutionalised foreign language learning we see that learners do not easily revert to their use and if they do, that their range of strategies is rather limited and their use of them rather laborious. It seems as if traditional foreign language teaching is not sufficiently communicative and too form-oriented to allow a natural process as the development of CpS in the foreign language to take place (Willems, 1987). We will, therefore, have to make our students aware of their CpS use and help them refine it in support of the further development of their own proficiency and as part of their pedagogic and didactic preparation as foreign language teachers. The nature of the exercises and the methodology used in the process may be a model for their later practice.

3.   It is of importance for all teachers who want to promote Europe and European citizenship to have a thorough knowledge of the idea of Europe and its origin and history. They should also, and this goes for foreign language teachers in particular, be sensitive to the uniqueness of the various European (sub) cultures as they are to be found in the variety of speech-communities in the European area. This knowledge and sensitivity may help liberate the mind from ethnocentrism and from the urge to stereotype other cultures.

In order for a school team of teachers to be able successfully to set up projects aimed at the development of a sense of European citizenship in their pupils it is necessary that they understand one another on the point of the project's purpose. They need a measure of shared knowledge and outlook concerning Europe and its future. Teacher education curricula, therefore, need to contain multi-disciplinary courses or projects on Europe. An important role in planning and organising these is to be played by foreign language departments. For, as stated above, it is only in contact with other Europeans, through the language of one of the participants or through a lingua franca, that one may become really aware of the otherness of the other culture. If one has been made conscious of these differences and has been prepared for dealing with them in a negotiating process, the communication may be ever so much more satisfactory. Materials and methodology geared towards this consciousness-raising process should be developed in training establishments to be used for their own students and in order to be shared with schools. Foreign language teachers in schools should likewise be prepared to play their role in Europe projects. Their training should have equipped them with the necessary knowledge and skills to do so to the benefit of all concerned.

Into the bargain, school teachers should be willing, in keeping with their linguistic education, to contribute ideas to preparing the pupils for fruitful exchanges with schools in other European countries. In view of obvious restraints on time that the training curriculum is subject to, this last claim, however, may need to be relegated to inservice training.

V. Conclusion

If the development of a "citoyenneté Européenne" in the student teacher and learner is taken seriously by training institutes and schools we should realise that not only the social sciences, history and economics have a role to play in the planning and organisation of projects or courses aimed at furthering this development. Also foreign languages have a clear-cut and very important contribution to make. They will only be able, however, to make such a contribution if they develop from mainly form and grammar oriented to communication-oriented disciplines. This implies that on a par with issues concerning the forms of the foreign language, the realisation of speech-acts and routines for the regulation of discourse must also be taken seriously and learners must be encouraged and helped to use compensatory strategies to make the interaction as satisfactory as possible.

It also implies that next to consciousness-raising regarding the differences between mother-tongue and foreign language in the morphological and syntactic field, serious attention should be given to study of the differences between how other speech-communities "do things differently with words" and have different ways of regulating discourse. Language teaching does not only become more efficient and effective in this way but it may also make a contribution to the development of an intercultural awareness in the learner, which makes for better communication across borders, and which is a pre-requisite for the Europeanisation of what are now still mainly nationalistic states. The development of the knowledge, skills and attitudes of the foreign language teacher that are necessary to help him play a stimulating role in the unification process of Europe, is a major task for language teacher education departments. They should work towards performing this task much more emphatically and explicitly than has been the case so far.***

NOTES:

* Sympathetic though I am to those who feel that the systematic use of "him" and "his" are sexist, I find myself unable to think of a stylistically acceptable alternative. I have tried to use the plural as often as I can, but this is not always appropriate when, as here, the learner as an individual is meant.

** It may be helpful to illustrate what exactly is meant here by means of a few examples:

— It is completely acceptable for German participants in a conversation, if I join a discussion during a meeting with: "Moment mal, Ich habe eine Frage." In an English company: "Just a minute, I have a question" as a formula to join in the discussion will be taken as rather direct and a bit boorish. Here: "Could I come in on this, I do not quite see..." would be a much more appropriate formula.

—   Something which is an anathema in an English setting, except when the tone of the discussion becomes decidedly unfriendly, is rejecting somebody's statement with: "oh, but that isn't true." Although not quite the summit of politeness, we hear from Germans that: "Aber das stimmt ja nicht" in German company, is not half as offensive and does not lead to the same amount of irritation between the interlocutors as in an English company.

—   "Can I use your phone, please?" uttered by a Dutch conference goer to an English secretary in her office, even if superiors have already given their permission for the call, could evoke a very bitchy reaction, rather surprising to the Dutchman. This is not the way to formulate such a request under the circumstances. "Excuse me, but could I please use your phone. I asked your boss and he said it was all right" would be a much more acceptable wording of the request.

—   And did you ever wonder about why the English, in conversation with the French, always think that the French are angry or have a bone to pick with them, when the latter are convinced that they are behaving quite normally? Or why the French never seem to notice when an English speaker is furious? It is the culture specific codes for (para) linguistic behaviour in communication that are at the bottom of this. Knowledge and awareness of these codes is essential for mutual understanding between speakers of difference languages. Such mutual understanding is, of course, vital if we are to work towards a more coherent Europe.

***   I am grateful to David Whybra for reading through the manuscript and correcting linguistic and pragmatic errors!

496

REFERENCES

Bell, G.H. (1990)
"Developing a European Dimension of the Teacher Training Curriculum." In: *European Journal of Teacher Education,* Vol.12/3.

Bruce, M. (1990)
"Teacher Education and the Erasmus Programme." In: *European Journal of Teacher Education,* Vol.12/3.

Coulmas, F. (1986)
"Diskursive Routinen im Fremdsprachenerwerb." In: Eppeneder, R. (1986).

Edmondson, W. (1968)
"Routinisierte Elemente im Fremdsprachlichen Diskurs." In: Eppeneder (1986).

Els van T.J.M. (1990)
Horizon Taal, Nationaal Actieprogramma Moderne Vreemde Talen, Ministry of Education and Science, The Hague.

Eppeneder, R. (1986)
Routinen im Fremdsprachenerwerb, Goethe Institut, München.

Faerch, C., Haastrup, K. and Pillipson, R. (1984)
Learner Language and Language Learning, Multilingual Matters, Clevedon.

Hatch, E.M. (1983)
Psycholinguistics; a second language perspective, Newbury House, Rowley, Mass.

Kasper, G. (1986)
"Interactive Procedures in Interlanguage Discourse." In: Eppeneder (1986).

Loveday, L. (1982)
The Sociolinguistics of Learning and Using a Non-Native Language, Pergamon.

Nattinger, J.R. and DeCarrico, J.S. (1989)
Lexical Phrases, Speech-Acts and Teaching Conversation. In: AILA Review, 1989.

Riley, Ph. (1989)
Learners' representations of language and language learning. In: Willems & Riley (1989).

Willems, G.M. and Riley Ph. (1984)
Communicative Foreign Language Teaching and the Training of Foreign Language Teachers, Hogeschool Interstudie, Nijmegen.

Willems, G.M. (1987a)
"The Dutch Disconnection : foreign language teaching and teacher (re)training in the Netherlands," *European Journal of Teacher Education,* Vol.10/2.

Willems, G.M. (1987b)
"Communication strategies and their significance in foreign language teaching." In: *SYSTEM,* Vol.15/3.

Willems, G.M. and Riley Ph. (1989)
Foreign Language Learning and Teaching in Europe, a book of readings for the language teacher, Free University Press, Amsterdam.

Willems, G.M. (1990)
"Foreign Languages for Communication; some new perspectives." In: *Bildungswissenschaftlichen Fortbildungstagungen an der Universität in Klagenfurt,* Böhlan Verlag, Vienna (forthcoming).

COOPERATIVE CURRICULUM DEVELOPMENT AND IMPLEMENTATION

Gertraud Havranek

Institut für Anglestik und Amerikanistik,
Universität für Bildungswissenschaften, Klagenfurt

1.   Introduction

Our situation at Klagenfurt University is probably not unlike that of many institutions training foreign language teachers, whose advanced language programs had started out with a structure-based syllabus some years earlier, prescribing work on nouns and adjectives for the first semester, verbs for the second semester, word order and subordinate clauses for the third semester etc.   When the concepts of communicative language teaching were introduced, the old syllabus was judged totally inadequate and unsatisfactory and was therefore abandoned.   However, this left us without a curriculum for the language program.   The official study plan specifies the number of classes the students must take but makes no recommendations as to their content.   Earlier attempts at a new curriculum had resulted in a change of the study plan in so far as hours were now divided between obligatory core classes and a number of options from which the students must choose a certain number.   The options were classes concentrating on specific skills. For students in the second part of their studies only options aiming at some form of specialisation were offered.

Our incoming students have had English for at least 8 years. They form a very heterogeneous group that can be classified as intermediate to advanced.   Language classes are a requirement for all of them, but within the overall program the language program has very little prestige.   Language is not really considered an academic subject.   At the same time it is the language program that is most often and most easily judged and criticised with regard to the graduates. Actually, the language proficiency of our graduates is often the only aspect of the program that outsiders *can* judge. Scholarly achievements in English linguistics or literature are not in general appreciated outside the university.

In many institutions the final exam includes a language proficiency test. At our university, however, only students majoring in English must take the final exam in English, which is an oral exam in either (applied) linguistics or literature conducted in English. Since the format of the exam varies and the exam is usually taken much later than the last language class, there is no examination syllabus that could substitute for a teaching syllabus.

The proficiency of the graduates was not always satisfactory and blame was invariably placed on the language teachers. An additional obligatory advanced language class was introduced a few years ago to ensure that the students did advanced work in a course integrating all skills. A curriculum for this course was not provided. The teacher was responsible for the class in terms of syllabus, method, materials, and assessment, as was the case in all other classes. No textbook was used in any of the classes. Continuity within the program depended exclusively on informal cooperation between the teachers which, for a variety of reasons, was not always possible. Despite repeated attempts towards a curriculum, the program remained fragmentary in many ways while at the same time inadvertently repetitive. It gave neither students nor teachers a sense of continuity. When recently new teachers joined the staff and found very little information to guide them in the preparation of their classes, the development of a new curriculum became mandatory.

2. Aims, Needs, Aspirations

Our program must attempt to achieve two aims at the same time. When our students leave the university, they must be proficient, flexible speakers, who can be models for their pupils. While they are at the university they must be able to do academic work in English, i.e. follow lectures, give oral presentations and write papers. This means that the program must aim at advanced general English, classroom language, and English for Academic Purposes.

We also realised that beyond those immediate aims the language program must serve as a model for future teachers and must help the students integrate the various fields of their course of study, in particular literature, linguistics and cultural studies. (The other subject attempting to integrate the program is language teaching methodology).

In addition to the students' needs, those of the teachers must be taken into consideration as well. The curriculum should help the latter concentrate their efforts and make their work more satisfying and, if possible, easier. It should also facilitate fair assessment of the students' work, and also permit evaluation of the teachers' efforts.

3. Curriculum decisions

It is obvious that the definition of what a curriculum is supposed to contain depends on the theories of teaching and of language learning on which it is based, and on the concept of what constitutes language proficiency or competence. If language learning is seen as the acquisition of a complex cognitive skill, the curriculum will specify which subskills (mastery of linguistic, sociolinguistic etc., rules) must be taught and practiced and in which order; if language learning is seen as a natural process following an innate syllabus which is independent of explicit instruction, the content can be specified in terms of desired language competence and in terms of opportunities for language acquisition, i.e. type of exposure to the language, learning environments and classroom activities, but not in terms of linguistic input. If proficiency is seen basically as the ability to use grammar and vocabulary correctly, grammatical structures will form the core of the curriculum. If proficiency is seen as including sociolinguistic and discourse competence as well, these will also be components of the curriculum. Additionally, a substantive or content component is frequently proposed to allow the learners to experience the language as a means of communication when it is used to teach a different subject (Brumfit, 1984; Allen, 1984). Stern (1984) would like to include a general language education component to allow the learner "to reflect about language, language learning, and culture in general." The form of the curriculum will also depend on who is responsible for, or involved in, the formulation of the curriculum, namely curriculum planners, teachers or learners.   The components of the curriculum reflect the function attributed to it.

Curricula are classified according to what constitutes the dominant organising principle of the content: grammatical structures, notions and functions, situations, skills and sub-skills, tasks or nonlinguistic content (Krahnke, 1987).   The choice of the organising principle again reflects a theory of language and of language learning.   The basic question is whether there is something like a universal competence underlying language proficiency, which can be tapped in new situations independent of how it was acquired, or whether a particular skill can only be acquired through specific practice.   Different curricula presuppose different types of transfer of learning.

4.   Cooperative curriculum development

4.1   Preliminary Decisions

We wanted a curriculum that clearly specified the proficiency deemed necessary:

(a)   for (future) teachers of English at a wide range of educational institutions;

(b)   for successful students at the university.

Thus the curriculum should be one for general English and EAP (English for Academic Purposes).   The curriculum should also be of help to the teachers by suggesting procedures and materials and defining relevant types of evaluation of the students' work.   It should ensure continuity within the program, and give teachers and students a feeling of progress.

We did not attempt to change the study plan, which prescribes core classes and options.   While the core classes aim at general language proficiency integrating all skills, each option concentrates on one specific area.   It was no longer clear whether they were supposed to be remedial classes or whether they were to lead to advanced competence in the area.   The original idea had been

502

that students would attend those options where they needed or desired additional work.   However, it had turned out that students were more likely to attend those options that they personally expected to be easier for them and avoid those where a weakness had been diagnosed.   The question will be addressed again when the curriculum is discussed in detail.

The two goals of the program, advanced general English and EAP made it clear that the curriculum had to be a combination of a structural, functional/notional and skill-based curriculum with the latter aspect receiving increasingly more attention.   Objectives had to be defined for each area.   While it was obvious that many topics would have to be treated in a spiral form rather than in a linear sequence, concentration on the same thematic content in consecutive classes was to be avoided.   Therefore themes in the sense of Yalden's curriculum design (Yalden, 1984) had to be included as well.   In addition to this comprehensive curriculum for the language program a content-based curriculum is in operation throughout the institute program, since all content classes in linguistics, literature, cultural studies, and methodology are taught in English.

4.2   Actual procedure

4.2.1.   *Participants*

In addition to all the teachers in the language program, the Head of Department, who is a linguist, and I were involved.   I was the new program coordinator, who was not teaching in the program but whose main responsibility was the methodology program and some classes in linguistics.   The language teachers expected help from the linguists.   They were thinking of a structural curriculum, to which the linguists should contribute in the form of, for example, an analysis of error frequencies.

The fact that the Head of Department took part in the meetings was appreciated by the language teachers.   They felt that it was an acknowledgement of the importance of their responsibilities within the program.

4.2.2. *Time*

Developing a curriculum is a time-consuming task. Since the development had to occur as an addition to the regular teaching assignments, it has been going on for two years now, and is not finished yet. Preparations began in the summer semester of 1988 when we met several times at irregular intervals. It was then decided that during the following semester a two-hour period for regular meetings should be set aside in the official timetable. For two years now we have met every Friday morning with very few exceptions. The slot has been kept free again in the schedule for the winter semester 1990/91.

4.2.3. *Considerations for staff development*

For the meetings, experience in Action Research as a powerful tool in inservice education of teachers, and some knowledge of Change Management proved useful. It was clear that we had to start from the existing program and from the teachers' experience. Every teacher has implicit and explicit theories concerning language, language learning and good teaching. Awareness of one's beliefs and assumptions, and of one's actual behaviour in the classroom, are a prerequisite to any innovation. Earlier work in Action Research had also taught me that we teachers often do things in our classrooms different from what we think and claim we do, and that teachers often mean different things (whether in reference to content, procedures, or activities) when they use the same term. In order to change anything, an analysis of what was actually happening, and of what the teachers thought they were doing, was necessary.

Change is often experienced as threatening. Change suggested to, or forced on, the teachers by some outside authority is likely to be interpreted as criticism and, therefore, resisted. The new curriculum and its implementation must be the concern of those involved and not that of some "expert" program adviser.

4.2.4.   *Steps towards a curriculum*

1.   Preparation

During SS 1988 the teachers were asked to collect all their materials, and record all activities for the classes they were teaching, and to try and find some form of organisation such as the level of language (phonology, morphology, grammar, discourse), or the skill(s) involved.   They were also asked to evaluate the activities and materials and to analyse the aims that an activity or material had been used for.   We were planning to arrive at the objectives through the tasks and activities used by teachers.

At the beginning of the winter semester 1988/89 we decided that we would like to run a research project following a group of students through the program.   The aim was to learn more about the effectiveness of the program or individual parts of it.   The students of the class of 1988 were to be tested at several stages of their career, while the teachers were expected to keep detailed records of the input the students received.   The diagnostic procedure at the beginning consisted of a cloze test, a multiple choice test and oral interviews with a native speaker.   Analysis of all three types of data was supposed to lead to a student profile, both for individual students and for the whole class.   However, only the written data were analysed fast enough to be used for diagnostic purposes in the first language class.   The oral interviews are only now being processed in detail and compared with later data.   While the project may still produce valuable results concerning the development of the students, the procedure was not rigorous enough to attribute any gains in language competence to a particular class.

2.   Defining the parameters of expected proficiency

An analysis of the language needed by teachers seemed both impossible and unnecessary.   A teacher in Austria is supposed to be as close to a native speaker as possible.   However, it was necessary to make explicit what such proficiency would consist of.   We turned to rating scales for language proficiency for help and arrived at fairly comprehensive lists of sub-skills for the four basic skills and translation, and at a structural component.   Additional categories were content, pragmatic function, and study skills.

In addition to OBJECTIVES for these categories, the "curriculum" also included the rubrics MATERIALS, ACTIVITIES AND ASSIGNMENTS, and ASSESSMENT.

This grid was presented to the participants as a suggestion open to change. It was accepted in that form, probably because everybody was overwhelmed by the number of categories and we lacked the experience to make any changes.

3.   Collecting what had been done

The original plan had been for the teachers to fill the grid in for one core class each for the following meeting and then to go through one class at a time. However, it soon became clear that it would make more sense to go through each category for all semesters if we wanted to see whether there was any progression, and do some cross-checking in addition.

Instead of a couple of weeks we spent a year "filling in the grid." Although the categories had been accepted by everybody right away, it turned out that —

(a)   activities, tasks and target behaviour were sometimes confused; while the idea was to collect what had been done, it often seemed necessary to include the expected standard of the target behaviour as well;

(b)   target behaviour had not always been specified for some classes; the activities sometimes seemed rather randomly chosen simply to provide an opportunity for conversation;

(c)   we did not always agree on what the categories meant;

(d)   we did not always agree on the particular competency at which a particular activity aimed;

(e)   some aspects of competence had apparently not been dealt with before, because the teachers had not been aware of them; or they were not aware of how they had tried to improve their students' performance in that particular aspect.

Despite the fact that these discussions took up much more time than expected, they were an essential part of the whole process. It was often quite difficult for us to understand each other because of background differences even though we were all language teachers. Sometimes it seemed hard to make explicit what had happened in a class. Some activities obviously work quite well, but it is difficult to explain to others what it is that makes the activity so valuable. Sometimes it was considered tiresome to split skills up into sub-skills. At other times we felt that teaching was based on intuition rather than on knowledge. This was true in the case of pronunciation, where the teachers were not aware of the characteristics of the local dialect, or even of standard German, and their influence on the students' pronunciation of English. Where possible such gaps were filled in at the meetings.

There were times when we felt that everybody would like to go back to their own classes and not worry about the program as a whole. But at the same time we felt that we were learning from each other and that we were learning to understand each other, to respect each other, and to work with each other. In addition to being a forum for the exchange of experiences and knowledge, the meetings provided a valuable opportunity to let off steam.

4.   Formulating objectives

We decided to formulate the aims of each class in terms of performance objectives for the structural component and skills, i.e. stating clearly what the learners were supposed to be able to do under what conditions. (Performance objectives have been criticised for subjects where the development of knowledge was the aim. They seem to be "a valid procedure" (Stenhouse in Nunan, 1988a, 60) for language learning.

The question was: "What must a student be able to do to complete a class successfully?" Skills and knowledge were defined in terms of function and context. The objectives for the most advanced language class, the target behaviour of the whole program, were formulated first and served as a model for the other classes. The objectives for each class were formulated by the teacher teaching the class at the moment or during the previous semester, using what we had compiled during the previous year. In some cases this proved a difficult task. Each individual curriculum was reviewed and revised by the group. In each case the form that assessment should take was also defined. The classes were all compared with each other to make sure we had covered everything we wanted to cover and had avoided repetition. We also had to come to some conclusion concerning the status of the options. It was decided to consider "Speaking" (the pronunciation of English) as mainly a remedial course helping students to achieve what was expected of them in the core courses. All the other skill courses include areas not dealt with in the core courses in such depth. However, mastery of what is taught there is definitely expected in the advanced language course. Therefore it is advisable for students to attend all the options, even at a later stage, if their language needs improvement.

We are aware of the fact that the curriculum at this first stage is more a plan for assessment than for teaching or learning. But further elaboration is on its way.

We did not ask our learners what they thought they needed. Learner needs (cf. Nunan 1988a) can only form the basis of the curriculum when the only responsibility of the program is to the learner. We are accountable for our graduates, to their future pupils and their parents, and to society as a whole as well.

But we also needed an instrument (=a public statement) that would make it easier for the teachers to explain to the students what level the students had to reach in order to pass a class and at the same time to make passing a class less dependent on particular teachers and their standards.

Moreover, we feel that students must also feel responsible for their language development. It is impossible to achieve the type of proficiency that we expect by attending a two-hour class once a week for three years. The courses provide opportunities and guidance for language learning. They offer practice in oral communication and exposure to the target language, and they give the students experience and guidance in the skills necessary in EAP. The classes can create an awareness of the language and thus provide help with two of the tasks of the learner identified by Klein (1986), i.e. analysing the target language and matching Learner Language rules against the target. The classes are also meant to help the students to learn to use various resources.

5.   Defining content

To develop the skills the students must have something to talk or write about. Our analysis of what had been done before had shown that the same topics tended to be used again and again in various classes. On the other hand, we had found that working with one theme for some time provided coherence to the class. Two conflicting points of view had to be taken into consideration:

(a)   teacher and students should be allowed to choose themes that they were interested in;

(b)   the same theme should not be the focus more than once to make sure that the language of a variety of topics was covered in the program.

Our decision was to set up a short list of topics for each core course, from which the class can choose one or more topics to base their work on. In addition they may choose one topic that they are really interested in. The teacher will then check with other teachers as to whether it has been dealt with recently. One topic that could always be included was Current Affairs.

6.   Developing materials

Attempts at making materials available to other teachers have not been very successful so far. Even if the material was there, it was hardly used in later classes, partly because the activity it had been used for was not explained sufficiently and partly because it was seen as too closely connected with the personality and teaching style of its developer. Furthermore it always seems too much work to go through somebody's material collection if one is looking for something specific. On the other hand teachers would like to have something to fall back on. We have come to the conclusion that materials created by other teachers must be treated like materials found in books — a source of inspiration that can be adapted to one's own needs.

We have decided to make use of modern technology. Materials and suggestions for each class will be stored on floppy disks. In this way access should become easy and adaptation should be no problem at all. At the moment a format is being developed.

7.   Implementation

We had to begin with the implementation of the objectives as soon as they had been formulated even though the accompanying procedures or the substantive content of the classes had not yet been specified. This means that the objectives have been considered "a public statement" that is binding for staff and students since last semester.

The procedure is the following:

At the beginning of the semester the students are given one or more tests in class to diagnose their strengths and weaknesses. I should add that we are still experimenting with a variety of tests. It is difficult to find a test that identifies a learner's strong and weak points and at the same time does not use up too much teaching time or take too long to score.

Then the objectives are presented to the students (i.e. they all get a copy), and discussed in class. Recommendations for remedial work, attendance of specific options or just additional work are made by the teacher.

8.   Next steps

It is clear that just telling a student to work harder is not enough. Therefore our next step will be to extend the small *self-access center*, which at the moment is used in self-access CALL project for our business students. In addition, a course in *study skills* for students of English will be offered next semester.

9.   Evaluation

We are still so busy developing the curriculum that we have not spent much time on the evaluation of what has been created. We are aware of the fact that every part of the curriculum — planning, implementation, and assessment — must be evaluated eventually. We are hoping that the objectives will enable us to specify where students make progress in the expected way and where progress does not seem to occur. We might then be able to introduce further changes either in the curriculum or in the program.

We have also begun to look at classroom procedures to find out whether they achieve what they are supposed to achieve and whether they are equally valued by teachers and students. One important question is whether the learners are ready to contribute, by working on their own, in order to meet the objectives of the courses. Their behaviour is yet to be studied.

5.   Conclusion

Developing a curriculum is an ongoing process. Having a clearly specified set of objectives has made our teachers' work easier and more satisfying. At the moment we cannot say whether it has also improved our students' English although there is some indication of that as well. At least it has improved attendance in optional classes even if the students do not get credit for the course. It has also made us aware of how much more work still has to be done, and of the limitations of any such program. In fact, one of the aims that was not stated in the curriculum, but which has become very important to me in the course of the curriculum discussion, is learner autonomy. Another one is guidance in learning how to learn.

Having meetings every week is very time-consuming. However, as a final point I would like to stress the importance of these meetings. They have improved communication within the department enormously and have created a new spirit and interest in professional development in all of us.

REFERENCES

Allen, J.P.B., (1984)
General Purpose Language Teaching : A Variable Focus Approach. In Brumfit (ed) 1984.

Brumfit, C. (ed) (1984)
General English Syllabus Design. Oxford : Pergamon.

Klein, W. (1986)
Second Language Acquisition. Cambridge : CUP.

Krahnke, K. (1987)
Approaches to Syllabus Design for Foreign Language Teaching. Englewood Cliffs : Prentice Hall.

Nunan, D. (1988a)
The Learner-Centred Curriculum. Cambridge : CUP.

Nunan, D. (1988b)
Syllabus Design. Oxford : OUP.

Stern, H.H. (1984)
Review and Discussion. In Brumfit (ed), 1984.

Yalden, J. (1984)
Syllabus Design in General Education : Options for ELT. In Brumfit (ed), 1984.

THE INFLUENCE OF TEACHERS' MOTIVATION FOR INSET ON TEACHER-PUPIL INTERACTIONS

Cveta Razdevsek-Pucko

Pedagoska Akademija, Ljubljana, Jugoslavija

Introduction

We cannot expect changes in school without changing the teacher. To change the teacher there must exist his/her inner need for change and for new knowledge. There are problems of needs assessment (B. van der Ree, 1983) and the problem of congruency between needs and INSET programme (N.Engels, 1988). Our starting-point is the assumption that the teachers should have positive attitudes to their own learning and changing (e.g. Cropley, 1981; Stein and Wang, 1988; Keiny and Dreyfus, 1989; P. Mortimore and Jo Mortimore, 1989). Only in this case can we expect real changes as a process of transformation (Darling-Hammond et al 1983), not conversion.

Problem

We were interested in the amount of teachers' needs for INSET activities and in the connections between INSET needs, length of teaching experiences and educational attitudes. We were also interested in the reflection of these needs in teachers' classroom teacher-pupil interactions and as a result, in the motivation of their pupils.

Method (sample and instruments)

The teachers (in one elementary school in Ljubljana) were given a questionnaire to answer some questions about which, and, how many INSET activities they would plan for one study-term (half a year). We have taken the amount and details in description of their plans as a degree of their needs for INSET.

(HD — high degree of INSET needs : teachers who were able to describe, in detail or just in general, a plan for INSET activities in one study term;

LD — low degree of Inset needs : teachers who were not able to make a plan for INSET activities).

The teachers were also given a questionnaire of progressive and democratic educational attitudes (modified and shortened MTAI). The total number of teachers was 50. 20 of them, 12 classroom-teachers and 8 subject-matter teachers (Slovene, mathematics, social sciences and environmental sciences), were included in the observation of their teacher-pupil interactions. We used a partly modified Flanders system FIAC.

The pupils of these teachers were given a questionnaire about school motivation.

(Four factors were extracted with factor analysis:

MOT 1 — extrinsic rewards from parents and teachers,
MOT 2 — achievement motivation, degree of aspirations,
MOT 3 — school grades as the extrinsic rewards,
MOT 4 — intrinsic rewards for school : curiosity and interest for learning).

16 classes (from 2 to 5) were included, totalling 362 pupils. The average scores on a questionnaire about school motivation for each class were computed and ascribed to the teacher of this class.

Sample:

Class	Number of classes	Number of pupils	Number of teachers	Number of lessons observed
2	4	82	4	32
3	4	98	4	32
4	4	91	4	32
5	4	91	8	16
Total	16	362	20	112

Results and discussion

1. Numbers (f) and percentage (%) of teachers with high (HD) and low degree (LD) of INSET needs:

	All teachers		FIAC teachers		Others	
	f	%	f	%	f	%
HD INSET needs	20	= 40%	13	= 65%	7	= 23%
LD INSET needs	30	= 60%	7	= 35%	23	= 77%
Total	50	=100%	20	=100%	30	=100%

We can see that teachers, included in FIAC observations and analyses, more frequently defined their programme for INSET activities. We may conclude that the analyses of their classroom-pupil interactions helped them to become aware of deficiencies of their knowledge and behaviour. The analyses of the observational data helped them to make a reflection of their work and to increase awareness, sensibility and willingness for new knowledge and changes.

2.   Correlations between the degree of INSET needs, some
      teacher variables and pupils' motivation:

	Degree of INSET needs
teaching experience (in years)	-0.23* (N = 50)
teachers' progressive educational attitudes	0.30* (N = 50)
FIAC categories:	(N = 20)
FL 1	0.36*
FL 2	0.51**
FL 3	0.51**
FL 4.3	0.48**
FL 8	0.65***
FL 10.1	0.45*
Motivational factors:	(N = 20)
MOT 1	0.57 **
MOT 2	0.13 n.s.
MOT 3	0.08 n.s.
MOT 4	0.71 ***
* $p < 0.05$	
** $p < 0.01$	
*** $p < 0.001$	

Teachers who have been teaching more than 25 years, very
rarely created their programme for INSET . It seems that they have
either no more needs for improvement of their work or they have
realised that the programme for INSET is none of their business —
the others (headmasters and school administrators) will take care of
it.

It is not surprising that progressive educational attitudes are positively connected with the degree of INSET needs. We can assume that teachers with more progressive and more child-centered attitudes probably have more needs for improving their work with children. Progressive educational attitudes mean that they are more open for novelties. They do not stick to traditional methods of teaching and are ready to accept a more democratic relation to children.

Teachers with more intensive needs for INSET activities can be described as more indirective teachers - the degree of INSET needs correlated positively with some indirective categories of classroom teacher-pupil interaction:

—   they accept the feeling of their pupils (FL 1);
—   they praise and encourage pupils (FL 2);
—   they use pupils' ideas (FL 3);
—   they ask divergent questions (FL 4.3);
—   pupils talk more and have more time for responses (FL 8);
—   pupils have more time for individual seatwork (FL 10.1).

Of course, this data are correlational. We cannot conclude that the needs for INSET cause more indirect behaviour, we could rather conclude that both variables relate to some more fundamental, but in our research unmeasured third factor, probably some personal characteristics, including attitudes. The most interesting, and we think also very important, data are positive correlations for the degree of INSET needs and some motivational factors of pupils.

The highest is correlation with the fourth motivational factor. It means that pupils, taught by teachers with intensive INSET needs, are more motivated for school work, they express intrinsic motivation for school. Their answers show that they like school and learning. We can say that they are motivated with intrinsic rewards.

This explanation is supported by the non-significant correlation with the third motivational factor, (MOT 3 - school grades as rewards).

It seems that teachers who have more intensive motivation for their own improvement have stronger influence on their pupils in the way that pupils like the process of learning, they appreciate learning and knowledge more than grades.

Positive correlation (0.57*) between the degree of INSET needs and the first motivational factor (MOT - 1) must also be mentioned. It means that pupils of teachers with a high degree of INSET needs (HD) are not just intrinsically motivated, they are also more sensitive to extrinsic rewards from their teachers and parents.

Concluding remarks

Our research confirms the idea of lifelong learning not only as a generator of changes in teachers' work, but also as an important factor of indirective classroom teacher-pupil interactions with positive influence on pupils and their motivation.

Teachers should have greater influence on their inservice courses. If not, their needs for improving decrease, they become more and more dependent on their superiors concerning both the content and form of INSET.

It seems important to emphasise the influence of teachers' needs for INSET on some pupils' motivational characteristics. As Cropley (1981) wrote, promotion of lifelong learning should be an important school activity. The goals should be to influence teachers and their work, and also to influence pupils in the direction of accepting permanent learning as a guiding principle and as a life style and worth-while value.

Summary

This paper describes one part of research about teachers' motivation for INSET and confirms the idea of lifelong learning not only as a generator of changes in teachers' work, but also as an important factor of indirective classroom teacher-pupil interactions with positive influence on pupils and their motivation.

Teachers with more intensive needs for INSET activities have a more indirective style of work - the degree of INSET needs to be correlated positively with some indirective categories of classroom teacher-pupil interaction.

Teachers, included in FIAC observations and analyses, more frequently defined their programme for INSET activities   Probably the analyses of their classroom-pupil interactions helped them to become aware of deficiencies of their knowledge and behaviour.

Pupils, taught by teachers with intensive INSET needs, are more motivated for school work, they express intrinsic motivation for school, they are also more sensitive to extrinsic rewards from their teachers and parents.

REFERENCES

Brophy, J.E. and Good, Th.L. (1986). Teacher Behaviour and Student Achievement. In : *Handbook of Research on Teaching,* Third Edition, Edited by Wittrock, M.C., Macmillan Publishing Co., New York, 328-375.

Campbell, R.J. (1982). Some aspects of INSET and subsequent curriculum change : a case study and discussion. Journal of Education for Teaching, Vol.8, No.3, 203-222.

Cropley, A.J. (1981). Lifelong learning : a rationale for teacher training. Journal of Education for Teaching, Vol.7, No.1, 57-69.

Darling-Hammond, L., Wise, A.E. and Pease, S.R. (1983). Teacher Evaluation in the Organisational Context : a Review of the Literature. Review of Educational Research, Vol.53, No.3, 285-328.

Engels, N. (1988). Teachers' need for permanent education. Paper presented at ATEE Conference, Barcelona.

Flanders, N.A. (1968). Interaction Analysis and Inservice Training. In : Morrison and McIntyre (ed). The Social Psychology of Teaching, Penguin Education, 63-74.

Kenny, S. and Dreyfus, A. (1989). Teachers' Self-reflection as a Prerequisite to their Professional Development. Journal of Education for Teaching, Vol.15, No.1, 53-63.

Mortimore, P. and Mortimore, J. (1989). School-focused In-service Training in England and Wales : the challenge to higher education. Journal of Education for Teaching, Vol.15, No.2, 133-139.

Razdevsek-Pucko, C. (1988). Motivacija uciteljev osnovnih sol za stalno strokovno izpopolnjevanje, posvet ob 30 - letnici enotne osnovne sole, zbornik, ZDPD Slovenije, Zavod SR Slovenije za solstvo, Ljubljana, 507-517.

van der Ree, B. (1983).   Schoolteam-based needs assessment : a
    minded area?   In : Issues in the In-service Training of
    Teachers, ed. by G. Chadwick, ATEE, Brussels, 10-23.

Stein, M.K. and Wang, M.C. (1988).   Teacher development and
    school improvement : The process of teacher change.
    Teaching and Teacher Education, Vol.4, No.2, 171-187.

TEACHER INSERVICE TRAINING AS ADULT EDUCATION

Dietlind Fischer

Comenius-Institut, Münster

My major concern in the field of teacher inservice education is in general to think about professionalisation or, in other words, about how to promote the development of schools and the learning of teachers by means of inservice programs.

The purpose of this specific contribution is to outline some trends of the current discussion of INSET in Germany, which are likely to indicate some elements of a theoretical framework of what teacher inservice education is, or should be, about. I am convinced that teacher inservice work needs to be cultivated as a certain educational environment, a milieu of mutual communication, working and learning, which is more than running different courses about whatever.

My background is a recent review of concepts, models or programs of the INSET run by public agencies, such as national or church institutions, from which I wanted to gain evidence about the specific accountability of Lutheran churches to the educational system (Fischer 1990).

In that study I made use of published articles or books and a great deal of occasional literature about inservice education. I did not use additional empirical methods such as questionnaires or interviews.

I would like to share the results of that study with those who work in the field of inservice education, because I think reflecting on the sense of what we are doing needs to be emphasised.

Teacher inservice training in the Federal Republic of Germany (FRG)

The system of teacher inservice training in the FRG is unique in the European context.

Every province has its own system, proceeding from the cultural autonomy of the country governments as well as from grown traditions and social structures. Some provinces organise the teacher inservice training in academies (e.g. Bavaria, Baden-Württemberg), some others in central institutions where the tasks of curriculum development, research on schooling and teacher training are linked together (e.g. Lower Saxony, Northrhine-Westfalia, Saarland). Some put strong efforts into the central training of teacher trainers in certain subjects, which are then located in regional districts (e.g. Northrine-Westfalia), some prefer regional teachers' centers (Hesse), expert counsellors (Lower Saxony) or counselling and service agencies (Hamburg). Sometimes the regional agencies of teacher inservice training are part of the school administration, sometimes they act fairly autonomously.

One might keep in mind that teacher inservice programs are not only offered by state agencies, but - according to the principle of schooling as a public affair — some communal (Nürnberg, Düsseldorf, Bremerhaven) or church institutions as well as universities, teacher unions, the army, companies, cultural institutions and so on. It is almost impossible to get an overview of this market.

Teachers voluntarily apply for and take part in teacher training courses. Most of the courses are addressed to help teachers to sustain or enrich teaching qualifications; they do not offer a certificate of formal qualification.

Individual teachers may demand up to 5 school days a year for their own training courses, sometimes more if they take part in state programs. There are no additional costs to the teachers, except in some programs in the free market.

In some countries (e.g. Lower Saxony, Northrhine-Westfalia, Baden-Württemberg) teachers are allowed to use additional collective study time of 2 or 4 days a year together with the staff. Apparently this collective study time tends to be broadened.

The role of the churches in the public system of education

Education in general is a worldly matter in the understanding of Protestants. So traditionally the churches participate as one factor in a pluralistic system of education, not to overwhelm education in a Christian manner, but to represent Christian understanding in worldly areas of working and living. Churches run kindergartens, youth centers, family and adult education houses, schools and institutions for the training and education of teachers and educators, mostly in religious subject matters, but even sometimes in general education subjects.

The inservice agencies maintained or financially supported by Lutheran churches offer programs that are sometimes not very different from those of the state institutions; some of them are additional programs in areas where state agencies do not yet work — e.g. integration of disabled children, cooperation of parents and teachers — and some programs are set up as a kind of compensation for different forms of instrumentalisation teachers find themselves in. If you look for a definition of the church connected activities in inservice education, you will find most people generally take the position that the role and personality of the teacher is that of an individual who asks for help and support. Some people inside the church communication think that the training teaching qualifications and competencies should be left to the state, but the care for the teacher's personality should be left primarily to the churches.

The need for didactic reflection and communication

Although you can hardly get an insight into what teacher inservice training practice is concerned with, you may notice some common problems to which different suggestions for solutions are discussed. I observed a threefold access to inservice theory:

1.   How can the needs of individual teachers and schools be met in a better way, when the organisation of courses is regionalised?

2.   How can inservice training become school-based, so that the development and innovation of individual schools may be improved?

3.   How can inservice training be shaped as a part of the educational system in which teachers are accepted as a d u l t learners?

One of the reasons why INSET has become a key issue in school politics since the early eighties is the ageing of teachers. In some countries, in fact, one generation of teachers did not get access to schools because, since the number of pupils and students diminished, they were not hired. Actually the average age of school teachers is about 50 years in many schools; in some schools the youngest staff member is 50.

But the challenges of social development — for example, the new information technologies, the multicultural life situation, the organisation of work, the international coherences — continuously urge for an appropriate change of schools. So teacher inservice education was increasingly treated as a bottleneck for the implementation of whatever the governments wanted to be implemented. I am sure teacher inservice training will never fulfill these expectations of omnipotentials (Nevermann 1988, 31) in reality, and a good thing it is too, but do we know enough about why and how INSET works under continuous attempts to instrumentalise it to purposes outside itself? What has to be thought of and done in order to conceptualise INSET as an area where education ("Bildung") happens?

1.   Under the term "regionalisation" of INSET, some policies are meant which should be pursued, such as:-

— *closeness* to the needs of teachers by local neighbourhood;
— *t ransferability* of problem solving into everyday work;
— *reachability* of teachers;

— participation of teachers;
— effectiveness of INSET;
— acceptability of reforms.

2.   The development of school-based or school-focused INSET is meant to support teachers' work in the specific social context of his/her school and school environment, to encourage the accountability of individual schools to the learning of its pupils, to help individual schools to improve their quality.

3.   Thinking about teacher inservice education as a certain form of profession-oriented adult education is a kind of grass-root movement among teacher trainers in which they search for an explication of their professionalism.

The latter is explained as follows:

Implications of relating INSET to adult education

Adult education is linked to everyday life in its private, professional and leisure area as well as in scientific, political, cultural or religious concerns.   Thus adult education is in general directed towards certain dimensions (Nipkow 1990, 567f).

1.   adult education helps to differentiate and/or broaden one's beliefs having regard to certainties and self-evidences which have been called into question;

2.   adult education works against monopolisation of opinion-making against political fiats, against functional determinism;

3.   adult education has its major concern in the field where cultural barriers, such as barriers between subcultures, expert terminologies, become mutually exclusive.

Teacher inservice training   which is limited to the qualification of teachers on the job for a specific function in their profession, will not be able to cope with these adult education dimensions.

Teacher inservice education will uphold the idea of the necessity for coherent thinking and acting as regulative moments of "Bildung" in the tradition of the modern enlightenment thought of the 18th/19th century.

In my opinion, we do not need teachers who are perfectly skilled technocrats, but we need well-educated teachers who are able to deal with the conflicts and antagonisms of schooling in modern societies, who are able to reflect on their own and their students' situation in a world of contradictions. How do teachers achieve education? How can INSET be established to support, motivate, enhance, keep in motion the self-education processes of teachers in the school context?

In fact, one does not achieve education by optimising information processing, but by adopting cultural traditions, by interacting, by negotiation of what gives sense to ones work and life.

Educational culture and teachers' work

The work of teachers in schools cannot adequately be described in terms of teaching, education, assessment, counselling, innovation, concerning which certain skills, techniques and attitudes can be defined to be learned in inservice courses. The work of teachers is also related to communicative, convincing, consensual work in a school community. His/her work is part of social activities, democratic participation, negotiation processes in a social network, as many research results on "good" schools have pointed out. Teacher inservice education has to be related to these descriptive factors of teachers' work as well as to the normative horizon of meaningful learning. The processes of organised inservice courses have to be related to experiences and actions, in search of coherencies in a reflexive reality.

"Bildung" can be defined as reflexive learning in the coherencies of tasks and problems of common interest. The contents of learning are substantive, meaningful to individuals and society.

Teacher inservice courses have to be addressed to future tasks of society, for example intercultural living together, peace, economy, North-South differences in the economy, sexism, racism and so on as key-issues of education (Klafki 1985). How can inservice training actually cope with requirements like these?

When we talk about "Bildung" in the context of inservice education or training we refer to a tradition of enlightenment from the 18th/19th century, in which "Bildung" is an autonomous, critical attitude differing from socialisation, education, learning, affirmation of a technological development. "Bildung" relies on a set of features/characteristics which cannot be ignored in any work with teachers (Nipkow 1990, 33-36).

—   "Bildung" in the classical tradition is linked to politics: integration of the personal and the public culture, reflecting the connection of "Bildung" and power.

—   "Bildung" has utopian/visionary potentials relating to an achievement of the future.

—   "Bildung" is connected with subjectivity and autonomy.

—   "Bildung" refers to tradition.

—   "Bildung" is realised in negotiation of mutual understanding, as a life of dialogue, overcoming national and international borders.

Thus teacher inservice work requires a great deal more attention as a domain of an educational culture which is in favour of processes of "Bildung."

528

REFERENCES

Fischer, Dietlind (1990). Lehrerfortbildung. Entwicklung, Positionen and Aufgaben aus evangelischer Sicht Münster : Comenius-Institut.

Klafki, Wolfgang (1985). Neue Studien zur Bildungstheorie und Didaktik. Weinheim : Beltz.

Nevermann, Knut (1988). Omnipotenzerwartungen. Was Lehrer/innen und Lehrerfortbildner/innen alles können müssen. In : Pädagogik, 40 (1988), 6, p.30-34.

Nipkow, Karl Ernst (1990). Bildung als Lebensbegleitung und Erneuerung. Kirchliche Bildungsverantwortung in Gemeinde, Schule und Gesellschaft. Gütersloh : Gütersloher Verlagshaus Gerd Mohn.

EDUCATION FOR EQUAL OPPORTUNITIES ON A ONE-YEAR POST-GRADUATE COURSE FOR TEACHER TRAINEES

John Coldron and Pam Boulton

Sheffield City Polytechnic

This paper describes the Sheffield TENET project. It aimed to integrate equal opportunities into the curriculum of an initial training course. The project is reported formally and in detail in the two reports published in 1989 and 1990 (Coldron and Boulton 1989; Boulton and Coldron et al 1990). The intention in this paper is to present the circumstances and considerations behind the project in the particular context of Sheffield City Polytechnic. It is a case study in the conduct of curriculum development. As such, we hope it will be of interest to those engaged in the same processes.

The Sheffield project was one of the many in a Europe-wide action research programme. It has run through two phases over two years. It began in October 1988 and is continuing into a third dissemination phase in 1990/91. Since October 1989 it has been the only TENET project in Britain.

The target groups for the project were the students of the Post Graduate Certificate of Education (PGCE) course. The PGCE lasts only one academic year. It trains students to teach in either Primary Schools (ages 5-11) or Secondary Schools (ages 11-16). There were two separate cohorts, each about 150 students; the first during 1988/89 and the second during 1989/90. There are three distinct elements of the course: *Applied Education* (approximately 150 contact hours) in which general pedagogy is taught; *Subject Studies* (approximately 150 contact hours for secondary and 260 for primary) in which pedagogy and content of constituent parts of the curriculum are taught; *School Experience* (approximately 450 hours) in which students practice teaching in schools. The contact time for Applied Education does not represent its importance. It, in fact, plays a coordinating and central role on the course and in the experience of the students. It is the only element that is common to all students. The tutors who teach on this element also have pastoral responsibilities for students and they are often the only tutors with whom contact is maintained throughout the course. In the planning of the first phase a number of considerations determined our choice of actions. The overall aim was to develop the course so that it better enabled students to promote equality of opportunity, not just on their teaching practice but when they had entered the profession.

Only two people made up the TENET team during the first phase. They were experienced on the course and had a reputation for hard work and high quality teaching but were not in a formally powerful position. Any influence they had was through persuasion on committees and at meetings. The course leader was sympathetic to curriculum development as were most of the core team of tutors on the Applied Education course. Nevertheless, there was a sense that colleagues might easily feel that too much was being made of the issue. Importantly, a policy document directly concerning equality of opportunity (gender, race, disability and class), had been drawn up by a group of students and staff and had been formally adopted by the course committee in 1986.

The two people who initiated the project had conducted an evaluation of the input on one aspect of equality of opportunity (race) on the course prior to involvement with the project (Coldron and Boulton 1988). This evaluation gave cause for concern. It threw doubt on the efficacy of a strategy of permeation. Permeation meant that an issue was considered to be so pervasive that it should, and would, "naturally" arise in all aspects of the course. It would be considered as it arose in other work. The method by which the issue of gender was tackled was permeation. Clearly the success of such a policy was highly dependent on the way tutors and students perceived the issue. However, there was no systematic attempt to ensure that it was regarded as important. While permeation is a defensible theoretical position, evaluation and experience showed that it was not working as well as it could. It led to the issue of gender being either dealt with patchily or not at all for some students. It had a comparatively low profile on the course. The powerful hidden message was that equality of opportunity was part of the rhetoric of professionalism but, in practice, students should deal with more important things first. The conclusion reached by the project team was that it was a priority that equality of opportunity should be fully legitimated as a prime professional concern and that it should feature more prominently in the PGCE course (Ginsburg, 1987).

There seemed to be two ways in which this might be achieved. Firstly, one could engage in a dialogue with all of the tutors on the course to ensure that the issue actually permeated the whole of their teaching. Secondly, one could ensure a kind of permeation by raising the profile of the issue through structural changes and by prioritising it explicitly in the common compulsory Applied Education course. The hope of the latter strategy being that if it was legitimated and problematised in one part of the course it would more likely be raised *by the students* as a natural part of all other work. These two strategies were not mutually exclusive but, in practice, the project team opted effectively for the latter for the following reasons.

Given the position of limited influence, and the constraint of time, the two people concerned could not mount a staff development programme that would ensure that the issue would be raised in the many subject areas where other colleagues traditionally assumed professional autonomy. Approximately fifty different tutors teach students during the course of the year. This number effectively ruled out the development of a consultative and collegial process of curriculum enhancement during this first phase.

Working through the committee structure of the course a number of small but strategically significant changes were introduced to try to make permeation work by raising the profile of the issue on the course. Firstly, a number of explicit core sessions focussing only on equal opportunity were timetabled and deliberately placed throughout the course. One occurred at the very beginning of the first term, one at the beginning of the second term and two towards the middle and end of the taught course. Secondly, the need to address equality of opportunity was made an inescapable part of two out of the three of the compulsory assignments in Applied Education. Thirdly, the ability to promote equality of opportunity in the classroom was one of the criteria against which teaching practice was assessed. This bolstering of low key permeation with a high profile in Applied Education and School Experience we called "focussed permeation."

Three points are worth noting about this process before gong on to describe the evaluation of the first phase. First, the existence of the written policy was an important feature that specifically legitimated the attempt to develop the curriculum to enhance equality of opportunity. Second, the evidence concerning the ineffectiveness of the permeation policy gave great strength to the arguments for change. It had been gathered in a systematic and adequately rigorous way and formally presented in an internal report. Third, the committee process leading to the introduction of the changes did not lead to a meaningful dialogue between colleagues, although it had been hoped that it would. This meant that the strategy itself was not adequately validated through peer criticism, nor was it properly owned by colleagues who would be partly responsible for operating the changes.

The first phase was evaluated by a questionnaire to all students and in-depth interviews with approximately 14% of the cohort. It was not possible to run a control group. The evaluation revealed that all students assimilated a concern with equal opportunity with good professional practice. This meant that virtually every participant stated categorically that to attempt to achieve equality of opportunity in his or her classroom was a professional duty. Overt and obvious forms of sexist behaviour were overwhelmingly disapproved of and were challenged by some students when encountered from either staff or peers. This commitment was part of the students' approach to school experience and they reported that they planned their lessons accordingly.

Significant differences of commitment were, however, revealed. A minority (approximately a quarter) of the students gave the impression that their commitment was extremely robust and would form a foundation for their practice on the course and in employment. Others (again approximately a quarter) voiced the rhetoric but tended to prioritise other issues over equality of opportunity and specifically gender. We speculated that such a view would effectively lead to the issue being marginalised in their practice. The majority of students fell between the two extremes. When students were asked to give examples of the kind of actions that they would take to enhance equality of opportunity in their classroom, those offered were often superficial. This suggested that the course as it was implemented in the first phase did not provide sufficient input for students to go far beyond an awareness of, and an attempt to eradicate, the more obvious manifestations of sexism.

The project tutors formed the opinion that there was a need for the development of materials and teaching strategies specifically designed to enrich students' understanding of the pervasive nature of the causes of systematic disadvantage and the role schools play in its reproduction. Such understanding was a priority because it was a prerequisite of informed commitment. That in turn was taken to be the only sound basis for critical reflection that would ensure development of practice. To set that *process* of learning in motion was the key to achieving the overall objective. Only a continually growing understanding would equip the students with confidence enough to maintain commitment and to make informed evaluations of their own practice. This was to be a main focus of the second phase.

The second phase also needed to address staff development (the first strategy outlined above) in the context of the structural changes achieved. Integration of the issue within the whole course could not take place without the commitment of those who taught on the course. At least a start needed to be made on this.

Further, some of the changes effected in Phase 1, although firmly in place, were not yet effective. An important innovation for the course was the introduction of formal assessment of the student's ability to promote equality on teaching practice. Examination of the School Experience reports gave rise to grave doubts as to how conscientiously schools and polytechnic staff filled in that category on the form. One school teacher of eight year olds wrote, "This kind of assessment is irrelevant for children of our age range." An experienced senior polytechnic tutor wrote "Not applicable" across that section. There was clearly a need in the second phase to make the assessment more effective.

Two other concerns shaped the plan for the second phase. Firstly, it was clear that two people was too small a team to ensure adequate discussion about fundamental strategies and issues. There was a need to involve more people. Secondly, it was essential to ensure that the issue was raised in the third element of the course—Subject Studies. So far this element had only been affected obliquely. It was already adequately present in some subject courses but not in others.

It was with these considerations in mind that Phase II was planned. All of the changes introduced in Phase I were carried over. The proposal was once again prepared and submitted by the two original project directors. It involved, however, a further eight people. These included seven tutors from four professional subject areas and a consultant from the Centre for Women's Studies. In addition an external evaluator was appointed. The chosen subject areas were Science, Design and Technology, English, and Mathematics. Each subject team and the project directors from Applied Education aimed to develop curriculum materials (in a broad sense of that term) mostly, with the exception of Applied Education which included students of primary education (5-11 yrs), for the students studying to teach in the secondary age range (11 yrs-16 yrs).

This enlargement of the team addressed the two needs of a larger consultation group and direct work in Subject Studies. It was a fundamental aspect of the conduct of Phase II that the team should act as a peer validation group. Monthly meetings were scheduled and members were asked to make these a priority. At these meetings each team's plans were presented and discussed, concepts clarified and joint decisions taken. The presence of the consultant from the Centre for Women's studies was intended to contribute intellectual rigour and an informed voice to the debate. The idea of a continuing critical dialogue was a central one to the whole process of the project.

Not all the subjects taught were included. This was partly because we were unsure as to how much money we could ask of the Commission. The positive criteria for choice were that three of these subjects formed the core curriculum of the newly introduced

National Curriculum and the fourth, Design and Technology, had a special need for curriculum development on this issue. The focus on developing curriculum materials was intended to meet the need to enrich students' understanding beyond the superficial. It was an explicit aim that the materials be designed to enable students to understand the nature of the problem and to present the opportunity to try out practical methods to counteract it in the classroom. The team's collaboration on the common task gave purpose to the dialogue through which much learning took place.

The need to improve the effectiveness of the assessment on teaching practice was a further concern of the larger team. There were two strands. One was the development of a computer program so that the use of the assessment forms could be monitored accurately. The other was the development of guidelines on what constitutes good practice. The method of development was consultation with all participants in the assessment process — students, teachers, and polytechnic supervisors. The end product of these consultations was a document to be distributed to students, schools and supervisors before teaching practice, to help in their assessments and self-evaluation.

The evaluation of Phase II was both formative and summative. Formative evaluation came from the team meetings and from the invaluable visits of the external evaluator. The summative evaluation was by a variety of methods tailored to specific subject groups, group evaluations with the whole cohort and in-depth interviews with 21 of the 151 students.

The curriculum materials devised were very diverse. They included materials to provoke discussion, a video to monitor gender issues in the classroom, student negotiated inputs. Full details are contained in the report and it is intended that as part of Phase III a publication will be made available presenting and, where appropriate, elaborating on these materials. It may be useful to present some of the conclusions reached at the end of Phase II.

Curriculum development in the subject specialisms is essential. The work done on equal opportunity in the four subject areas was perceived by the students to be highly relevant. They felt that it equipped them with practical ideas for implementation in the classroom. This perceived *relevance* may have contributed to what was perceived to be a more robust commitment to the professional centrality of the promotion of equality of opportunity.

Generalised work undertaken in Applied Education was an important feature of the course and complemented work in subject studies. It gave a conceptual overview of gender issues and allowed for exchange of ideas with students from other subject areas, and with students who taught different age-ranges of pupils. This facilitated understanding of developmental and pervasive aspects of the issues.

Peer tutoring and discussion is an effective method in this area. The success of student-led seminars on equal opportunity issues was striking. Students reported that they were often affected more by statements made by peers than by tutors.

Concepts of sexism and anti-sexism are enhanced by consideration of other sites of disadvantage. The introduction to equal opportunity on the course encompassed race, class, and disability as well as gender. Although specific input was generally within these discrete areas, inter-relationships and common aspects were highlighted where possible.

Tasks and projects which were required to be carried out in schools were especially useful. Aspects of the project which made demands on the students while they were in schools included observation, monitoring of practice, designing and implementing pupil projects. Success in these was only partial and allowance needs to be made for contextual constraints. Nevertheless, this strategy is invaluable as a way of helping students translate intentions into actions.

The Applied Education model that linked contextual relevance with the exploration of personal value systems was effective. The initial input in the first week in Applied Education on equal opportunities emphasised the professional necessity of effectively promoting equality of opportunity in the classroom. It was coupled with research evidence on teacher expectations making the point that teachers often *unwittingly* fail to fulfill this professional requirement because of unexamined assumptions. This was seen by the students as a high profile, yet non-threatening, introduction which implicitly established the rationale for exploration of personal values and attitudes. Addressing personal values is challenging and needs sensitivity but is essential for real change to occur (Kelly 1985). Establishing the need for such challenge is an important aspect of curriculum design. Students may need to face and, in some cases, alter attitudes and values in which there is great social/personal investment. Experience has shown us that a strategy of simplistic confrontation is often fruitless. It is likely to lead to polarisation and entrenchment where the possibility of real personal change is remote and meaningful dialogue almost impossible. The alternative adopted at Sheffield was in effect the strategy underlying the whole of the TENET project. It was based on the view that what mattered was the *whole* experience offered to the student by the course. An educational "environment" had to be created where every aspect contributed to establishing the necessity for vigilance concerning the gap between intention and practice and facilitated an informed response. Establishing such a necessity was precisely what was meant by "legitimation." Given that the importance and associated difficulty of the issue were universally accepted, reflection could be encouraged and a challenge made to personal and professional values.

The emphasis on peer collaboration and peer group challenge maximised the possibility of meaningful dialogue where the intervention of tutors in an authoritative role might have inhibited. It was vital that facts and information were provided and this was done through conventional lecture formats, workshops and required reading in both Applied Education and Subject Studies.

In short, this process seeks to reveal cognitive and affective dissonances with acknowledged professional duty. Against a background that legitimates concern about the issue, it facilitates informed discussion so that these dissonances can be articulated and examined within the peer group. Opportunities are provided throughout for students to test ideals against practice.

An unexpected result of considerable importance came from

the process of consultation about the assessment guidelines. It had already been established in Phase I that formal assessment emphasised the importance of the issue to students, polytechnic tutors and teachers in schools. It was a necessary feature of a permeation policy. Phase II established that such assessment provided invaluable support for teachers in schools who were themselves implementing equal opportunities policies. The development and dissemination of guidelines was welcomed as a potential catalyst to discussion within schools. It had some impact coming as it did from the outside institution for initial teacher training. Teachers expressed appreciation for the support it would give them in school.

The experience of the TENET project has been overwhelmingly positive. We started with a policy of permeation that worked very patchily. We have moved to a point where, during the course of the year, students receive the unmistakable message that it is a central professional concern and have a great deal of help to implement this in their practice.

The gap between rhetoric and practice is not accidental. We are all of us aware that disadvantage is a deep feature of our educational system even though we may characterise the causes differently (Lynch, 1989; Sharp and Green, 1975; Apple, 1979, 1986; Spender and Sarah, 1980). We are also unsure how far initial teacher training courses affect the practice of teachers. It is possible that under workplace pressures new recruits may not develop their practice positively (Zeichner Tabachnick and Densmore, 1987). Considering the immensity of the task, what we have done during the last two years is little enough. How can one avoid despair?

We each committed, more or less, to a particular context and role in our chosen workplace. My experience of the places in which I have worked has been of a lively coalition of different worldviews. They are necessarily sites of contradiction and struggle. In each of our specific areas we engage in a dialogue where we work to make our particular voice heard. In the process of defending or advocating important principles we refine our world view. This is then reflected in our practice (Giroux, 1989). The consequences of that continual process are significant for the people immediately affected. At Sheffield we have for the moment been successful in taking a lively and productive part in this important dialogue.

To end on a practical and hopeful note. For the first time we have gained some support from the Department of Education and Science for the year 1991. We hope to be able to convert this, as yet modest, support into more substantial help to extend the work within other institutions. The legitimacy that this would confer would be invaluable.

REFERENCES

Apple, M. (1979)
Ideology and Curriculum, London, Routledge and Kegan Paul.

Apple, M. (1986)
Teachers and Texts : A Political Economy of Class and Gender Relations in Education. Routledge and Kegan Paul, London.

Boulton, P. Coldron, J. et al (1990)
Integrating Equal Opportunities in the Curriculum of Teacher Education. (TENET) Phase II Report for the European action-research project on integrating equal opportunities in the curriculum of teacher education. Sheffield City Polytechnic.

Boulton, P. and Coldron, J. (1988)
Multicultural Education in the PGCE. Internal Report Sheffield City Polytechnic.

Coldron J., Boulton, P. (1989)
The implementation and evaluation of an action plan to develop the PGCE curriculum. Project Report (Phase I) for the European action-research project on integrating equal opportunities in the curriculum of teacher education. Sheffield City Polytechnic.

Ginsburg, M. (1987)
Reproduction, Contradiction and Conceptions of Professionalism : The Case of Pre-service Teachers. In Critical Studies in Teacher Education (ed, T.S. Popkewtitz), Falmer Press.

Giroux, H. (1989)
Schooling for Democracy : Critical Pedagogy in the Modern Age, Routledge.

Kelly, A. (1985)
    Changing Schools and Changing Society : Some reflections on the Girls Into Science Project. In Race and Gender : Equal Opportunities Policies in Education (ed M. Arnot), Pergamon Press.

Lynch, K. (1989)
    The Hidden Curriculum : Reproduction in Education, an appraisal. Falmer Press.

Sharp, R. and Green, A. (1975)
    Education and Social Control : A study in progressive primary education. Routledge and Kegan Paul, London.

Spender, D. and Sarah, E. eds (1980)
    Learning to Lose : Sexism and Education. Women's Press, London.

Zeichner, K., Tabachnick, Densmore, (1987)
    Individual, institutional and cultural influences on the development of teacher's craft knowledge. In Exploring Teacher's Thinking (ed J. Calderhead) Cassell.

THE INTEGRATION OF GENDER
IN SCHOOL GEOGRAPHY

Claire Lane

Thomond College of Education, Limerick, Ireland

Introduction

This paper investigates the need for the examination of gender issues in second level geography school content. It explores the nature and content of geography as a male dominated discipline and subject area, and examines the attempts made by a particular TENET project to integrate a feminist perspective into school geography content.

As a discipline, the concern of geography with places, spatial analysis and interactions, and the relationships between human beings and land, gives it a unique and important role among the social sciences. Geography approaches problems in terms of the relationships between people and land, and thus is more readily understood by, and identified with, a large proportion of the population. Given this unique position of geography, it is important that as a body of knowledge, and as a research discipline, it should be free from biases, and particularly those which serve to reinforce the traditional gender roles of women and men, and thus distort the insight which is obtained.

Geography has long been seen as the study of "man and his environment." Textbook titles such as *Man and the Land, Man, Space and Environment,* and, *Man's Role in changing the Face of the Earth* represent the content of much of the materials available to geographers. Geography generally assumed the word "man" as a generic term. However, on examining its content more closely, it is found that women's issues are generally ignored. It may not be the case that geography can be accused of being actively or consciously sexist.[1] As gender and gender roles are socially constructed and maintained, knowledge is also socially constructed and transmitted. The type of knowledge which emerges from a discipline depends largely on who produces the knowledge, what methods are used to obtain it, and the purposes for which it is required. The number of women involved in generating that knowledge is also an important factor in determining the type of knowledge produced.

Geography has been, and is still, predominantly a male profession.[2] With the division of labour which has prevailed within the profession, men have largely been in control of geographic research and curricula, and women have chiefly played a supportive role. Women are far outnumbered by their male colleagues in every area of geographic endeavour, apart from undergraduates where females dominate. In short, most academic geographers have been men and have structured their research according to their concerns, their goals and their values, all of which reflect their experience. It is important, therefore, that women seek to elect themselves to similar positions of influence, and assert themselves in achieving a fundamental shift in emphasis in the nature and content of the discipline at all levels.

The spatial interactions between human beings and their environment, which are a central concern of human geography, are undoubtedly gendered. However, without corrective measures, many of the students who are introduced to the discipline through existing texts, resource materials, and methods of study will never know this fact. Because geography traditionally emphasised male activities, the discipline has tended to assign women to marginal status. Geography students are currently being initiated into the discipline in ways that reinforce the illusion of women's marginality.[3]

Geography has for too long generalised the male to be the norm. The integration of gender issues within school geography is fundamental in providing an accurate analysis of human geographical phenomena, in order to enhance our understanding of society and space. It is not enough to say that women's views add colour to the data. They may be different, or contradictory, and require a totally different theoretical and methodological framework for study. A substantial body of work has shown that women's spatial behaviour, and perceptions of the environment are often different from those of men, and that ignoring these differences has meant that much traditional "genderblind" theory is at best partial, and at worst, simply incorrect.[4]   A geography course should provide female students with the same understanding of the social, economic, and spatial processes in which women interact, as it gives male students of the processes in which men interact.   Female students must be given the opportunities to view themselves as agents of social and landscape change, as male students are frequently given.

The question, therefore, becomes one of how school geography can most easily accommodate the recent insights which feminist research has brought to light.   In response to the raised consciousness of geography teachers about equality of opportunity and feminism, the most basic changes that can be made would be to eliminate, as far as possible, sexist behaviours and texts from the classroom.   While such changes represent a beginning, a more substantial shift in the angle of geographic vision is required. Further degrees of development involve the addition of something positive, such as the recognition of women's contributions to society or to a field of study, and supplementing course content with materials which emphasise such accomplishments.   There are also a number of examples of courses which focus on a "geography of women" in an attempt to reduce the invisibility of women in the discipline, which, while certainly a move forward, the problem remains of reconciling women and geography within "mainstream geography" courses.

A more sensitive handling of women's issues is essential to developing a more human geography.   There is a need to include recent feminist research findings in school geography content, to demonstrate the inadequacy of many existing concepts and methods for interpreting the worlds of women and men.   The launch of the ATEE/TENET projects in 1988 provided an opportunity to investigate how this might be achieved, and how it might affect teacher education.   This particular project was entitled *The Examination of Equal Opportunities Through Second Level Geography Education,* and was initiated by Thomond College of Education, Limerick, as one of the six Irish responses to the programme.

Project Objectives

The project attempted to redress the balance of equality education in two ways:

1. It was an attempt to provide junior cycle geography teachers, now facing a new syllabus in which gender issues are an integral part, with a secure and thought provoking set of resources from which to approach an area with which they may have hitherto been unfamiliar.

2. It was hoped to provide students with a stimulating learning experience through which they might become more aware of the existence, and potential problems of gender issues, and thus develop their sensitivity towards them.

Layout of the Resources

The project materials took the form of three self contained, but not mutually exclusive sets of resources, on three geographical themes, identified through prior research as being particularly useful in the exploration of gender issues:

1. Third World Development.
2. Residential, service and industrial patterns in the layout of large urban areas.
3. Economic geography.

Each pack contained ten individual resources, each designed under the following headings:

- Title,
- Objectives of the resource,
- Evaluation possibilities,
- Activity procedures,
- Suggestions for follow-on activities,
- Resource materials.

The resources attempted to extend over as broad a range of teaching and learning situations as possible, thereby providing both the teacher and the students involved with a worthwhile learning experience. The resources were designed to be flexible and adaptable to meet the demands of individual teachers, and school situations. Participating teachers were asked to keep detailed records of the students activities and assessment procedures employed, on the basis of which, the success of the materials could be evaluated, and modifications made for the dissemination of the project materials at a later stage.

Evaluation of the Project

Evaluation procedures were focused on two separate avenues of enquiry, the first being the success of the project materials, and the second, the worthwhileness of the project as a vehicle for teacher education.

Throughout the duration of the project, in both its first and second phase, participating teachers were encouraged to maintain an accurate and detailed record of all assessment procedures utilised, and general class responses to resource materials and activities. Students in some schools were invited to keep class journals of their activities, and record their opinions and attitudes in them. These journals, along with other assessment procedures, for example: essay work, semantic structure diagrams, and teacher records of questioning and discussion responses, formed the informative basis on which an assessment was made on the success of the project materials.

The teachers' responses to the project were evaluated by means of informal interviews based around a series of leading questions during the second inservice courses of both phases. This was an attempt to gauge how much teachers had learned about gender issues through their involvement in the project, any particular skills and insights which they might have gained, any additional confidence in dealing with gender issues, and their thoughts on the value and possibilities for inservice courses, or preservice courses, on gender issues in the future.

The project materials were designed with the new Junior Cycle Geography syllabus in mind, which incorporates into its objectives:

"an awareness of the dangers of all types of
stereotyping and prejudice, and to contribute to
students' understanding of important issues and
problems in our society."

Phases of the Project

The project was initially planned for a one year duration,
but was later extended to include a second year. In the first phase of
the project, initial background research was undertaken to establish
the areas of concern, and to design the resource materials bearing
these in mind. Six teachers were identified for participation, and
initial contact was made with them in November, 1988. The first
inservice course was held in January, 1989, during which the
resource packs were distributed and examined in detail. From this
point, until the end of April, 1989, teachers applied the resources in
the classroom, and frequent contact was made between them and the
project team members to monitor their progress and provide help
with any problems that may have arisen. The second inservice
course was held at the end of this period at which an attempt was
made to evaluate the success of the project based on the criteria
previously mentioned. Modifications were then made to the
resources based on the information provided from the participating
teachers, and ongoing research, in preparation for the second phase.

The second phase of the project took place during the school
year 1989/90, and was very similar in design to that of the initial
phase which was deemed to have been successful in achieving its
aims. This phase involved a much larger number of teachers, thirty
one in all, in a total of twenty six schools. Some schools undertook
the project as a team effort involving whole geography departments,
and in some cases, inter-departmental involvement was successfully
applied. Because of the greater number of teachers, and their wider
distribution across the country, two locations were chosen for
inservice courses. The administration of the project was similar to
that of the initial phase in every other respect. Modifications to the
project materials included format revisions such as the addition of a
resource index, pagination, a list of the names and addresses of other
participating teachers. Some textual changes were also made to a
number of the resources themselves.

Issues emergent during the project

The project inspired many questions on the issue of equal opportunities in teacher education. Most of the teachers involved expressed an interest in gender issues prior to the commencement of the project, but a very low number of these felt that they had previously tried to build this into their normal teaching programme. Others felt that they lacked the confidence and the background factual information necessary to approach such issues. The possibilities for providing such advice and information on how to tackle these issues are great at both preservice, and inservice levels. After the second evaluatory inservice course of both phases, the general consensus was that given a secure base of information and encouragement, such as the project provided, there was every reason to believe that many teachers would integrate a gender awareness perspective in their teaching and, not just in geography, but across the curriculum.

It was found also that participation in the project benefitted the teachers and students in a number of ways. In general the teachers felt that their confidence in dealing with gender issues was greatly increased, but they also experienced an increase in confidence in tackling other new issues, and in employing varied and innovative teaching methods. Many of these innovatory approaches were suggested by the material, but often the teachers saw the material as a trigger mechanism which encouraged them to try new strategies. The use of groupwork in learning was an example of an approach whose attractiveness became greatly enhanced to the teachers. Groupwork is frequently suggested in the resource materials and the teachers in general found it very successful. Many had previously avoided its use, having viewed it as a "luxury" and "time consuming." After their involvement in the project they found that their organisational skills in groupwork were greatly increased and it was a teaching method which proved very productive.

The students' response to the resources was in general very positive. Most enjoyed the variety incorporated within the resources, and many of the teachers believed that the materials acted as a trigger for the students to think more in depth on gender issues, and that it was certainly successful in raising their consciousness in the area of equal opportunities. However, in general, male students were less likely to analyse their views than were female students.

Conclusions and recommendations

One of the most important findings of the project over the two phased period was the need for a substantial body of relevant resources for teachers, either provided through inservice courses, or developed through preservice programmes. Many of the teachers are unfamiliar with such issues and the means of approaching them, and the provision of a flexible, reliable set of resources may encourage them to integrate this particular theme more fully into their teaching.

Due to the constraints of time necessarily placed upon the project, a significant change in students' attitudes could not realistically be expected. However, it was expected that the resources could successfully be employed to create an awareness of gender issues among students. It is believed from the evidence provided from the teachers, and through examination of students' journals and other evaluative instruments, that their level of consciousness of such issues was substantially increased.

Thus, to state the case positively, there is every reason to believe that, with some planning and insight, geography may be able to provide the female students with the opportunity of perceiving themselves as agents of social and landscape change, and to explore models of analysis that would be more applicable to their experiences, as male students are frequently allowed. To do so, geography would help to halt the process of generalising the male norm to be the experiences of all people, and would greatly increase girls' self image and esteem, as they view themselves visibly in interaction with men, which must inevitably lead to a questioning of equality of opportunity, and the realisation that their potential is as great as that of any male counterpart.

REFERENCES

1. Zelinsky, W., Monk, J. and Hanson, S.
   Women and Geography : A review and prospectus.   In
   Progress in Human Geography, 6, p.317-366, 1982.

2. Institute of British Geographers, Women in Geography
   Group. *Geography and Gender : An introduction to
   Feminist Geography.* London : Hutchinson, 1984.

3. Monk, J.
   Integrating Women Into The Geography Curriculum.   In:
   Journal of Geography, Vol.82, No.6, p.271-273, 1983.

4. McDowell, L., and Bowlby, S.
   Teaching Feminist Geography.   In *Journal of Geography
   in Higher Education,* Vol.7, No.2, 1983.

LA RÈFORME DE L'ÈDUCATION : EVALUER POUR INNOVER

I. Bordas

Facultad Pedagogía, Université Barcelona

M. Montané

Generalitat De Catalunya

Pendant l'année 1989 et les premiers mois de 1990 s'est réalisé en Catalogne l'évaluation ponctuelle d'une Réforme de l'Education qui a été exécutée experimentalement dans 40 centres scolaires.

Dans la 14th *Annual Conference de l'ATEE* — Kristianstad — au paragraphe 11 nous avons exposé le modèle qu'on allait suivre.

Comment on a fait cette évaluation?

L'évaluation s'est réalisé dès la perspective de différents secteurs: Dans le *secteur académique* se sont évalués non seulement les aspects qui ont une influence immédiate sur les apprentissages et sur le développement de structures mentals et des valeurs des élèves- comme le curriculum, l'orientation scolaire et professionnelle, les travaux et les activités d'enseignement, apprentissage—, mais encore tous les élèments qui y interviennent directement — gestion, direction, coûts économiques, etc. On a obtenu l'information moyennement des questionnaires et des entretiens avec les directeurs des centres, des professeurs, des élèves, des parents et d'autres personnes qui interviennent au procés de l'education.

Dans le *secteur professionnel* les évaluateurs se sont intéressés aux facteurs qui aideront l'élève à développer sa profession dans un futur plus ou moins proche. C'est à cause de cela quón a examiné les tà ches scolaires qui se projettent au secteur — orientation professionnelle, contenus et objectifs des matières par rapport à la réalité du domaine professionnel, les pratiques et les valeurs les plus significatives dans ce secteur, etc. Et que la commission a visité et a eu des entretiens avec les responsables des institutions du monde du travail de tous les secteurs professionnels.

Les stages des élèves aux entreprises se sont mis spécialement en valeur. Le caractère obligatoire des stages aux entreprises des élèves de l'étape 16-18 s'est considéré très avantageux et a contribué à prioriser l'aspect formatif plutôt que le productif.

Valorisation du procés d'évaluation des élèves, comme axemple

Dans le secteur académique se sont analysés différents aspects du curriculum: l'adequation des objectifs généraux des matières fondamentales aux capacités des élèves, la cohérence du curriculum entre les différentes étapes, les possibltés interdisciplinaires des nouveaux curricula, les adequations "curriculaires," l'individualisation de l'enseignement selon les besoins des élèves, la fonction de l'optionalité dans un curriculum équilibré, l'adequation des curricula au milieu où est placé le centre, l'analyse du procés d'évaluation des élèves, etc. En nous cernant à ce dernier aspect nous remarquerons trois aspects:

1. Pour la pluspart ils considèrent qu'ils *ont été évalués correctement dans la majorité des matières* des nouveaux curricula. Il n'y a à peine de différences entre les différentes étapes qui se sont évaluées (12-16), 16-18, cicle superieur d'Education primaire et 14-16). La plupart des élèves ont dépassé la note de "passable/et sont situés entre cette note et le "très bien," avec des pourcentages très pareils, entre le *passable* et le *très bien,* aux quatre étapes. Malgré cela, il faut observer la forte descente des pourcentages relatifs à l'excellent. Il faut observer aussi que les notes les plus élevées s'assignent à l'étape 16-18 — baccalauréats — c'est à dire, dans l'enseignement non obligatoire, ce qui confirme que dans cette étape il y a déjà eu une selection de l'effectif scolaire.

2.   La plupart des élèves des étapes évaluées disent qu'il y a *une évaluation par trimestre,* et dans peu de cas de deux. Cette distribution d'une évaluation par trimestre correspond à la structuration du cours par trimestres, et à la structure des matières en blocs.

3.   Les élèves coincident à affirmer que l'évaluation se fait surtout à partir des *questions, des thèmes, des sujets et des travaux écrits* et que s'evaluent peu les procédés et encore moins les attitudes, les valeurs et les normes.

La forme plus fréquente d'évaluation est la correction des travaux écrits, soit des activités qui se font souvent dans les cours, soit des preuves d'aspect plus formel. D'après les élèves la correction doit avoir une valeur de diagnostique et de support. Les élèves apprécient qu'on leur signale les erreurs, mais non seulement d'un simple signe mais d'une explication de la nature de l'erreur, ou bien en lui indiquant de parles avec le professeur pour qu'il le lui explique. D'un autre côté, ce style de correction permet au professeur de constater les erreurs les plus fréquentes et pouvoir préparer les cours selon ces fautes.

Dans les centres qui ont expérimenté la Reforme on constate des différences aussi dans le temps que dans l'effort que les professeurs consacrent *à la correction des travaux des élèves.* Dans quelques cas, la correction est du type diagnostique et formatif que nous avons signalé... Dans d'autres cas on le fait d'un manière plus routinaire, sans guère d'explication sur la nature des erreurs.

Quan la correction est peu fréquente, les élèves répètent les mêmes erreurs à cause du manque de compréhension d'un concept déterminé, ou bien on fait peu de travaux à cause du manque du temps pour les corriger. En général, ce n'est pas possible ni souhaitable de corriger tous les travaux. Il faut trouver un équilibre entre le temps qu'on consagre à corriger et le temps qu'on consagre a préparer les cours. Les élèves apprécient qu'il leur soient rendus les travaux corrigés le plus tôt possible.

D'un autre côté les "curricula" devraient expliciter davantage les orientations, et devraient contenir des indications sur la manière de résoudre les problèmes spécifiques d'avaluation de chaque matière.

4.   Il faut signaler l'effort que les centre on fait dans *la préparation des "modules" d'objectifs généraux.*

Il n'est pas toujours facile de trouver des sujets qui répondent aux besoins des élèves, et de les élaborer aux niveaux du rendement des élèves.

Il n'est pas aussi facile de trouver l'équilibre entre les faire trop faciles ou trop difficiles, de manière que dans un cas comme dans l'autre, ils ne soient pas utiles comme un instrument de mesure.

Il est important que ces preuves soient suivies d'un dialogue avec les élèves, de manière que ceux-ci aient l'oportunité d'expliquer leurs raisonnements, correctes ou non, pour pouvoir commenter les difficultés qu'ils ont rencontrées.

5.   Il faut signaler enfin les résultats des élèves des centres de la Réforme aux cycles 12-16, 16-18 et aux preuves d'accès a l'Universite.   Ceux-ci sont plus positifs que dans les centres ordinaires.

EDUCATION AND COMMUNICATION

Teresa Levy

Dept. de Educacoa, Lisboa

It is our contention that classrooms should be viewed as communicative spaces where those involved participate in the effort to establish common meanings and referents. In consequence, we want to stress the importance of considering the communicative interactions between teachers and students for an adequate approach to education. A view of communication as shared pragmatic and semantic work undertaken by all those involved influences our conceptions of personal relations and their fundamental importance for the realisation of human beings always in process and such conceptions will have, in turn, a bearing on our educative practices. Within this context, dialogue appears not just as another means to promote learning but as a quest for meaning, responsibility and truth which both students and teachers should pursue in their educative endeavours.

According to Jacques (1982, 1985) human sociality involves primarily two relational dimensions: the collective dimension which links individuals to a group or groups and an interpersonal dimension, revealed in relations of reciprocity, bringing a person to another, regardless of the instituted groups to which they belong. It is this last dimension which enables encounters between persons of different groups and prevents the complete closure of groups, which would have as a consequence the ascription of fixed places to the individual by the collectivity in a rigid network of social relations.

A systematic approach enables us to understand certain effects of group structuration, the ways in which the collectivity ascribes places to individuals who must, therefore, learn certain types of behaviours so that they can become integrated within the group and relations can be stabilised, by virtue of constraints exerted on the individuals. Acceptable individual behaviours prescribed by social rules are programmed and organised in systemic and viable patterns and must be learned by the members of the community, as well as the ideology that comes with them. This is the force of the social tissue which keeps each individual in a given place in a system of places. Thanks to this system, men entertain with their community a relation of belonging. From this collective perspective, society demands conformity and tends to avoid independence. In this collective reality the information that circulates becomes inseparable from the system of instituted communicative relations and the channels through which that information is disseminated. If those are established in a tendentious fashion, power relations tend to appear by means of the interplay of interconnected hierarchies within the complex communicative situation. Subtly, power permeates everything involving discourse formation and its reproduction.

If belonging to a group provides the individual with a set of predicates identifying his/her place within the group, personal relations, help to constitute one's personal identity which is irreducible to those predicates. When somebody is linked to some others by love, work, friendship or some type of interest requiring mutuality, we do not have here a series of totalisations but a moving dispersion of reciprocities.

Undoubtedly, the systemic approach can be applied to schools and classrooms, viewed from the perspective of their collective functioning. Still, if this approach is pertinent it is not the only one, nor can it claim epistemological primacy. It is not unique, given the existence of personal relations, at least in principle, even though they often suffer erasure, given the weight of the mass collective. Moreover, the systemic approach has no epistemological priority, since human systems are essentially open systems where relations must be able to transform themselves in the sense of reciprocity. It may be worthwhile to insist that a system in order to integrate relations among persons in a dynamic, interactive mode must not remain close in itself. Only in a closed system are relations completely cohesive but they also tend to degenerate in power relations, in oppressive forces, in parasitism. Individuals pay for such a closure becoming strangers to themselves and to those confined by it. True, that reciprocity or mutuality do not totally protect men against reification: relations which were reciprocal are sometimes recovered by relations they sustain and which are themselves repressive or reified. Still, they do fight closure that turns a system in a rigid structure where there is no possibility of transformation of rules and relations, no man's control over the system. In that sense, relations of reciprocity enable a change of the conditions of the type of belonging to a group. Relations of reciprocity must not be confused with relations of assimilation or rivalry of the same with the same, nor with relations of solidarity existing among members of a same group which are the complement of their situation of interdependence. However, without interpersonal reciprocity, we would not even know solidarity. Based on belonging, social relations would be reduced to relations of domination or competition among individuals or sub-groups. It is reciprocity which enables the generation of a constitutive division in a social situation so there can be a plurality which prevents a totalitarian representation.

In most of our concrete discursive dealings in social contexts, we find ourselves constrained to speak both as members of a given speaking community and as persons being involved in an interlocutory exchange. Thus, in a social usage of speech, the enunciative contract receives a double determination which entails special processes in the production and understanding of meaning. Because of the social framework, the question who speaks? or to whom am I speaking? is, in general, implicitly or explicitly, addressed in order to know the speaker's or interlocutor's place in a network of social roles, their conceptual and cultural codes, the ways in which they are supposed to be addressed or address others. At the same time, because the other is an interlocutor, we enter in some kind of interpersonal relation so that the discourse comprises a certain degree of dialogism, here understood as a relational condition of significance, insofar as the constitution of meanings is produced in discourse. This dialogism is responsible for a certain overcoming of the individual's place and its displacement to a differentiation as persons in a universe of communication where a shared participation of the semantic work is required in the face of a world to be spoken. Discourse takes place in between persons, the prefix- *dia* - representing both a distance and its overcoming by the institution of an interlocutory relationship. Thanks to it, the surpassing is made in the hope, shared by both participants, that it is possible to go to the end of the journey until mutual understanding is reached.

In other words, as a social phenomenon, every discursive act is at the intersection of a double determination, its value being determined by a double register, the institutional dimension which proceeds from the relation of belonging of the speakers to a given community, and the personal interactive dimension, regulated by an interlocutory reciprocity.

Let us insist: human systems are open systems if they are to allow their own life and renewal, and such a condition allows the transformation and modification of the relations and rules existing in them, since individuals have a certain possibility, by their activity of communication, to shift from the place to which they are ascribed in an instituted community of communication to a position in a regime of canonical communication. In particular, there is much that could be said about the capacity of persons to meta-communicate, that is, about the processes by means of which members of a speaking community communicate about communication to displace it or to transform its rules, which are determinant here. Meta-communicative discourse introduces a disposition of freedom in the social contract. Persons, do not only speak about interpersonal relations or comment on them, but are also able to change the rules, thus creating new communicative frameworks. Among all the changes in the formation and reformation of human relations, during all the vicissitudes which they undergo during negotiations and renegotiations, the most interesting processes are probably those by means of which the subjects institute among themselves common and accepted rules used to create and mutually understand messages. These common rules will serve as frame for the deployment of new relations.

Thus, not only are interlocutory relations, gaining body and life in discourse, essential for the conferring of a personal identity to human subjects but they have, in a sense, priority over systemic integrative approaches. True, that relations only find stability and identify within a system of compatible and articulated relations but belongs to the interlocutory relations the initiative to force the opening of social systems and the managing of conflicting situations in a satisfactory manner.

All that has been said applies, with some qualifications, to the life in school and in a classroom which are social contexts with diverse organisational rules and given operative instituted relations where each one has his/her place ascribed by a set of social criterion, some of which are imposed from the outside by those who have power over the educative system.

From a macroscopic point of view, each student is a student among others, all members of a class. The teacher, when he/she is in class, addressing the entire class, speaks to all in the same manner. However, this standard pedagogy is often doubled, or can at least be doubled, by interpersonal relations. Under an apparent monologism there can emerge a multiplicity or dialogic relations.

It is clear that the one-to-one relation between master and disciple is located in a larger context. As said, the school is not an abstract place; it is a concrete human place where the teacher is a teacher in and of his or her class, which behaves like a social group. All teaching deploys itself against a background of a community of wills and action. The particular relation established with such and such a student emerges from this communitary background, from a space saturated with presences which provide a common reference. More generally, the dialogue between master and disciple is located within the vast horizon of culture, in its process of construction by shared participation, within a vast patrimony of languages and traditions to which the master has to introduce the student, so that he/she can critically evaluate them and be prepared to participate eventually in their change, taking up his/her share of responsibility in the course of worldly events.

Within such framework, by a convergence of wills, the master and the disciple discover each other as such in the relation that binds them. The truth of each one of them depends on the relation with the other. It is a truth in reciprocity, found in dialogue.

The word of the teacher is not simply spoken in front of a class; it is a word that must resound through the class. More deeply, to teach implies to speak to, for with someone; it implies a reciprocity of perspectives. In spite of all ignorances, precautions and relational distortions, speech is a pact and presupposes a tacit agreement of mutual engagement and involvement of existences. Each word is a meeting place of involvement of existences. Each word is a meeting place of awaiting beings; they have the possibility of constructing a world in common, even if each one has the power to deceive such a project by non-participation or rejection, or to fulfill it.

Perhaps the ultimate justification of teaching is to be found in a communicative ethics. Each member must possess a communicative competency, comprising the capacity to meta-communicate, so that rules may be changed and relations transformed, having in view the search for better paths which might enhance mutual understanding whose horizon is given by the exigence of unconstrained, emancipatory communication aiming at consensus, respectful of the plurality and distinctiveness of human subjects.

In fact, the deepest, most paradigmatic reality of education, conceived as a search for humanity, a quest for a meaningful personal life, is centered around those dialogic instances during which two human beings of different ages and with different positions with respect to experience and knowledge, face and confront each other, so that each one of them becomes, in his or her own way, as witness before the other of human possibilities.

Even if teaching should not be confused with education, all teaching should have educational value. To instruct means, in Latin, to build, to edify. The school is one of the most influential places where a personality is edified. The milieu concurs for this edification. The mute presence of things, the presence of others, the teacher's discourse, all this orients, at each moment, the students' awareness. The possible encounter between teacher and student, the dialogue they may carry on, is not a dead dialogue in a space without contours, according to immutable liturgies. A man calls another man, a man addresses other men in their becoming, and they all are testimonies of humanity. The word culture reveals here its peasant roots: it is a life and a landscape. Each epoch has the culture it deserves. Ours, with all the means of communication, in general, of mass communication at its disposal, which, it would seem, would diminish the distance among persons, has done very little for the establishment of real closeness, or for the opening of a public space, brought forth by authentic dialogue. Also, if we are already headed to a civilisation no longer of work but of leisure, this cannot be seen, as it is usually, as an escape from work and as contributing to man's distraction of himself. In particular, culture, and the coming into culture cannot mean evasion and escape, but the enjoyment of a common pursuit for meaning and knowledge within an ever expanding horizon of possibilities.

Education is, as we have said, above all a human relationship, whose meaning may vary with the age, experiences, knowledge and interests of those involved. Existence forms and informs itself in contact with other existences that surround it, being a knot in this web of human relations. Within such relations we can include, as one of the most privileged, that established between the master and disciple, to the extent that the master is able to reveal to the disciple the requirement of the search for meaning and value of life and to orient him or her in that search. In confrontation with the master, students, in search of themselves, are awakened and moved to choose themselves, under the guidance of someone recognised by them as being able to provide what they lack. There are no neutral moments or steps in a life, in spite of the many efforts made to banalise events, to take away what they have of singularity, so as to diminish the possible risks involved. Encounters are possible risks because they can displace and recompose us. The word of the master opens for the disciple a field of infinite possibilities among which he/she must find his/her way. A discourse with an audience can then appear as a test for the one who speaks and the ones who are silent. Beyond concrete questions, a larger question can arise, a question each one may pose to himself/herself and that puts the questioner in question.

The smallest experience of an exchange of words attest to the fact that our existence is ceaselessly open and permeable to the other, and does not really know that self-possession so dear to a certain philosophy. A personality is especially alive when it encounters another personality and not if it remains closed in itself in some sort of apathy. The presence of the other, be it a messenger of similitudes or differences, is a privileged occasion of awakening and enrichment. In the encounter, two existences reveal themselves to one another and to themselves, because we only really discover ourselves and the others in the risk and test which the presence of the other constitutes.

Let us emphasise here that the relation of the master and the disciple is not, or must not be, a specular relation or any type of identificatory projection. They are looking not at each other but, together, in the same direction, aiming higher and further than before. The relation of the master with the disciple as well as that of the disciple with the master is characterised by a subtle dosage of intimacy and distance, of distance in intimacy and intimacy in distance.

It is in the encounter that master and disciple make one another authentic as interlocutors. From then on, there is no question of avoiding or escaping the other; together, they must go to the end of a certain exigence. In the debate that is maintained each one is exposed to the danger the other may represent and no one can tell in advance how the joint adventure is going to end. A bond, an alliance is formed, justified by the recognition of a non-predetermined yet common goal. Undoubtedly, in some sense, this is not an alliance among equals, between persons of the same age, similar experiences and knowledge. It is well to keep in mind this difference so that the teacher does not negate his/her responsibility, masquerading its avoidance with the assumption of some mystifying "maitre-camarade" position. There is in fact a gap between the positions of the master and that of the disciple. There is, however, a convergence of wills which communicates at that point in the horizon where their intentions are joined. Coming from different places, master and disciple participate in the same adventure, looking ahead in the same direction. Thus, in spite of actual hierarchic different places, we assist in the present of a reciprocity of positions which comprises the project of a future at the birth of an affinity, a fraternity of souls in spite of all possible gaps. This is why, says Gusdorf (1960) pedagogy is always secretly a form of friendship while adding, that friendship is, perhaps, always a form of pedagogy.

If the necessity of dialogue is recognised this signifies the end not only of a certain ontology, that of monologue and monopoly, but also of a certain pedagogy which looks only for the macroscopic appearance of education. This last one trusts the efficiency of a standard language with which all the students can be taught. However, no language is that impersonal, and the language of education least of all, since it is a privileged means of communication and self-formation. If the teacher's word mobilises the whole of the teacher, the discourse that is heard and the knowledge learned summons the whole of the student, requiring his/her active participatory answer. The dialogue between the master and the disciple is, as we said, a privileged one, to the extent that what is at stake is truth itself. This truth, let us repeat, is not already there at the disposal of everyone. It affirms itself as the common horizon of an interpersonal relationship, forms and transforms itself in the reciprocity which links the one who teaches and the one who learns. This truth, or its search, is the third term of the relation which involves and engages master and disciple, sustaining their union and preventing a complacent mutual contemplation. The influence of the master takes the form of a call to being in a world of possibilities.

564

BIBLIOGRAPHY

Gusdorf, G. (1961). *Pourquoi les professeurs?* Paris : Payot.

Jacques, F. (1982). *Difference et subjectivite.* Paris : Aubier-Montaigne.

Jacques, F. (1985). *L'espace logique de l'interlocution.* Paris : PUF.

TEACHERS' KNOWLEDGE AS BOTH THE LOCK AND THE KEY TO PROFESSIONAL DEVELOPMENT AND PLANNED CHANGE IN THE NINETIES : TESTING A PROPOSED FRAMEWORK

Ciaran Sugrue

St. Patrick's College of Education,
Drumcondra, Dublin, 9

Introduction

It is a truism to say that there will always be tensions in the field of education. There will be uneasy relationships between the demands made on the system by society for change in programme direction and content, and what the individual teacher thinks is best in his classroom for his pupils, not to mention what the pupils themselves might have to say were they consulted. Parents are insisting more and more on having a voice on behalf of their children.

Governments increasingly demand greater accountability from educators as pressures continue to grow to balance already overtaxed budgets at the local and state level. Meanwhile, pressure groups become more numerous and more vociferous, if not justifiable in their demands for greater portions of a shrinking national cake to be disbursed to their particular programme. This can only happen at the expense of another, perhaps even more deserving project. As health care and "high tech" medicine become more of a reality, as well as an expense, while actuarial predictions act as accurate predictors of creeping longevity in our communities, then, our educational system is more likely to have to get used to the idea of change, certainly without expansion, if not with contraction. The formal system of compulsory schooling may well be contracting, but there is an ever increasing demand for second chance, and re-education from the adult community, which in turn places extra demands on finances. These statements are not intended as a plea for leniency or special category status for educational programmes. Rather, changes which are necessary to improve the quality of the service of education, while at the same time improving its cost effectiveness, cannot be made simply appealing to the better nature of the individual teacher or administrator. In saying this, I do not wish to underestimate the importance of goodwill, merely to indicate that, it is no longer sufficient to bring about system-wide change in a complicated and complex system such as education.

Some indications from research

There is a growing volume of literature which indicates that, after fifteen to twenty years of research on educational change and implementation, more is known about the factors of success than many care to recognise (Huberman and Miles, 1984). In more recent research, various attempts have been made to systematise the benefits of these accumulated and accumulating findings, and to apply them in a systematic manner so that the problems can be re-conceptualised in terms of organisational design as problem-solving (Jones and Leithwood, 1989; Leithwood and Jantzi, 1989; Leithwood, Cousins and Trider, 1988; Leithwood, Farquhar and Boich, 1989; Marsh and Bowman, 1989; Leithwood, 1988; Leithwood, 1986; Gordon, 1984; Seashore Louis, 1989; Farrell, 1989; Crandall et al 1986). If a common theme can be identified in this research it is that much greater consistency between organisational needs and individual needs within the organisation can and must be planned to bring about greater congruence, thus improving organisational effectiveness, while at the same time, enhancing career patterns and the professional development of the individual teacher. However laudable a task this may be, it is a tall order. The bigger the scope of the operation, whether the initiative for change is at school, district, province or state level, the more varied, and in some ways also, the more variable are the factors which need to be influenced. It is at least worth postulating whether or not the level of control over the system, and consequently over individuals, implied in the literature is either desirable or attainable (Jones and Leithwood, 1989). In saying this, I do not wish to cast doubt on the veracity of those who wish to tackle this demanding and somewhat elusive task. Rather, I wish to draw attention to the enormity of the task and its remoteness from the reality of the classroom while not doubting that some of these factors do, despite their apparent remoteness, impinge directly or indirectly, for good or ill, on the quality of teaching and learning.

Proposing a framework to develop teachers' knowledge

This paper accepts that it is possible to improve organisational factors which in turn will reflect positively on teaching and student outcomes. The paper wishes to highlight the fact that none of these organisational factors are sufficient to bring about significant change at the level of the classroom. The pivotal factor of change in the school context, remains the teacher in his or her classroom as solo performer and team member. There are some dangers I submit, in focusing on the organisation as a unit of design such as attempting to combine the problem-solving strategy of Leithwood (1986), Ross (1985) and others, with the idea of organisational design (Leithwood, Steinbach, 1989). Both these approaches attempt to combine the lessons of twenty years of research to bring about improvements in both the effectiveness and the efficiency of education as a system. There is evidence that greater cohesion and consistency (Jones, Leithwood, in Press) can bring about these desired changes in organisations but there is the significant risk of strait-jacketing everyone in the process. The greater the cohesion at the organisational level, the greater the need for flexibility at the local level. Our experience of organisations to date has tended to see these two notions as conflicting or incompatible. Even with the apparent conflict between consistency and flexibility, there is still the need to facilitate the teacher to enable him to be able to reconcile them in practice. What then is the next step to be taken in attempting to capitalise on what is known about planned change? To give some context to the thesis being developed in this paper, it will be necessary to broaden the scope of the literature referred to above, to give it a greater contextual and theoretical base.

Epistemology and Cognition : cornerstones of the proposed framework

There are essentially two parts to this framework. There is an epistemological dimension and there is a portion which deals with

information processing. I will begin with the epistemological issue.
Donald Schon (1983, vii) informs the reader that there are many
"institutions committed, for the most part, to a particular
epistemology, a view of knowledge that fosters selective inattention
to practical competence and professional artistry." As a
consequence of this, he postulates that "practitioners usually know
more than they can say. They exhibit a kind of knowing-in-practice,
most of which is tacit" (vii). For a decade or more now, some
educational researchers (Elbaz, 1983; Clandinin, 1986; Clandinin
and Connelly, 1988) have been attempting to describe this tacit
knowledge in some detail through the use of rules, principles,
images, metaphors within a collaborative research design framework.
This approach rests on a particular epistemological perspective,
articulated with particular cogency, by Polanyi (1958). If it is
accepted within his framework that teaching is the practice of an art
form, then the relationship between the rules of the art form and the
practice of the art form become crucial. Polanyi (1958), p.50) says:

> Rules of an art can be useful, but they do not
> determine the practice of an art; they are maxims,
> which can serve as a guide to an art only if they
> can be integrated into the practical knowledge of
> the art. They cannot replace this knowledge.

The import of this dictum, though simple enough to
comprehend, has quite profound implications for bringing about
planned change. What is being said essentially is that organisational
planning at a system wide level is very important, but while new
prescriptions, rules and principles may set the ball of change rolling,
sooner or later it becomes the responsibility of the teacher to decide,
to change or not to change? Reformulating this question in Polanyi's
terminology, it becomes; how can the new rules and principles being
prescribed by a new programme, be integrated into the practical
knowledge of the teacher? Looked at from this perspective,
teachers' knowledge is both the problem and the solution, the lock
and the key to change.

Administrators at various levels within the educational
organisation, may believe that the latest proposal is most laudable,
necessary and timely. At a conceptual level everything seems more

than acceptable and the only wonder is why this is not already part of established practice. If it is to become part of established practice for staff who do not regularly practice in classrooms, all that is required is a shift in their conceptual frameworks to accommodate the new ideas. Changes may also require the reorganisation of timetables or other rules of procedure. What is required of non-classroom personnel is *accommodation* rather than *adaptation*.

For the teacher who has the responsibility of putting the plan into practice, much more is required than a mere conceptual shift. Where a significant change of practice or instruction is envisaged in a new plan, the practitioners' rules and principles of classroom practice must undergo significant alteration at the conceptual *and* the practical level. This is borne out by recent research which indicates that the proposed change has got to be sufficiently distant from teachers' current practice before they will consider it worth their while attempting to change (Huberman, Miles, 1985). This could be rephrased to say if teachers think they can, like the administrators, accommodate a newly proposed change into their existing practice frameworks, then adoption into existing practice, as opposed to adaptation of it, is all that is required of them. It is time to add a number of other elements to the context and elaboration of the proposed framework.

Elements of Teachers' knowledge

Huberman (1983, p.480) provides a detailed classification of knowledge which is a further refinement of the two broad categories which I have outlined above; theoretical or conceptual in addition to practical knowledge. The knowledge which teachers possess is primarily "recipe knowledge" or "craft wisdom." This in turn has three pertinent dimensions: locus, format and derivation, so that there is a very strong tendency for teachers to favour sources of knowledge close to them rather than depending on outside help in the form of consultants or journals (Huberman, 1982, pp.482-483). Cousins and Leithwood (1986, p.356) lend further weight to this perspective when they point out that:

Working knowledge, a term attributable to
Kennedy (1983, 1984) and derived from personal

experiences, beliefs, values, interests, and goals, was shown to be a powerful competitor with evaluation data. Several studies showed that knowledge derived from personal observation reduced the importance of evaluation for decision-making.

More recently, Huberman (1986, pp.604-606) has returned to this issue and again reinforces the craft, recipe nature of knowledge through referring to "ownership" and how it is influenced by positive, local institutional factors. The more personal, local and informal the help and support the greater the likelihood of ownership and of institutionalising change.

Changing Recipes

At this point the reader may be inclined to ask: what is all the fuss about? Is the process of change not the relatively simple matter of exchanging one recipe for another? Unfortunately, the heat of the classroom kitchen does not drive the consumers out as they are a captive audience. The teacher as recipe maker, is very much like the low income family or the old woman who lived in the shoe; essentially she could not change the diet as she lacked the resources to purchase alternative ingredients. It is in the nature of recipe knowledge, even when alternative ingredients (resources, materials) are provided, to cook them in the same old pot and in the same old way. This has the effect of cooking the nutrition out of the new materials so that the level of nutrition received by the learners (achievement outcomes) remains unaltered as the delivery system (recipe) and the manner in which it is cooked also have important significance for the eventual outcomes.

You may protest that many proposed programme changes in recent years have attempted to improve the delivery system of incorporating the accumulated wisdom of research into support programmes for the change initiatives. However, during this period also there has been growing pressure to cut the funding of such projects as their impact is said to be marginal (Farrell, 1989). One of the reasons for this has been a failure to distinguish between skill and judgement, particularly as these two terms are applied to teachers and teaching. Attempts to implement innovations have focused on the materials (ingredients) or the recipe (teaching skills) or the more recent model, in an attempt to give recognition to the knowledge and expertise of teachers, as well as to save money, is to present the conceptual framework (course on cooking, without breaking eggs) of the innovation, leaving it to individual teachers and schools to work out the details for themselves. Failure to distinguish between skills and judgements provides some of the explanation as to why support for innovation has been so selective.

Chambers English Dictionary defines the term skill as follows: discrimination, expertness: expert knowledge, a craft or accomplishment. By comparison, the explanation of the term judgement is significantly broader, while there is some degree of overlap with the term skill. The term judgement is defined in the same lexicon as follows:

> act of judging: the comparing of ideas to elicit
> truth: faculty by which this is done, the reason:
> opinion formed: discrimination: good taste.......

At one extreme, the simple routine application of rules to classroom situations is the total recipe approach, whereas, others point to the continuous need for making judgements through reflection in action (Schon, 1983). Grundy (1987, p.59) shows the relationship between the two when she says:

> Rather than simply claiming that the knowledge
> and application of sets of rules is a sufficient basis
> for action, hermeneutics reminds us of the
> importance of making decisions about the meaning
> of rules and the situation in which they are to be
> applied before action is taken.

Some implementation of innovations in the past have attempted to substitute one recipe for another. Even when support for innovations has included some element of conceptualisation and reflection, by and large the action element has been ignored. This seems rather strange when one turns to the literature on curriculum development.

The distinction between cognition and cognitive skill is pertinent to an understanding of this issue. Posner and Rudnitsky (1986, p.206) describe cognition as: "an idea that is intended to be learned" and a cognitive skill as "the ability to use or apply cognition." Pratt, (1980, p.312) develops this distinction further, when he says that while knowledge is necessary for skill development it is not sufficient. This distinction means that neither the simple prescription of a recipe or the conceptualisation of a proposed change is sufficient to bring about the change in practice. "The twin pitfalls of skill training are," he says (1) "neglect of relevant knowledge and (2) over-reliance on it." To accommodate to both the need for cognition and skill it is necessary to identify "three main stages in skill learning.... cognition, fixation and automation." This latter requirement will probably require overtraining as without this the value of many skills is extremely limited (p.314). Translated into the school context of innovation, this means that unless the initiative includes a knowledge component as well as skill identification and practice to the point of overlearning, the existing teaching recipe being employed by the teacher is unlikely to alter in any significant way. Is anything further required to improve the possibility of implementation leading to institutionalisation? Yes.

There are two additional ingredients of refinements which I would like to add to this pot pourri. To complete the framework that I am developing I am dependent on the Kolb (1976) learning style inventory as it has been adapted by Hunt (1987), particularly in what the latter calls the create or recreate cycle. When this is added to the need for demonstration in skill mastery and guided practice to provide support and feedback through the transition phase (Pratt, 1980, p.313), the following schema for institutionalisation of programme change suggests itself. In the same way that children have to creep before they walk, neglect of any one element in the schema will inevitably detract from the success of the implementation initiative, and in more usual circumstances lead to reversion to an earlier, less developed practice. If each element of the process can be seen as a notch on the key to teachers' knowledge, then each serration on the key is necessary to unlock the concepts, rules, skills and judgements to produce new recipes and different learning outcomes for both teacher and learner.

TEACHERS' KNOWLEDGE FRAMEWORK : ANALYSIS OF IMPLEMENTATION STRATEGIES

	Skill				
	Demonstration	Reflect	Concept	Practice	Feedback
Innovation Unfreezing					
		Refine			
Implement Changing					
Institutionalisation Refreezing			Autonomous Automation/Reflection		

(This grid is based on an adaptation of the curriculum development literature [Fullan, 1982; Rowntree, 1982; Pratt, 1980] and the Kolb [1976] learning cycle, particularly as it has been adapted by Hunt [1987]).

The labels on the left hand column are readily identifiable as the three phases through which a proposed change must go, to become part of the fabric of teachers' knowledge and practice. The five columns labelled across the top of the page are a variation on the Kolb cycle. The first column, skill demonstration, would begin with the concrete experience of the proposed change in operation. This would be followed by reflection (column two) on this proposed new practice and how it differs from what each teacher is currently practicing. This would lead naturally to column three and in systematic conceptualisation (Kolb; Abstract Conceptualisation) of the proposed change. The next step in the cycle, the practice phase (active experimentation) is probably the one that is most frequently ignored in implementation strategies. Much support is needed initially or participants will give up. It is significant that teachers are expected to develop new skills, judgements, concepts and expertise in front of their most critical audience, their own pupils, without the benefit of any dress rehearsal. This is why the additional column has been added to the Kolb cycle as being of particular importance, particularly at the initial stages as moral support, encouragement and feedback are vital for the refinement of concepts and skills. Indeed, it could be argued that to expect teachers to do this without any semblance of a safety net is to almost guarantee a luke-warm enthusiasm from all but the most daring of risk takers who probably need the programme least.

After sufficient time has been allowed for the change to occur, bearing in mind that some will take longer than others to adapt and adopt for a whole plethora of reasons, it should be possible for the teachers to dispose of columns one and five as they come to refine their skills and concepts and rely on their own reflections and judgements to do so rather than on the aid of a third party. It is important, therefore, to have an ordered retreat rather than sudden abandonment. This should probably be a joint decision of teachers and support staff rather than simply the termination of funding which is the more usual. This approach could probably save funds in many instances. Of course, as the innovation passes through various stages to the institutionalisation phase, the various elements of the schema will be in a dynamic relationship as the teachers create new menus through bringing about different blends of old and new recipes (Hunt, 1987).

If the framework, as it has been outlined above, has validity, then, the most successful innovations will be those which most closely conform to all the elements in the schema. Conversely, those innovations which consist of only some of the elements will be less successful, with those containing few or only one element of the framework, being least successful.

Testing the Framework : searching the literature

In an ideal world, the planning of an innovation would include the framework outlined above, as part of its structure. In the absence of this ideal, it is necessary to search recent research for evidence which would help in the evaluation of the usefulness of such a framework. What was I looking for? The literature would have to report on innovations that were designed to have impact at the classroom level. The innovations would also have to include an instructional change of some significance for the teachers, an alteration of old recipes so that long established rules of procedure, skills and judgements, well honed through practice, would have to be reconceptualised in a different context (innovation) with the consequent need to define, practice and automatise these, into new classroom routines.

The search of the literature began with the ERIC database, using the following descriptors: curriculum implementation, instructional innovation, case studies. As I was unsure as to the extent of the response to this request, the time limit put on the search was very generous, dating from 1970 to the present. Once the printout was received, which contained 56 studies in all, I put a five year limit (1984-1989) on any other searches which would be undertaken because I wished to limit the study to recent research. Also, the fact that in the early seventies little was known about implementation as a problem was a further encouragement to look at more recent literature (Fullan, 1982). Using the same descriptors and the names: Connelly, Leithwood and Fullan, a search of the CSSI[1] was conducted. This yielded a disappointing list of only three studies. Following this, a manual search of *Curriculum Inquiry, Alberta Journal of Educational Research* and *Canadian Journal of Education* was undertaken. At this point also I had decided to limit the studies to the primary school sector as that is my major area of interest, as well as the fact that some recent studies indicate that different sets of variables are at play in the secondary domain (Firestone, Herriott, 1982). On completion of the various searches there were sixteen studies which seemed to be relevant to the issue. Another framework was then used to do a preliminary analysis of these sixteen studies. This framework has been successfully employed elsewhere for the purpose of organising large quantities of research information (Leithwood, with assistance from Batcher, 1987; Leithwood, Lawton, Cousins, 1989). In the context of this paper, the purpose of the analysis was to group the studies according to major focus, as well as to discover the detail of the support structures which were provided in each case for the innovation which each study was evaluating.

METHODOLOGICAL CHARACTERISTICS OF THE SELECTED STUDIES

Authors	Categories of Dependent Variables	Designs and Procedures	Sample : Nature of Instruments	Data Collection Procedures
1* This is the Canadian Social Science Citation Index				
1. Vanderveghte, R. (1988)	School Principal behaviour	Principal intervention effects on implementation	275 Elementary schools interater reliability	Interview
2. Vandervegt, R. (1988)	Principal and teacher	Conceptualise implementation	21 Schools	Case Study: observation & Interviews
3. Hall, G.E. (1988)	Principal, teacher interaction	Principal as leader of change facilitating	9 Schools taxonomy of intervention	Concerns based adoption model
4. Butt, R.L. (1984)	Supervision: professional development. Collaboration	20 Teachers	Case study	
5. Ellis, N. (1986)	Collaborative : support for teacher change	Focused observation : targeted feedback	13 Teachers, 5 schools	Checklist, observation
6. Bratlie, M.P. (1987)	Principal influence: teacher autonomy	School : loosely coupled principal as leader	Principal and 19/26 staff	Interviews

METHODOLOGICAL CHARACTERISTICS OF THE SELECTED STUDIES (continued)

Authors	Categories of Dependent Variables	Designs and Procedures	Sample : Nature of Instruments	Data Collection Procedures
7. Stokking, K.M. (1988)	National Policy : support	Support for implementation and renewal	4 Major projects. Netherlands, 1975/88	Questionnaire : statistics, analysis
8. Ellis, N. (1987)	Level of teacher interaction	Supportive atmosphere specific feedback	13 teachers, 5 schools 3 school districts	Questionnaire, observation, interview
9. Erickson, G. (1988)	Teachers perspectives: innovation	Mandated change: teacher responses	4 Senior high schools 2 Junior high schools	Participant observation
10. Smordin, C. (1984)	Personal contact : degree of implementation	Inservice, feedback, participation	4 Schools, 130 5th grade teachers	Questionnaire: self-reporting, interview, document analysis
11. De Acosta, M.C. (1988)	School, classroom : effects on implementation	Computer literacy	3 Schools, different SES	Case study
12. Martin, L.M.W. (1988)	Outside classroom variables	System-wide factors influence implementation of inquiry	82 Teachers, 32 schools, inservice : workshops	Questionnaire, interviews, observations

METHODOLOGICAL CHARACTERISTICS OF THE SELECTED STUDIES (continued)

Author	Categories of Dependent Variables	Designs and Procedures	Sample : Nature of Instruments	Data Collection Procedures
13. Guskey, T.R. (1987)	Teacher self-concept: influence on implementation of mastery learning	Effective teachers : effective implementers	120 Elementary and Secondary teacher inservice	Questionnaire
14. McRadu, K.A., Allison, D. & Gray, R.F. (1985)	Central development : local implementation	Language arts programme	115 Teachers, 6 schools randomly chosen	Questionnaire
15. Larocque, L., Coleman, P. (1985)	School board policy : school response	Community relations : "logic of confidence"	36 Elementary, 9 Secondary	Interview : formal, informal
16. Sharman, R.G. (1987)	Teacher level of use and fidelity of implementation	Organisation support : consistent with implementation	155 Elementary teachers	Correlational design study

Having analysed the material in this manner, it was possible to group the studies into three general categories. Eight of the sixteen studies focus directly on implementation and classroom practice and these form the major focus for testing the validity of the proposed framework (Ellis, 1986, 1987; Erickson, 1988; Smorodin, 1984; De Acosta, 1988; Martin, 1988; Guskey, 1988; Sharman, 1987; Butt, 1984). The second focus for analysis is the interplay between the staff and the school principal as a crucial factor in enhancing implementation (Bratlie, 1987; Hall, 1988; Van Den Berghe, 1988; Van Der Vegt, 1988). The third category of information which will be examined in the light of the proposed framework is the impact of policy, regional and/or national, at the local level (Stokking, 1988; McRadu, Allison & Gray, 1985; Larocque,Coleman, 1985). The first and second groupings are much more important to an assessment of the value of the proposed framework and this will be reflected in the analysis which follows.

Framework : Focus on Changing Classroom Practice

It is appropriate at this point to clarify more precisely, the terminology of the framework. Planned change, as it is used in this context implies growth (Leithwood, 1986) within the system. Also implied in the process of implementation, from innovation to institutionalisation is, the idea of this process occurring over time (Leithwood, Fullan, Taylor, 1987; Fullan, 1982). Consequently, it is necessary for teachers to develop the "necessary implementation procedures" (Saunders, McCutcheon, 1986), to see teaching as a "decision-making process" (Bacharach, Conley, Shedd, 1986), to develop greater collegiality (Zahorik, 1987), and to recognise that teaching is also filled with "routine activities" (Barakett, 1986). Teachers must also recognise that these routines or recipes are the entithesis of reflective teaching (Schon, 1983) and if they, (teachers), are to engage in a process of change then they must be open "to confusion, to not-knowing, hence to vulnerability.... and to defensive strategies designed.... to protect against vulnerability" (Grimmett, Erickson, 1988, p.23). The framework is, therefore, generally supported by the literature which says that grwoth in teachers occurs over time, in an atmosphere where risk-taking is encouraged and vulnerability is cushioned by a positive and supportive environment which includes the provision of feedback. Closer analysis of the processes involved is necessary, if the proposed framework is to be tested further.

While retaining the three groupings already arrived at as a result of the analysis of the studies conducted above, the proposed framework was then applied to each of these three groupings. The original numbering of the studies is retained so that the numbers no longer appear in sequence but in the groups to which the earlier analysis has assigned them.

Proposed Framework : classroom change

It becomes very obvious, with even a cursory glance at the following table that, no matter how closely related to the routine practices of teachers, none of the studies treat all aspects of the knowledge framework of teachers in a systematic manner. The most impressive study (Martin, 1988) also becomes disappointing when it is realised that all the activities in the first five columns were confined to a one week workshop framework. The study concludes that "teachers are learners" and "this learning happens in the workplace" (p.6) so that it becomes vital for staff developers to have contact with teachers in their classrooms (p.9). This general thesis is supported by Butts (1984, p.11) when he claims that much of what has passed for curriculum implementation strategies have only served to "disenfranchise teachers" rather than to promote the concept of ownership and expertise at the classroom level. Both studies conducted by Ellis (1986, 1987) provide very good evidence that local support is vital if teachers are expected to trade old recipes for new ones. This support must consist of a theoretical framework for the proposed change, targeted feedback to classroom performance, provision for participants to meet and discuss with colleagues as well as technical support where necessary. Where there is contact between a programme developer and participating teachers, the amount of contact, its nature and duration, become very important (Smorodin, 1984,; Sharman, 1987).

KNOWLEDGE FRAMEWORK APPLIED TO THE SELECTED STUDIES

Authors	Skill Demonstration	Reflect	Concept	Practice	Feedback
4. Butt, R.L.		*	*	**	**
5. Ellis, N.				**	**
8. Ellis, N.					**
9. Erickson, G.	Focus on	conducive	enviorment	for	change
10. Smorodin, C.					**
11. De Acosta, M.C.				**	
12. Martin, L.M.W.	**	**	**	**	*
13. Guskey, T.R.	Teacher	self-concept	central to	effective	implementation
16. Sharman, R.G.				Evaluation, supervision	staff-development
6. Bratlie, M.P.				Support from	principal
3. Hall, G.E.				Principal as team	leader
1. Vanden-Berghe, R.				Principal:	styles of leadership
2. Vander-Vegt, R.					
7. Stokking, K.M.					
14. McRadu, K.; Allison, D.; Gray, R.					
15. Larocque, L., Coleman, P.					

[Key: Where two ** appear, this indicates that this aspect of teacher knowledge is the major focus of that particular study; where one * appears, some evidence is provided in the study to indicate that the focus has had some influence on these other areas of teacher knowledge also. where a particular study could not be categorised using this framework, a cryptic sentence is provided as an alternative].

All these factors, on their own, are not sufficient to ensure that teachers institutionalise change or trade old recipes for new. It is necessary for these strategies to be undertaken in a conductive atmosphere (Erickson, 1988). Further evidence of the need to work closely with teachers, in a collegial manner is provided by Guskey (1988), p.67) when he says: "teachers who express a high level of personal efficacy.... also appear to be the most receptive to the implementation of new instructional practices." Even more support becomes necessary for less confident and less accomplished teachers. There is also evidence that implementation strategies that ignore the need for conceptualisation of the proposed changes, reduce the effectiveness of the change to nothing more than "tricks for teachers" (De Acosta, 1988). Substituting one recipe for another is not sufficient.

These studies are disappointing from the perspective of the proposed framework, as they do not supply any substantial information on the duration of support for the various initiatives or the intensity of the support. Obviously this would have to be tailored to the needs for the teachers and the nature of the proposed change. It may also be the case, although this is not confirmed by any of the evidence in the studies under discussion, that for some proposed changes at the classroom level, it may not be necessary to include all elements of the proposed framework. However, the more likely interpretation is that attempts to date at implementing change have been too narrowly focused to the detriment of the change process itself and to the development of teachers' capacities to improve their powers to process knowledge so as to improve their expertise in a cumulative fashion. There is growing evidence from the literature and from some of the studies analysed in this context that the school principal is of pivotal importance in supporting and bringing about change at the classroom level.

Proposed Framework : School Principal and Classroom Change

Apart from a maturing literature on school effectiveness (Purkey, Smith, 1987), there are also indications, as has been suggested above, that the school principal is a key player in this process (Leithwood, Begley, Cousins, 1989, in press). It is against this broader background that the studies already identified, will be analysed with the specific focus of the extent to which the school principal plays a key role in enabling and facilitating teachers to develop their knowledge processing capabilities.

Bratlie (1987, pp.12-13) identifies a series of steps whereby teachers change their knowledge; what he calls: four quasi-sequential phases:

(a) seeker/missionary interface,
(b) encapsulation,
(c) implementation, and
(d) maintenance.

The principal with a clear sense of mission is more likely to provide the other elements which Bratlie deems to be necessary for successful classroom change. These phases seem to be remarkably similar to the basic structure of the framework being proposed in this paper. Further refinements of this Bratlie structure is provided by some of the other studies. Van Der Vegt (1988) identifies: direction, concept clarification, directional pressure, latitude definition (where the teacher is given enough autonomy to work things out for himself), assistance and support in the form of social and emotional support, technical support as well as operational power to remove blockages, as important elements in the process. This notion of a highly developed local network is developed a little further by the idea of a team with the class teacher, principal, vice-principal and curriculum consultant or other outside professional (Hall, 1988). The essential point is that the task is too complex for the teacher to undertake in isolation. The style of leadership of the principal is significant, with those with a capacity for planning and good communicating having a clear advantage over more managerial, less innovative leadership styles (Van Den Berghe, 1988).

All this evidence I take to be broadly supportive of the proposed framework with room for possible refinements and adjustments dependent on local context. The evidence generally strengthens the perception of knowledge processing as a dynamic interaction. It also lends support to the idea to see it as a cynical process (Hunt, 1987). This becomes even more important when it is realised that the recipe nature of knowledge in classrooms is so embedded that coercion (positive) through very strong local vision and support is necessary to get adults to adjust and change their practices. With an ageing teaching force this becomes even more important. It should also be clear from this evidence that national or state prescriptions must be undertaken with flexibility and respect regarding local needs and problems.

Proposed Framework : planned change at the provincial or national level

While the studies which are analysed in this final section have the specific focus of the proposed framework, it is also important to locate them in the context of an emergent and expanding literature. This literature has set itself the ambitious task of attempting to develop the effective school literature further by applying it to the system as a whole. There is a growing awareness through it of the need, not only, to disseminate the benefits of accumulated research findings but to try to present this information in a manner whereby it can be processed effectively into the classroom recipes of teachers (Leithwood, 1989; Farrell, 1989; McClean, 1989; Huberman, 1987; Odden, Marsh, 1987; Cousins, Leithwood, 1986; Fullan, 1986). Looked at in this light, the challenge to the system is the seemingly contradictory one of creating system-wide support structures which make the system more efficient and more effective, while at the same time being flexible and responsive to local needs and problems. It is also true to say that practice lags along way behind the accumulated wisdom of current and past research. It is a very real and a very important challenge to the system to improve the information processing capacity of the practitioners.

How is this to be done? Stokking (1988) points to a developing consensus among researchers, in Europe as well as in North America, of consistency in research findings with regard to what is needed at a system-wide and local level. At the heart of this is a need for clarity of policy, realistic deadlines, (this will help to eliminate overload) as well as personal contact. Of course the list is more extensive than this but none of the items contradict the basic structure of the proposed framework. This is further reinforced by McRadu, Allison and Gray (1985, p.198) when they say that: "the majority of the teachers (in their study) felt a need for more assistance than had been provided at the local level." Other evidence (Larocque, Coleman, 1985) suggests that coercion does not work at the classroom level as teachers who do not subscribe to policy initiatives will not implement them. Another way of describing this phenomenon is to say that teachers only process that information which they consider to be of value and of consequence for their teaching. This suggests that whatever is done to streamline the system, the information processing capacity of the teacher continues to be the barrier as well as the gateway to effecting growth at the personal and system levels.

Conclusion

All aspects of the framework which this paper proposes have been highlighted by the research which has been analysed as essential elements in implementing change at the classroom level. The fact that there has not been a systematic attempt to address the issues of personal or recipe knowledge as a major barrier to programme change would seem to indicate that planning in this regard has been short term, associated with specific initiatives only. These initiatives always seem to have a fixed timescale, which is usually too short, before the curriculum specialist or Government Minister launches yet another initiative. It would also seem to indicate a clear need for a policy which has teacher development, rather than particular curriculum initiatives as its primary focus. From a policy perspective, putting the cart before the horse is neither fair to beast or burden and serves only to retard the development of the transport system.

The research is disappointing in so far as it does not indicate why, or in what way the various aspects of the proposed framework are important. Future research will have to concentrate on a more systematic treatment of embedded rules, principles and beliefs of practitioners. This requires a more long term commitment to professional development than the system has been prepared to provide to date. However, it may be the only long-term investment that will pay an appropriate dividend for planned programme change.

Teachers' knowledge will certainly have to be unlocked if

the system is to be able to respond to the accelerating pace of change. There is sufficient evidence to suggest that the framework which has been proposed here would assist in that process. It may well be that the school principal in cooperation with staff, as well as other local support, is the one who holds the key.

REFERENCES

Bacharach, S.B., Conley, S.C., Shedd, J.B. (1987)
"A Career Development Framework for Evaluating Teachers as Decision-Makers." *Journal of Personal Evaluation in Education 1*, pp.181-194.

Barakett, J.M. (1986)
"Teachers' Theories and Methods in Structuring Routine Activities in an Inner City School." *Canadian Journal of Education*, Vol.11, No.2, pp.91-108.

Boich, J.W., Farquahar, R.H., Leithwood, K.A. (1989).
The Canadian Superintendency.   Toronto : Ontarion Institute of Studies in Education Press.

Bratlie, M.P. (1987)
"The Conversion of Teachers : Principal Influence and Teacher Autonomy."   A paper presented at the Annual Meeting of the AERA, (ED 302 877).

Butt, R.L. (1984)
"Curriculum Implementation, Classroom Change and Professional Development : The Challenge for Supervision." A paper presented as CSSE, Guelph, Ontario (ED 269 853).

Clandinin, D.J. (1986)
Classroom Practice.   Great Britain : The Falmer Press.

Coles McRadu, K., Allison, D., Gray, R. (1985)
"Implementing a Centrally Developed Curriculum Guide." *The Alberta Journal of Educational Research,*   Vol.31, No.3, pp.191-199.

Connelly, E.M., Clandinin, D.J. (1988)
Teachers as Curriculum Planners Narratives of Experience. Toronto : Ontarion Institute of Studies in Education Press.

Cousins, J.B., Leithwood, K.A. (1986)
"Current Empirical Research on Evaluation Utilisation." *Review of Educational Research,* Vol.56, No.3, pp.331-364.

Crandall, D.P., Weisman, J.W., Seashore Louis, K. (1986)
"Strategic Planning Issues that Bear on the Success of School Improvement Efforts." *Educational Administrative Quarterly,* Vol.22, No.3, pp.21-53.

De Acosta, M.C. (1988)
"The Impact of Schoolwide and Classroom Elements On Instructional Computing : A Case Study." A paper presented at the Annual Meeting of the AERA, New Orleans, (ED 301179).

Elbaz, F. (1983)
TeacherThinking : A Study of Practical Knowledge. London : Croom Helm.

Ellis, N. (1986)
"Collaborative Interaction as Support for Teacher Change." A paper presented at the Annual Meeting of the AERA, San Francisco, (ED 283 812).

Erickson, G. (1988)
"Teacher Perspectives and Educational Innovation." A paper presented at the Annual Meeting of the AERA, New Orleans, (ED 3029).

Farrell, J.P. (1987)
International Lessons for School Effectiveness : the view from the developing world. In M. Holmes, K. Leithwood, D. Mussella (Eds). *Policy Development for Effective School Administration.* Toronto : Ontarion Institute of Studies in Education Press.

Firestone, W.A. & Herriott, R.E. (1987)
    Effective Schools : do elementary prescriptions fit
    secondary schools. In R.V. Carlson, E.R. Ducharme (Eds).
    School Improvement — Theory and Practice. Lanham,
    M.D., University Press of America.

Fullan, M. (1982)
    The Meaning of Educational Change. Toronto : Ontario
    Institute of Studies in Education Press.

Fullan, M.G. (1986)
    School Improvement Effort in Canada. Prepared for the
    council of Ministers of Education, Canada as part of the
    International School Improvement Project (ISIP),
    CERI/OECD.

Gordon, G. (1984)
    The Myth of School Self Renewal. New York : Teachers
    College Press, (Ch.6).

Grimmett, P.P. & Erickson, G.L. (Eds)
    Reflection in Teacher Education. New York : Teachers
    College Press, 1988.

Grundy, S. (1987)
    Curriculum : Product or Praxis. England : The Falmer
    Press.

Guskey, T.R. (1987)
    "Teacher Efficacy, Self-Concept, and Attitudes Toward the
    Implementation of Mastery Learning." A paper presented
    at the Annual Meeting of the AERA, Washington, (ED
    281838) and published in *Teaching and Teacher Education,*
    (1988) Vol.4, No.1, pp.63-69.

Hall, G.E. (1988)
    "The Principal as Leader of the Change Facilitating Team."
    Journal of Research and Development in Education,
    Vol.22, No.1, pp.

590

Huberman, M. (1983)
"Recipes For Busy Kitchens. A Situational Analysis of Routine Knowledge Use in Schools." *Knowledge : Creation, Diffusion Utilisation,* Vol.4, No.4, pp.478-510.

Huberman, M. (1987)
"Steps towards an Integrated Model of Research Utilisation." *Knowledge : Creation, Diffusion, Utilisation,* Vol.8, No.4, pp.586-611.

Huberman, M. & Miles, M.B. (1984)
"Rethinking the Quest for School Improvement : Some Findings from The DESSI Study." Reprinted by permission of Teachers College Press from *School Improvement Research Craft and Concept,* Teachers College 86, No.1 (Fall 1984) pp.35-54.

Hunt, D.E. (1987)
Beginning with Ourselves. In Practice, Theory and Human Affairs. Toronto : Ontario Institute of Studies in Education.

Kolb, D.A. (1976)
The Learning Style Inventory. Boston : McBer & Co.

Larocque, L. & Coleman, P. (1985)
"The Elusive Link : School-Level Responses to School Board Policies." *The Alberta Journal of Educational Research,* Vol.31, No.2, pp.149-167.

Leithwood, K.A., Jones, L.B. (1989)
"Draining the Swamp : A Case Study of School System Design." *Canadian Journal of Education,* in press.

Leithwood, K.A., Lawton, S.B. & Cousins, J.B. (1989)
The Relationship Between Selected Characteristics of Effective Secondary Schools and Student Retention. A paper presented at the International Congress for School Effectiveness, Rotterdam, The Netherlands.

Leithwood, K.A., Cousins, J.B. & Trider, D.M. (1988)
The Process and Substance of Curriculum Reform in Canada. In J.Y.L. Lam, *Canadian Public Education System : Issues and Prospects.* Toronto : Kagan and Woo Publishers.

Leithwood, K.A. (1986)
"Planned Change as Problem-Solving." A paper presented at International Symposium about Theoretical Models and Strategies for Educational Innovation, Murcia, Spain.

Leithwood, K.A. (1986)
Planned Educational Change. A Manual of Curriculum Review, Development and Implementation (CRDI) Concepts and procedures. Toronto : Ontario Institute of Studies in Education Press.

Leithwood, K.A. Fullan, M. & Heald-Taylor, G. (1987)
School Level CRDI Procedures to Guide the School Improvement Process (SIP). Prepared for the Ministry of Education, Ontario School Improvement Project.

Leithwood, K.A., Begley, P.T. and Bradley-Cousins, J. (1989)
"The True Causes and Consequences of Principals' Practices : An Agenda for Future Research." *Journal of Educational Administration,* in press.

Leithwood, K.A. (1987) [With assistance from Elaine Batcher]
A Review of Research Concerning Characteristics of Exemplary Secondary Schools. A Working Paper Prepared as part of the Research Project : Student Retention and Transition.

Leithwood, K.A. (1989)
School System Policies for Effective School Administration in M. Holmes, K. Leithwood, D. Musella (Eds). *Policy Development for Effective School Administration.* Toronto : Ontario Institute of Studies in Education Press.

592

Marsh, D.D., Bowman, G.A. (1989)
"State-Initiated Top-Down versus Bottom-Up Reform."
Educational Policy, Vol.3, No.3, pp.195-216.

Martin, L.M.W. (1988)
"System-Wide Factors in Sustaining Technology-based
Inquiry Environments." A paper presented at the Annual
Meeting of the AERA, New Orleans, (ED 301171)

McClean, L. (1989)
Lessons for Administrators from Large-scale Assessments
of Teaching and Learning. In M. Holmes, K. Leithwood,
D. Musella (Eds). *Policy Development for Effective
School Administration.* Toronto : Ontario Institute of
Studies in Education Press.

Odden, A.R., Marsh, D.D. (1987)
How State Education Reform Can Improve Secondary
Schools. Policy Paper No. PCC87-12-14-SDE.

Polanyi, M. (1958)
Personal Knowledge. Towards a Post-Critical Philosophy.
London : Routledge and Kegan Paul.

Posner, G.J. & Rudnitsky, A.N. (1986)
*Course Design. A Guide to Curriculum Development for
Teachers.* London : Longman.

Pratt, D. (1980)
Curriculum Design and Development. Toronto : Harcourt
Brace Jovanovich, INC.

Ross, J.A. (1985)
"Program Evaluation as Problem Solving. Implications of
a Metaphor." *Evaluation Review,* Vol.9, No.6, pp.659-679.

Rowntree, D. (1982)
>   *Educational Technology in Curriculum Development.*
>   London : Harper & Row Ltd.

Sanders, D.P. & McCutcheon, G. (1986)
>   "The Development of Practical Theories of Teaching."
>   *Journal of Curriculum and Supervision,* Vol.2, No.1,
>   pp.50-67.

Schon, D.A. (1983)
>   *The Reflective Practitioner. How Professionals Think in
>   Action.* New York : Basic Books, Inc., Publishers.

Seashore Louis, K. (1989)
>   The role of the school district in school innovation. In M.
>   Holmes, K. Leithwood, D. Musella (Eds). *Policy
>   Development for Effective School Administration.* Toronto
>   : Ontario Institute of Studies in Education Press.

Sharman, R.G. (1987)
>   "Organisational support for implementing an Instructional
>   Innovation." *The Alberta Journal of Educational
>   Research,* Vol.33, No.4, pp.236-245.

Shuell, T.J. (1986)
>   "Cognitive Conceptions of Learning." *Review of
>   Educational Research,* Vol.56, No.4, pp.411-436.

Smorodin, C. (1984)
>   "Why Teachers Implement : An Examination of Selected
>   Variables." A paper presented at the Annual Meeting of the
>   AERA, New Orleans, (ED 249622)

Stokking, K.M. (1988)
>   "National Educational Policy and External Support Systems
>   as Conditions for Curriculum Implementation." A paper
>   presented at the Annual Meeting of the AERA, New
>   Orleans, (ED 300869).

Trider, D.M. Leithwood, K.A. (1988)
"Exploring the Influences on Principal Behaviour."
Curriculum Inquiry, Vol.18, No.3, pp.289-311.

Van Der Vegt, R. (1988)
"The Role of the Principal in School Improvement :
Steering Functions for Implementation at the School Level."
Journal of Research and Development in Education,
Vol.22, No.1, pp.

Van Den Berghe, R. (1988)
"The principal as Maker of a Local Innovation Policy :
Linking Research to Practice." *Journal of Research and
Development in Education,* Vol.22, No.1, pp.

Wideen, M.F. (1987)
"School Improvement in Canada." Qualitative Studies in
Education.

Zahorik, J.A. (1987)
"Teachers' Collegial Interaction : An Exploratory Study."
The Elementary School Journal, Vol.87, No.4, pp.385-396.

TEACHERS AND INNOVATION

PRE AND INSERVICE TRAINING STRATEGIES FROM THE FIRST AND SECOND EUROPEAN ACTION PROGRAMMES ON TRANSITION FROM SCHOOL TO ADULT AND WORKING LIFE 1979-88

Gerry McNamara

Dublin

This paper examines the implications for pre and inservice teacher training provision of the First and Second European Community funded Action Programmes on Transition from School to Adult and Working Life. The paper begins by describing briefly the work of the two Action Programmes and stresses the crucial importance assigned to methodology and teaching skills as elements in curriculum reform. It goes on to outline the most important additional teaching skills identified in the transition literature and finally it offers an account of the main pre and inservice training strategies developed to equip teachers with these additional skills.

**The First and Second Transition Programmes :
a brief description**

The Second European Action Programme, 1983-1988, which followed the First Programme 1979-1983, placed great emphasis on teacher pre and inservice training. Two significant reports on this topic were produced, *Staff Development for Workers with Young People* and *Teacher Training Strategies from the Second Transition Programme.*[1] Both reports are at pains to stress that the implementation of the extraordinary array of initiatives developed in the course of both action programmes is entirely contingent on significant reforms in teacher pre and inservice training.

The two programmes, involving more than sixty projects in twelve countries, originally intended to target the educationally disadvantaged, the low achiever, the remedial pupil and the unmotivated, early school leaver, and also to tackle special problem areas such as gender equality, education for the handicapped, migrants and other "risk groups." In the course of the projects, it became increasingly apparent to those involved that a much wider range of pupils, in essence all of those leaving school to seek employment as opposed to entering third level, required new programmes significantly different to those on offer at present. Thus the project evaluators eventually concluded that "the projects should be regarded as experiments which provide the foundation of fundamental changes in existing education and training systems."[2]

Some of the "fundamental changes" suggested include —

1. greater use of the out of school environment for learning purposes,

2. integrated modular courses to allow students to progress at different rates,

3. structured home-school and home-community links,

4. involving pupils through a process of negotiation in decisions about their own programmes,

5. new modes of assessment such as profiling,

6. new and much closer pupil teacher relationships through concepts such as the "transition tutor,"

7. greater flexibility in the curriculum allowing for teacher involvement in curriculum planning, implementation and evaluation,

8. the implementation of measures to combat sex stereotyping,

9. a methodological approach with the emphasis on activity based learning in the form of discussion, project/group/individual work, work experience and so on.[3]

The influence of this thinking has already had a significant impact on programmes outside of the mainstream curriculum. Teachers involved in "alternative" programmes such as VPTP and Youthreach 'in Ireland, YTS and TVEI in the UK, Arbeitslehre in Germany, etc. have become aware of these changes and have adapted their programmes and teaching methods as best they can with little inservice help.[4] However, this *ad hoc* situation is not satisfactory and will become less and less so as elements of these initiatives begin to influence the "mainstream" educational programmes to a greater extent. Examples of this development can be seen in the spread of "active learning" methods such as work experience/project work/mini companies and so on, particularly on the Continent and in the UK and indeed also in several aspects of the new Junior Certificate in Ireland.[5] An equally significant pressure for improvement in teaching methods and skills is the growing discipline problems in our schools and levels of alienation and dropout in many educational systems. The experience of the two Action Programmes demonstrates that, particularly in the area of methodology, effective curriculum reform requires an adequate training response.

Transition Theory and Teaching Methods

The vast quantity of literature produced by the two European Action Programmes stresses several major themes but the one most often emphasised is undoubtedly the centrality of teaching methods in curriculum reform. The following quotation is one of many that could be chosen to illustrate the point.

> The Programme showed conclusively that the key to successful courses lay in the methods used. In preparing young people for adult life the knowledge content — at least in the form it is usually offered them — is less important than experiences which are aimed at the development of personal and interpersonal competencies. This experience is gained from doing things and interacting with people. In other words, *learning methods not content are of most importance.*[6]

The crucial importance allotted to methods in transition education theory is a function of the type of competencies which are deemed to be needed by young people. For example, competencies in the realm of personal development such as independence/initiative or in the realm of logical ability such as problem solving, are said not to be susceptible to acquisition through traditional didactic teaching strategies. An alternative methodology is, therefore, essential — "most of these competencies can be learned only through experiences of situations; they cannot be taught — they are learned through action, not through absorption."[7] Any curriculum reform implemented without regard to the central importance of methodology could not, it is argued, result in the acquisition of the required competencies and would be of little benefit — "to substitute a new curriculum, however appropriate its content seems to be, without changing radically the methods of learning and the social context is of little value."[8]

This emphasis on alternative methodology leads logically to two further major themes in the transition literature. The first is the definition of the pedagogic skills required to implement the alternative teaching strategies effectively. The second is the development of appropriate pre and inservice training approaches which will enable teachers to acquire the skills defined.

The Identification of Teaching Skills for Innovative Programmes

The First Transition Programme *Final Programme Report* contains the sub or "special theme" report on staff development referred to previously.[9] There were only two such reports (the other on Work Experience) and this is a good indication of the extent to which teacher training and re-training came to be perceived as crucial to the development of transition education.

This report argues that the adoption of active learning strategies — the project method, integrated studies, individual/small group learning, use of the out-of-school environment as a learning resource, and so on — requires a range of teaching skills far greater than those necessary to implement more traditional subject-centred, classroom-based curricula. These new skills, it is suggested, can be isolated by means of analysing active learning strategies in action and can then be acquired by staff through appropriate pre and inservice training. The report goes on to identify the main areas in which additional skills are required and finally offers a fairly detailed account of those considered to be most important.

The first category of additional skills identified is in the area of curriculum development. Active learning involves a significant departure from traditional, well-defined subjects to the development of programmes of integrated studies. Therefore, the role of the teacher as curriculum developer will be much greater than heretofore, as will the related skills required. For example, the teacher, it is suggested, will be actively involved —

> in considering ways of working out the philosophy of a programme for young people, selecting the approach appropriate in the circumstances, establishing guidelines for the content of the programme, developing the learning/teaching situations to be generated and initiating modes of assessing the progress achieved, all of which involves team work, pooling of ideas, sharing of experience and careful thought.[10]

In addition, he must play a role in "the development of appropriate materials and the introduction of new institutional policies where required."[11]

Secondly, in implementing the programme which he has helped to develop, the teacher will find himself requiring other new skills. He will have to work as part of a team, and be responsible for the organisation of activities and experiences which will almost certainly be new to him. For example, "a spell with responsibility for audiovisual methods may be followed by another as organiser of residential periods, or perhaps acting as a negotiator for work experience placements." Finally, having developed "the necessary personal qualities, he can be considered for leadership of the team."[12] the organisation of appropriate learning situations and experiences, in particular those designed to utilise the out of school environment, also requires new skills — "an extensive knowledge of the local environment, the skill to identify potential learning situations, a real understanding of the working world and some knowledge of the home and social backgrounds of the young people."[13]

If many of these skills above appear primarily organisational or instrumental in nature, purely pedagogic skills are not neglected. Active learning situations cannot, it is suggested, be handled by a "chalk and talk" approach, but require skills in areas such as group organisation and animation, individual learning activities, project and survey planning, enquiry/discovery methods, simulation, games, discussion development and facilitation, brainstorming, role-play, negotiation with learners, and so on. The exercise of these "student centred skills" must logically, it is argued, involve teachers in the use of yet further new skills such as creative questioning, the introduction of pupils to research and enquiry methodologies, and reflection and action upon data and experience.

The examples given above of "skills necessary for the successful implementation of transition education schemes" represent only a fraction of the formidable array mentioned throughout the transition programmes' staff development document. In order to reduce them to more manageable proportions, the report concluded by identifying the chief categories of skills which should form the basis for teacher training and re-training.

These are:

1. the ability to plan and implement integrated programmes, involving close inter-staff cooperation, including team teaching;

2. the use of participative teaching/learning methods and the ability to design experience based approaches to teaching;

3. the counselling of and negotiating with learners about their programmes;

4. the use of resource-based learning and teaching methods;

5. the construction and use of profile records of attainment;

6. the ability to take part in group design and evaluation of the curriculum;

7. the improvement of the "social context" of learning through interpersonal and group animation skills;

8. the ability to work against a check list rather than through a syllabus, emphasising the process of learning as well as covering content;

9. the planning and operating of residential periods and work experience placements;

10. the development of new approaches to vocational work based on the broad skills area rather than on the demands of particular employment.

With each of these categories, more detailed check lists of basic skills and sub skills are identified.[15] In some cases this process of identification is carried to extreme lengths. Some of the skills identified appear meaningless or even ludicrous. For example, in the publication *Inventory of Recruitment Criteria and Training Needs of Staff of Youth Programmes*, which influenced the skill categories identified in the *Staff Development* report, the author specifies "knowledge of self and development of own attitudes and capacities" and "knowledge and understanding of society" as being among "the vital skill needs of transition staff."[16] The notion that such general terminology has anything to do with the idea of a skill represents a misuse of the term and confuses skill with knowledge, personal qualities and attitudes in a most alarming way.

The strong emphasis in the transition literature on the importance of teacher skills has resulted in charges that transition theory tends to see teaching and learning in a narrowly behaviourist way. David Carr, for example, suggests that to stress skills to this extent may result in the teacher coming to be perceived as "a craftsman, one who plies a trade analagous to that of a plumber or farmer."[17] Richard Smith is one critic whose position is fairly representative of others.[18] Smith does not deny the necessity of teaching skills as such, but argues that they are inseparable from the other aspects of the activity of teaching. The analogy he cites is that of driving a car. It makes no sense, he argues, for the learner driver to be told not to worry about looking out for pedestrians but to concentrate on changing the gears. The two elements are logically inseparable parts of the activity of driving. This is undeniable, but the point Smith misses is that it is possible and indeed sensible to practice changing the gears on a closed road or in the driveway before venturing out in public. Mastery of the gears, a skill which can be attained in isolation from, for example, watching for pedestrians, will allow the teacher greater opportunity to develop what Gerry Gaden defines as the professional aspects of teaching — commitment to the subject and care for one's pupils.[19]

While the skills and professional components of teaching are inseparable in terms of defining the nature of the activity, it is perfectly possible to isolate necessary pedagogic skills and train teachers in their implementation. Therefore, the emphasis on skills in the transition literature, while over-elaborated on occasion, is largely justified. It acknowledges the vital connection between pedagogic skills and curriculum reform and correctly identifies the lack of adequate skills training which many teachers receive in pre and inservice education.

The important role assigned to methodology and teaching skills in transition theory led inevitably to a consideration of current pre and inservice teacher training practices in European Community countries and to recommendations for reform. The final part of this paper offers an account of the ways in which it is suggested that the providers of teacher training might develop new approaches designed to meet the changing needs of their clients. The emphasis which emerges tends to lie more in the field of inservice rather than preservice training, since most projects were situated in schools and used established school staffs. This is a positive advantage, since it is now widely accepted that with limited openings into the teaching profession in most European countries, resources and action should be shifted from pre to inservice training. Nonetheless, a good deal of what has emerged could also be profitably considered in the preservice training sector.

Teaching Skills and Staff Development Strategies

The range of innovative teaching skills considered necessary for the implementation of curriculum reform appears to require that pre and particularly inservice training is not just seen as a matter of the acquisition of a few new specific skills such as, for example, word processing or basic computer literacy. Neither can it be seen as just a matter of keeping up with developments in one subject or as a brief introduction to the content of a new syllabus. These "conventional needs" remain important but in *Teacher Training Strategies* the process is described as "more fundamental.... to do with roles, self perceptions and behaviour of the teachers as individuals and as professionals in the changing context of their schools."[20] This wider view is described as embracing the acquisition of new knowledge but also as involving "the acquisition of new professional skills such as how to organise student centered learning, or continuous assessment, or how to run a work experience scheme" and beyond this again as involving "opportunities for personal development, for instance to gain more self confidence and to become more aware of sex-stereotyping."[21] These broader concepts are considered as going beyond training and become "staff development." Strategies designed to deliver this wider goal are considered at length in the action programme reports on staff training.

One suggested strategy for effective staff development which has become an accepted model in several European countries is "market led" or "consumer oriented" or "school focused" inservice training.[22] In effect, this involves the provision of a staff development budget to individual schools. Each school is then responsible for producing a coherent plan to meet its own inservice needs, appointing (in some cases) a post holder to oversee the plan's implementation and is free to "buy-in" staff development services from a range of providers.

School focused staff development of this type has been shown to possess several advantages over more traditional models. For one thing the involvement of a school staff as a whole in the processes of analysing the needs of the institution often of itself provides an ideal opportunity for project-led staff development.

Secondly, this model, by providing an opportunity to involve the entire staff of a school, reaches many teachers who may have evaded previous staff development organised on a voluntary subject centered basis. It also allows schools to tackle non curricular staff development issues such as school discipline, teacher stress and so on, and consequently to bring expertise from a range of providers — sociologists, psychologists, management experts, — which has been little utilised in the past. The provision of resources to the consumers also of course allows inservice providers — teacher training colleges, teacher centres, management institutes and so on to specialise in particular inservice packages and to sell these to schools.

The emphasis placed on school-focused staff development is also reflected in a second strategy widely used in the transition projects. Variously entitled "action research" or "project led staff development," it included very extensive in-school training programmes for the project teams involved.[23] Particular stress was placed on the induction of new members into the project team and the opportunity to learn the skills required through observation and participation. This usually involved the team leader or another team member acting as mentor to the new recruit and providing what is described as "the most important form of support for teachers trying new approaches.... the opportunity to see a colleague doing it and being able to discuss the problems of making the change with them."[24] In most projects the mentor system was augmented by other skills analysis and development techniques including micro teaching, team teaching and interaction analysis and action research projects on the use and effectiveness of particular skills.

Clearly the extent of induction provided by the pilot projects reflected the considerable resources available and would be beyond the scope of most individual schools at present. However, the projects have demonstrated the value of more systematic induction in acquiring both basic and advanced teaching skills. It is possible that the present reduction in numbers in preservice training and the consequently greater resources for inservice may allow the "mentor" or "cooperating teacher" approach to be greatly expanded in the future and action research/interaction analysis to become a regular tool in improving the skills of the serving teacher.

Both strategies mentioned to date are essentially school focused in nature. However, pilot projects also demonstrated the need for much greater sharing of experience among staff from various institutions as an essential component in staff development. This process, designated "networking," emerged as the third important strategy advocated and, similarly to the others discussed, networking models of various types are becoming increasingly widely utilised.[25]

Networking simply involves bringing together groups of staff from various institutions, providing time and resources, and allowing them to share experience and knowledge with or without the help of outside facilitators. At the most basic level, the network may consist of teachers of a particular subject or a principal or vice principal support group. The organisation of such networks can easily be undertaken through teacher education departments, teacher centres or even by groups of cooperating schools. More complex networking was developed by several projects to enable team members to obtain relevant experience in other organisations. For example, the Zeeland project in the Netherlands developed local liaison networks to provide opportunities for transition course teachers and guidance counsellors to obtain short periods of work experience in placements similar to those being offered to pupils. This scheme is now being spread to other Dutch provinces.[26] Other projects developed networks serviced by a liaison officer to provide for staff exchanges and sharing of experience between schools and such agencies as training bodies, technical colleges, the social services, voluntary organisations and so forth. In several cases, the networks and the liaison staff have been retained after the completion of the project.[27]

The provision of this range of experience outside of the school is closely connected to a conception in the transition literature of each teacher as taking responsibility not only for the learning needs but also for the personal and vocational guidance of a small group of children. In this context networking with many outside agencies becomes indispensible. However, even within the more restricted teaching role operated at present, networking at the very least provides a long needed opportunity for teachers to emerge from the isolation of the classroom and share information and insights with their colleagues.

Conclusion

The work of the First and Second Action Programmes in the fields of methodology and teaching skills can be summarised as follows. New curricula are essential, not only for the less able and "risk groups" but for most pupils. However, unless these curricula involve a more pupil centered teaching methodology they will bring little success. Teachers, due to inadequate pre and inservice training, do not by and large have the skills or indeed the confidence to adopt more pupil centered methods. To remedy this problem, the necessary skills must first be identified and the appropriate pre and inservice training strategies be put in place to equip teachers with them. Most of the sixty pilot projects which comprised the two action programmes found it necessary to follow this procedure—

new curriculum > new methods > identify necessary skills > train staff.

In the training field, many new strategies have emerged which for reasons of space I have condensed into three broad areas — school focused staff development, induction through team working and action research, and networking. Within each of these broad areas a range of specific methods were developed which are described in detail in the staff development documents produced in the course of the action programmes. These broad strategies and specific methods may well have a significant impact on the emerging shape of pre and particularly inservice teacher training in the European Community in the years to come.

REFERENCES

1. European Community, First Transition Programme, *Final Programme Report, Theme Reports; Staff Development for Workers with Young People,* (Brussels: IFAPLAN, 1983); European Community, Second Transition Programme, *Teacher Training Strategies from the Second Transition Programme,* (Brussels: IFAPLAN, 1986).

2. European Community, First Transition Programme, *Final Programme Report Part A, Synthesis Report,* (Brussels: IFAPLAN, 1983), p.21.

3. For detailed accounts of the conclusions of both Action Programmes, see First Transition Programme, *Policies for Transition,* (Brussels: IFAPLAN, 1984) and Second Transition Programme, *Final Summary Report,* (Brussels: IFAPLAN, 1988).

4. For an example of the impact of these ideas on "alternative" courses in Ireland, see Kevin Williams and Gerry McNamara, *The Vocational Preparation Course: An Educational Appraisal and Practical Guide,* (Dublin: ASTI, 1986).

5. The influence of Transition Programme thinking on proposed changes in the Junior Cycle Curriculum in Ireland can be seen in the Curriculum and Examination Board's document *In Our Schools* (Dublin: CEB, 1986), and in Aine Hyland, "The Curriculum and Examination Board: A Retrospective View," Gerry McNamara, Kevin Williams and Donald Herron, (eds), *Achievement and Aspiration: Curriculum Initiatives in Irish Post Primary Education in the 1980s,* (Dublin: Teachers' Centre, St. Patrick's College of Education, Drumcondra, 1990).

6.   European Community *Education for Transition: The Curriculum Challenge*, (Brussels: IFAPLAN, 1984), pp.12-13.

7.   *Staff Development*, p.67.

8.   *Policies for Transition*, p.13.

9.   *Staff Development*.

10.   *Staff Development*, p.24.

11.   Ibid, p.24.

12.   Ibid, p.22.

13.   Ibid, p.46.

14.   Ibid, pp.48-50, p.97.

15.   Ibid, pp.97-98 (this list of skill categories is largely based on a report entitled *ABC in Action* produced in 1982 by the Further Education Unit in Great Britain in connection with the piloting of the pre-vocational scheme "A Basis for Choice."

16.   Dudley Plunkett, *Staff Training and Development for the New Youth Programmes: A Comparative Study of Policy and Practice in Western Europe*, (London: European Institute for Education and Social Policy, 1982), Appendix 3.

17.   David Carr, "Education, Professionalism and Theories of Teaching" in the *Journal of Philosophy of Education*, Vol.20, No.1, 1986, pp.118-119.

18.   Richard Smith, "Teaching on Stilts: A Critique of Classroom Skills," Maurice Holt, ed., *Skills and Vocationalism, the Easy Answer*, (Milton Keynes: Open University Press, 1987), p.44.

19.   Gerry Gaden, "Professional Attitudes," *Irish Educational Studies*, Vol.7, No.1, 1988, pp.33-38.

20.   *Teacher Training Strategies*, p.13.

21.   Ibid, p.13.

22.   Accounts of this model appear in *Staff Development*, pp.40-43; *Teacher Training Strategies*, pp.33-39.

23.   Accounts of this type of staff development work are to be found in *Staff Development*, pp.16-25; *Teacher Training Strategies*, pp.27-30.

24.   *Teacher Training Strategies*, pp.33-39.

25.   *Staff Development*, p.34; *Teacher Training Strategies*, p.14-23.

26.   European Community, Second Transition Programme, *Innovations No.22*, (Brussels: IFAPLAN, 1987), p.1.

27.   See *Innovations*, Nos.7, 28 and 30.

PUPIL FEEDBACK FOR STUDENT TEACHERS :
AN AID FOR THE TEACHER EDUCATION INSTITUTE

Harrie G.B. Broekman and Peter Bannink

University of Utrecht, The Netherlands

Summary

First of all in this paper we will discuss what the original reason was behind making a study of pupil feedback. This is followed by a report of an investigation carried out at a teacher education institute in the Netherlands, on the use made of pupil feedback within different school subjects. We interviewed representative institute supervisors of every school subject, the central question being *what* role pupil feedback has in teacher education. The ideas that lecturers have on pupil feedback is also discussed. We have also had a literature search carried out, whereby the following questions were of primary importance:

— can pupils give valid feedback?
— is it possible for a (student) teacher to elicit feedback from pupils, and assimilate it, during and after a teaching session?

Based on indications from the literature studies, and from limited investigations carried out at the above mentioned institute, some conditions are given for a worthwhile use of pupil feedback in a teacher education program. When these conditions are met, we are of the opinion that it would be wise to include pupil feedback in the teacher education program.

Introduction

At our institute workshops are held regularly, during which the lecturers exchange views on various aspects of the training. An example of this would be a workshop spent on assessment, the school teaching practice, education research carried out by the students themselves and meso-macro. In response to the workshop on school teaching practice, pupil feedback also came under discussion. Pupil feedback had, for most of the teacher educators, a place at the end of the teaching practice, it was considered to be part of the final evaluation in the class. The lecturers on mathematics and mother-tongue found this surprising, since both of them broached the subject with the question "how can we teach future teachers to be open to the questions sent out by pupils and how can we teach future teachers to do something with them." In mathematics these questions arose, to a certain extent, from a changed vision of learning and teaching, whereby pupils' own constructions are considered to be very important. For example, Freudenthal (1983) gives some examples concerned with *unlearning* wrong ideas and methods; "notice that often too little attention is paid to the potential and need of unlearning the instruction. " Streefland (1990) expresses it as follows: "What matters is that pupils' constructions and free productions are used for building and shaping the teaching course." Based on the differences ascertained between the various lecturers, a project group was set up in order to survey the role played by pupil feedback in the teacher education program. This project group was made up of subject teachers of mother-tongue and mathematics, supplemented by a student assistant. Little incentive to continue with pupil feedback emerged from the survey; there was too much scepticism about the facility of student teachers to be able to cope effectively with pupil feedback.

1. Pupil feedback in a teacher education institute

We have investigated how the subject of pupil-feedback is handled within the university teacher education program. This was conducted by holding interviews with nine education lecturers in as many different school subjects. Only one lecturer was interviewed in the French, German, English and Spanish group, since these subjects have a common program. In all cases a post-graduate training is involved, which is the professional preparatory element of the teacher education program for the regular subjects in secondary education.

1.1. *Methodology*

The project group opted to work with half-open interviews, whereby the respondents had the opportunity to give as much relevant information as possible. An itemised list was also used (Appendix 1). The interviews took between 30 and 90 minutes, the average being 45 minutes. The interviewer had followed training in this method of interviewing and had carried out a trial interview twice amongst the members of the project group.

1.2 *Results*

In this paper we will restrict ourselves to the difference between requested and spontaneous feedback and the value of pupil feedback according to the lecturers.

The interaction between teacher and pupils receives regular attention within the various programs, even if indirectly. It is an indisputable discussion point. In the first instance, it comes up for discussion in the more theoretical part of the study. This means that emphasis is put on the patterns of communication in the class and/or the conscious or unconscious influence the teacher has on the pupils. Some programs maintain that interaction in the classroom is the central theme within the curriculum. Others consider the subject by discussing a topic such as "group dynamics in the classroom situation," and by discussing the skill of "observation." Practically all the programs make use of a model to study teacher behaviour. This model is based on a model devised by Leary (cf. Wubbels, 1987).

Of course pupil feedback comes up during the school-based components of the course: teaching practice and the one-to-one lessons (see Vedder and Bannink, 1988). The respondents state that during follow-up and supervising discussions, the matter of interpreting pupil behaviour comes up and is discussed. Here use is made of video or audio recordings, roleplay or the incident method. The idea generally is that the lecturer should introduce the subject in order that students pay attention to it.

A particular method or approach of working is regularly promoted within the interviews, motivated, in fact by one or more presumptions. The general view is that pupils are able to give feedback, but the opinions on the value of that feedback are not unanimous. On the one hand, there is the idea that pupils can give very clear, but also very personal feedback; on the other hand, the value of feedback is denied. It is also suggested that it can be "too hard." The student-teachers are not able to do much with this. Therefore, the feedback is less effective. It is also possible for feedback to be less effective since it is given at inopportune times. Feedback may also be less valid since the pupils view the student-teacher as a guest who gives them lessons on a temporary basis only, and any feedback holds, therefore, little advantage for them. There are respondents who doubt whether pupils are able to give honest feedback at all, since it is also the teacher's task to evaluate the pupils. One lecturer stated that the student-teachers would prefer feedback on the content of the lesson, whereas pupils are more willing to show whether they find a student agreeable or otherwise: pupils give feedback on the individual. Finally, the atmosphere within the class or during a lesson is also quoted as being a relevant factor. Where the atmosphere is good, the pupils are able to give succinct feedback (provided it is requested), but it was considered difficult for students to control and reverse their insecurity.

It was emphasised that it is difficult for a student-teacher to react to pupil behaviour during a lesson, or to stop the lesson and enquire what the problem is. It was remarked that a student in front of the class pays more attention to the pupils' verbal reactions, whereas fellow students observing the lesson concentrate more on the non-verbal reactions. It is generally held that students find it difficult to make contact with the pupils. One lecturer added that, in many schools, there is little obvious contact between the teacher and pupils. Follow-up discussions on a lesson with the pupils was considered less useful, since this discussion would take place in exactly the same style as in a lesson which had gone wrong; no useful information would be provided — according to the lecturers interviewed.

The interviewees point out that students do not readily seek contact with pupils. It was stated a number of times that the lecturer must formulate explicit tasks to be carried out by the students to prevent them from not progressing beyond the level of just giving lessons. Examples of some of these tasks are: students should set a test paper and analyse it; collect and analyse the content of pupils' exercise books; discuss a particular subject with individual pupils; observe all the lessons of one particular class for a whole day; carry out a verbal or written final evaluation with the pupils; carry out ad hoc evaluations with pupils; establish the initial knowledge level of pupils; at least once, allow pupils to evaluate a lesson that has been given with regard to content and performance.

1.3 *Interpretations*

Here we shall discuss three points which came to light during the interviews:

— interaction in the class between teacher and pupils,
— the role of pupil feedback in the teacher education program which is possibly related to preconceptions of teacher educators,
— the tasks the student teachers have to perform in their teaching practice periods.

The questions posed in the interviews were answered readily, but because of the half-open nature of the interview, the opportunity was taken to discuss further a number of matters associated with pupils' reactions, etc. From this part of the interviews it appeared that spontaneous feedback from pupils during a lesson was considered to be part of interaction and was not thought to be pupil feedback as such. However, we consider that it does belong to pupil feedback, since the student learns to relate pupil behaviour to his own behaviour. Little attention was paid in the various programs to requesting pupil feedback. Performing a number of tasks in their teaching practice (already mentioned in 1.2), does not necessarily guarantee that the students are actually confronted with pupil feedback or that the students have an opportunity to do anything with that feedback. This is not the case, however, during the final evaluation period, which is usually required during the last teaching practice lesson. Another comment is that the feedback does not necessarily have to be valid. This does not have to be related so much as to what the pupils say, but more as to what kind of questions the student asks. In other words: a task to perform an evaluation with pupils can receive less valid information if the student does not know what kind of questions to ask, or if she asks the wrong questions (content or formulation). It appears generally that the teacher education program pays little attention, or none whatsoever, to the content and formulation of questions.

One important category of comments is connected with *how the lecturers estimate the students.* It has been said that the students are not yet ready:

> "At the beginning of teaching practice, pupil-feedback will not contribute to the student's learning process. The student is more concerned with "how to survive." After that, the subject matter of the lesson is all important, followed by the pupils and only then the educational theory. Therefore, it is difficult at the start to pay attention to pupil-feedback," and

> "Pupil reaction, even when positive, is considered, at the start, to be something of a nuisance."

Two of the lecturers also state that the situation where pupil-feedback is given to student teachers should be dealt with separately. The student teachers usually enter an already existing class situation, for either a short or longer period of time. For the pupils this means a disturbance to their established conditions. This can influence the feedback which the pupils give. As a consequence, student teachers are not particularly motivated to maintain systematic contact with the pupils. Only when they have done this more than once are they able to see the usefulness of feedback.

It is possible that student presumptions on learning and teaching play a part. However, those interviewed did not comment on this. With hindsight it is a pity that no questions were asked on the way in which teacher educators themselves cope with feedback from their own students. It is possible that this also plays a role.

Teacher pupil interactions have an indisputable role, but pupil-feedback is not a structural component of the teacher education

616

program of this institute.   We are of the impression that this is partly
related to the ideas and presumptions held by lecturers on students,
pupils and school life.   These presumptions may form the basis of
particular traditions within teacher education, where the emphasis
lies on feedback from the lecturer, the supervisor within the school,
and fellow students.   Pupil-feedback is usually only "referred" to
during discussions on the observations with those mentioned above.
Very little is done to teach the students to elicit valid feedback from
pupils.

"Education's *okay, but I'm not crazy about school as a delivery system.*"

2. An investigation into the literature

The questions we have investigated are as follows:

—   why pupil feedback?
—   can pupils give valid feedback?
—   is it possible for a (student) teacher to elicit feedback from
        pupils, and assimilate it, during and after a teaching session?

With the above questions in mind, a search in the ERIC
database was carried out.   From amongst the results of this

investigation the large number of "older" publications from the sixties and seventies was significant.

2.1 *Why pupil feedback?*

Different authors provide arguments as to why pupil feedback is so important. One important reason is to be found in the fact that the future teachers, during teaching practice, are primarily supervised by the cooperating teacher and the university supervisor. Both sources are limited by the quantity and quality of feedback (e.g. Freiberg and Waxman, 1988). The information provided by the pupils should not be dismissed. Besides, the use of pupil feedback has several advantages according to these authors:

(a)   they are relatively inexpensive to administer,
(b)   they can be administered at a convenient time during the class,
(c)   they can be standardised,
(d)   they can be designed to maintain anonymity,
(e)   they are a way of observing the prospective teacher on many occasions under normal conditions,
(f)   they can pick up a wealth of data in a very short time.

It must be clear that above mentioned authors are speaking of using self-report instruments or rating instruments.

2.2 *The value of pupil-feedback*

This section concentrates on the question of whether feedback given by pupils can actually bring about a behavioural change in the (student) teacher. The literature formulates a number of criteria, for feedback in general, which have always been related to manifest (and verbal) feedback. Kieviet (1972) maintains that feedback should be as *objective* as possible. The actions should be reflected as fully and reliably as possible. Buis (1978) agrees with this, but adds that feedback should be *specific* and, as a result, qualitative. The message which is fed back should be so specific that whoever receives the information should be capable of directing his attention and effort at any flaws and weak points. Grell (1976) believes that feedback should never be directed at a teacher's behaviour alone. The feedback should provide functional and relatively objective information on the teacher's behaviour, rather than opinions and value judgements.

Whether requested or not, pupils generally give their opinions or let them be known (non-verbally) on whatever a teacher is doing. Usually, there is no compliance with the requirements placed on feedback, such as, "being related to actual observed behaviour," or "the recipient should be able to do something with the feedback." It is, rather, more a question of a signal being communicated, of which the specific how and why can only be guessed at.

Grell (1976) concludes that pupil behaviour is hardly an objective measure of the quality of teacher behaviour. One of the reasons is, that over a period of time, a familiarising process may take place between teacher and pupils. A consequence of this could be that the standards become eroded. It is also possible that a pupil behaves in a certain way because of factors outside the classroom and which is, therefore, not a reaction to the teacher's behaviour. Finally, a number of pupil behaviour patterns are reactions to long established circumstances, and consequently, cannot be considered as being feedback.

Freiberg and Waxman (1988) conclude that "(..) students' judgements about their teachers' behaviours agree significantly with the judgements of experienced classroom observers." Rohrkemper (1985) agrees with that for older pupils, who can emphasise better and deeper than younger pupils. They are able to indicate the different ways in which teachers will react to various pupil behaviour. They see teacher characteristics and motives more as a result of the specific demands of the profession than of the personal traits of the teacher. Pupils also indicate that teachers not only consider pupil behaviour but also pupils' ideas.

Tuckman and Oliver (1968) ascertained that pupil-feedback changes a teacher's behaviour more than no feedback at all, or supervisor-feedback alone. Supervisor-feedback combined with pupil-feedback does not result in more change than pupil-feedback on its own. Supervisor-feedback alone can actually have a negative effect i.e. resulting in a change in direction other than the one recommended.

Other investigations have also confirmed the positive value of feedback. Levinson-Rose & Menges (1981, p.411) state: "There seems to be enough evidence to conclude that feedback from students' ratings leads some instructors to improve their subsequent ratings. However, the effect is not reliable judging from the inconsistency of the findings across studies." Research carried out by Gage et al (1963) attempted to answer the question of whether a teacher changes his performance if he obtains written information from pupils on:

(a)   his performance in the class as perceived by the pupils;
(b)   ideal teacher performance as the pupils would wish it.

The results show that a teacher's behaviour does indeed change in the desired direction, but also that the accuracy with which the teachers perceive the pupils' opinions also improves.

In addition to the requirements to be placed on feedback in general, there are also conditions to be attached to the recipient of the feedback, i.e *the extent to which teachers are actually open to feedback*. Beckman (1973) is the most negative on this matter. He concludes that teachers often seek the cause outside themselves. A teacher will attempt to ignore any insight into his own behaviour. Basically, a teacher is satisfied with himself when the pupils cooperate, but is dissatisfied with the pupils when they do not become involved in the lesson. The number of years teaching experience also has a significant effect on a teacher's openness to pupil-feedback.

Schildwacht (1981, p.31) states three factors which influence the way in which student-teachers handle feedback viz. their attitude towards themselves, anxiety and dogmatism. The results of various investigations into these three factors are not always in agreement. Schildwacht draws the following conclusion: certain kinds of feedback will serve to strengthen the picture someone has of himself. Research shows that students who are reasonably satisfied with themselves before watching a video recording, give themselves higher scores as teachers after having watched it. This also holds, mutatis mutandis, for students with a low opinion of themselves. Anxiety appears to interact with the effectiveness of feedback.   The more anxious students tend to dismiss feedback.

According to Schildwacht, a little anxiety can have a favourable effect, since it helps to set processes in motion.   Finally, in comparison with less dogmatic personalities, dogmatic persons feel more readily threatened by feedback, and ignore any information which differs from their own opinions.

During all the above mentioned investigations, observers acted as intermediaries between pupil and teacher, and interpreted the information.   It involved feedback requested of the pupils by a third party.   Accounts of the investigations do not make it clear whether the teachers, after the research, had acquired the skills to request feedback from the pupils, or whether they were able to handle it.   However, it is clear that feedback in general, and pupil-feedback in particular, can under certain circumstances and for certain teachers, have an effect.

2.3 *The handling of pupil feedback*

In the large amount of literature available on pupil feedback very little attention is paid to the way in which this feedback can most effectively be obtained.   By means of questionnaires, often administered by a third party and sometimes by the teacher, investigation into pupil feedback is carried out.   Sometimes teachers have discussions with pupils.   There is very little reported on obtaining spontaneous feedback from pupils.   A number of science-articles appear on pupil feedback in the literature on teaching methodology.   This is mostly involved with mathematic-didactics which study protocols of discussions between pupils themselves and between pupils and teachers (such as Van 't Hul et al 1989; Carpenter et al 1989).   There is also the investigation carried out by Wubbels et al (in press), who concentrated on the study of the teacher-pupil relationship, in which they focus on interpersonal teacher behaviour in classrooms.

In their research, interpersonal teacher behaviour in classrooms is investigated from a systems perspective, following the theory of Watzlawick, Beavin and Jackson (1967) on communication processes.   This theory was adapted for use in classroom communication research (see Wubbels, Creton and Holvast, 1988). Within the systems perspective on communication, it is assumed that behaviours of participants influence each other mutually.   The behaviour of the teacher is influenced by the behaviour of the students and in turn influences student behaviour.   Circular communication processes develop which not only consist of behaviour, but which also determine behaviour as well.

With the systems perspective in mind, Wubbels, Creton and Hooymayers (1985) developed a model to map interpersonal teacher behaviour on the basis of a model by Leary (1957).   In their adaptation of the Leary model, teacher behaviour is also mapped with the help of a proximity dimension (Cooperation, C — Opposition, O) and an influence dimension (Dominance, D — Submission, S).   These dimensions can be represented in a coordinate system divided into eight equal sections (see Figure 1). Every instance of interpersonal teacher behaviour can be placed within the system of axes.   The closer the instances of behaviour are in the chart, the more closely they resemble each other.   The sectors are labelled DC, CD, etc. according to their position in the coordinate system.   For example, the two sectors CD and DC are both characterised by Dominance and Cooperation.   In the DC sector, however, the Dominance aspect prevails over the Cooperation aspect, whereas the adjacent sector CD includes behaviour of a more cooperative and less dominant nature.   The sections of the model describe eight different behaviour aspects: Leadership, Helpful/Friendly, understanding, Student Responsibility and Freedom, Uncertain, Dissatisfied, Admonishing and Strict.   To clarify the concepts covered by each sector, Figure 1 shows typical behaviour for each sector.

622

FIGURE 1 — (copied from Wubbels in press)

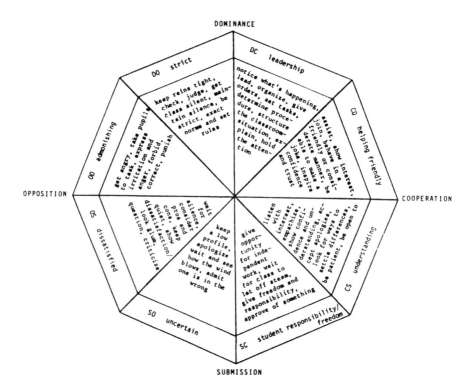

In line with the learning environment research tradition, interpersonal teacher behaviour was investigated by our research group through the use of student perceptions. We added to this the use of teacher perceptions. An instrument to measure secondary students' and teachers' perceptions of teacher behaviour was developed in the Netherlands in several studies in the early eighties; it was called the *Questionnaire for Teacher Interaction* (QTI; Wubbels et al 1985). Designed according to the model for interpersonal teacher behaviour, it has eight scales, each consisting of about 10 items and corresponding to one of the eight sections of the model. The 77 items are answered on a five point scale. Based on the Dutch version, Wubbels and Levy (1989), developed an American version consisting of 64 items, Table 1 gives a typical item and the number of items for each scale.

TABLE 1 — Number of Items in the Dutch and American Version and a Typical Item for the Scales in the Questionnaire on Teacher Interaction (QTI)

Scale	Number of Items		Typical Item
	Dutch	American	
DC Leadership	10	7	S/he is a good leader
CD Helpful/friendly	10	8	S/he is someone we can depend on
CS Understanding	10	8	If we have something to say s/he will listen.
SC Student responsibility/freedom	9	8	S/he gives us a lot of free time in class
SO Uncertain	9	7	S/he seems uncertain
OS Dissatisfied	11	9	S/he is suspicious
OD Admonishing	9	8	S/he gets angry
DO Strict	9	9	S/he is strict

C Cooperation; O Opposition; D Dominance; S Submission

(Copied from Wubbels in press)

We have gone into more detail on the example of Wubbels et al, not only because they are colleagues of ours but also because they give one of the few examples of ways to obtain spontaneous pupil feedback which can actually be used by a student teacher. Also the literature on coping with preconceptions (see, for example Van 't Hul et al 1989) gives examples of opportunities for evoking and using spontaneous pupil feedback. It is indicated in this literature how, by means of confrontational — possible conflict — situations meaningful pupil feedback is to be obtained. Another source which we cannot fail to mention is the literature on preconceptions (student) teachers which we discussed in 1989 at the ATEE conference (Broekman et al, in press). By bearing in mind student teachers' preconceptions, use is made of confrontational situations in order to obtain meaningful feedback from the pupils and in this case from students. As a last source we want to mention the literature on "teacher development," which is discussed by Paul R. Burden in the 1990 *Handbook of Research on Teacher Education* (Burden, 1990).

Discussion

Based on the results from the interviews and the literature, we have amended the curriculum for, amongst others, mathematics teachers with respect to pupil feedback. Attention is now being paid to it in different places, whereby our general starting point in our program is, first and foremost: teaching is helping to learn. The students should, during the teacher education program, be taught to elicit explicit feedback from the pupils, and how to observe and interpret signals given by pupils. How to handle any feedback received is, in our opinion, something that has to be learned. We consider that not only desirable, since the student obtains more (and effective) feedback on his teaching performance, but also since it especially involves skills which promote the growth of every individual teacher. In the following we give a description of how we want to accomplish this in our mathematics teacher education program. A program in which we try *not* to ignore the situated nature of cognition, because we do not want to defeat our goal of providing usable, robust knowledge (Brown, 1989).

3. Our training

We shall now proceed to give a number of phases in our training where we pay explicit attention to (obtaining) pupil feedback.

DIAGRAM OF THE TRAINING

(a)   During the university training of one particular subject, there is a full-time two-month course called "orientation on the profession of teaching." Parts of this orientation course are the one-to-one lessons, institute practicals, and a one week orientation in a school for secondary education.

(b)   The post-graduate one year course is structured as follows:
    (i)   Introduction (2 weeks)
    (ii)   Trio-stage (block, or parallel program) (16 weeks)
    (iii)   Re-orientation (6 weeks)
    (iv)   Individual Final Teaching Practice (12 weeks)
    (v)   Research and conclusion (8 weeks).

This is shown in the diagram below:

FIGURE 2 — Summary of the 12 month Teacher Education Program at the University of Utrecht (starting in January)

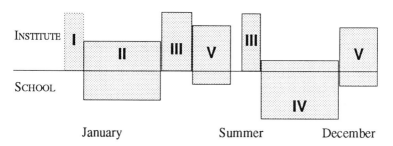

A.   One-to-one lessons

Before the student-teachers start their actual teaching practice, they teach one individual pupil one hour a week for a number of weeks (see Vedder and Bannink, 1988). These lessons are audio-recorded for further analysis. During these lessons the student-teacher is confronted with spontaneous feedback, which is presented in a non threatening way. Only one pupil is involved (the student-teacher does not have the feeling that he will be ridiculed by the group) and furthermore, he is able to listen to his recording at home in his own time. Besides that, a fellow-student listens to his recordings and they have to write down what they noticed. The recordings are then discussed with the institute supervisor.

B.   Institute practical

In all teacher education programs time is spent on observing and interpreting pupil behaviour on videotapes. This is important for learning to recognise signals from the pupils, and for interpreting them. To be able to handle feedback it is important that students request feedback from the group, which occurs in a less threatening situation than in the class. It is, of course, desirable that the institute supervisor himself is a good example in respect of this, to his own students. A way of observing is stimulated which can be seen as a kind of *progressive focussing.* Every observation "has" to progress along the following lines:

> judgement about teaching behaviour;
> description of observed teaching behaviour in general terms;
> description of observed teaching behaviour in concrete terms;
> descriptions of student's reactions.

C.   Teaching practice

In the interviews with the institute supervisors a number of methods of obtaining explicit feedback were mentioned.   Of these we use those for which a follow-up is possible, e.g. performing a written evaluation halfway through the teaching practice or collecting pupils' exercise books, followed by discussion on anything significant in them.   Also, the students have to prepare jointly a questionaire for evaluation in the class.   By discussing the questions they have generated themselves, they can gain a clearer insight into what they themselves consider important.

The follow-up discussion forms another important component of teaching practice.   Paying more attention to pupil feedback can mean a shift of emphasis.   We do not have in mind that students should have follow-up discussions with pupils, but that student-teachers should attempt to elicit feedback from the pupils themselves, rather than this being solely provided by fellow students, cooperating teachers, and institute supervisors.   The manner in which students handle feedback should also be discussed more often.

3.2   *Implementation*

From theories on teachers' preconceptions (see for example Broekman et al, in press) including lecturers, it appears that preconceptions contribute towards how people think about pupil feedback.   If a change in preconceptions is to be effected, then objective data should be produced, but in particular a confrontation should be made with these preconceptions.

Therefore, based on our research we organised another workshop, where the lecturers were confronted by statements made by fellow lecturers and the relevant literature. This resulted in them changing their minds on part of the aims of the training. This last workshop resulted in the tasks in the teaching practice periods, for a number of subjects, being directed more at individual pupils. Scepticism on the student teachers dealing effectively with pupil feedback remained, but did result in stimulating the student teachers to become more receptive to the signals from pupils. This was to be carried out by structured teaching practice tasks, whereby specific attention was to be paid to pupils' reactions. Furthermore, more attention was to be given in the training to the most effective way in which pupil feedback is to be obtained.

REFERENCES

Adams, E. (1980)
The Ford teaching project,. In: Stenhouse, L. (ed), *Curriculum research and development in action*. London, p.229-239.

Barone, T.E. (1987)
Educational Platforms, Teacher Selection, and School Reform : Issues Emanating from a Biographical Case Study. In: *Journal of Teacher Education,* nr. 2, pp.12-17.

Beyer, L.E. (1984)
Field Experiences, Ideology, and the Development of Critical Reflectivity. In:*Journal of teacher Education,* nr. 3, pp.36-41.

Beckman, L. (1973)
Auswirkungen von schulischen Leistungen auf die Kausal-attribuierung von lehrenden und beobachtenden Personen. In: Hofer, M. and F.E. Weinert (Hrsg.), *Pädagogische Psychologie 2. Lernen und Instruktion.* Frankfurt A.M.

Broekman, H.G.B., P. Bannink and J. Vedder (in press)
Taking account of preconceptions of student teachers. In Voorbach, J.T. and L.G.M. Prick (eds), *Teacher Education 6.*

Brophy, J.E. (1979)
Teacher behaviour and its effects. In: *Journal of Educational Psychology,* nr. 6, pp.733-759.

Brophy, J.E. (1983)
Research on the self-fulfilling prophecy and teacher expectation. In: *Journal of Educational Psychology,* nr. 5, pp.631-661.

Brophy, J.E. and T.L. Good (1974)
Teacher-student relationships : Causes and consequences. New York.

Brown, John S., Allan Collins and Paul Duguid (1989)
Situated cognition and the culture of learning. In: *Educational Researcher,* 18, 1, pp.32-42.

Buis, P. (1978)
Het functioneren van terugkoppeling in het wetenschappelijk onderwijs. Amsterdam.

Burden, P.R. (1990)
Teacher Development. In: Houston, W.R. (ed), *Handbook of Research on teacher Education,* MacMillan, New York, London.

Carpenter, Thomas P. and Elizabeth Fennema
Building on the knowledge of students and teachers. Paper delivered at the 1989 Conference of the International Group for the Psychology of Mathematics Education (published in volume 3 of the proceedings).

Corporal, A.H. (1979)
Micro-onderwijs. In: Kieviet (red.), *Nieuwe methoden in de opleiding voor onderwijsgevenden.* Groningen.

Freiberg, H.J. and H.C. Waseman
Alternative Feedback Approaches for Improving Student Teachers' Classroom Instruction. In: *Journal of Teacher Education,* July-August, 1988, pp.8-14.

Gage, N.L. et al (1963)
Changing teacher behaviour through feedback from pupils : an application of equilibrium theory. In: Charters, W.W. and N.L. Gage (eds), *Readings in the social psychology of education.* Boston.

Grell, J. (1976)
Training van onderwijsgedrag. Groningen.

Heider, F. (1958)
The psychology of interpersonal relations. New York.

Heinen, H., H. Heuschen e.a. (1979)
Lehrer ausbilden — aber wie? Düsseldorf.

Hul, F.E. van, W.R. van Joolingen en P. Lijnse (1989)
Begripsverandering en microcomputers, praktijkervaringen met kracht en beweging. In: *Tijdschrift voor B-didactiek,* 7, 3.

Jeu, J. de (1984/1985)
Onderwijsverbetering op basis van studentoordelen? In: *Universiteit en Hogeschool,* 10, pp.349-361.

Kepler, K.B. (1977)
Descriptive feedback : increasing teacher awareness. Paper presented at the Annual Meeting of the American Educational Research Association. New York.

Kieviet, F.K. (1972)
Microteaching als methode in de opleiding van leerkrachten. Vaassen.

Korthagen, F.A.J. (1982)
Leren reflekteren als basis van de lerarenopleiding. Harlingen.

Leary, T. (1957)
An interpersonal diagnosis of personality. New York.

Levinson-Rose, J. and R.J. Menges (1981)
Improving College Teaching : A Critical Review of Research. •
In: *Review of Educational Research,* nr.3, pp.403-434.

Marsh, H.W. (1984)
Students' Evaluations of University Teaching : Dimensionality, Reliability, Validity, Potential Biases and Utility. In: *Journal of Educational Psychology,* nr. 5, pp.707-754.

Payne, P.D. (1984)
Interrelationships among college supervisor, supervising teacher and elementary pupil ratings of student teaching performance. In: *Educational and Psychological Measurement,* pp.1037-1043.

Renniger, K.A. and S.S. Snijder (1983)
Effects of cognitive style on perceived satisfaction and performance among students and teachers. In: *Journal of Educational Psychology,* nr. 5, pp.668-676.

Rohrkemper, M. (1985)
Individual differences in students perceptions of routine classroom events. In: *Journal of Educational Psychology,* nr. 1, pp.29-44.

Schildwacht, R. (1981)
Feedback in nagesprek en begeleiding. Utrecht. SOVA-groep (1978), *Samen werken, samen leren.* Bloemendaal.

Tuckman, B.W. and W.F. Oliver (1968)
Effectiveness of feedback to teachers as a function of source. In: *Journal of Educational Psychology,* nr. 59, pp.297-302.

Vedder, J. and P. Bannink (1988)
The development of practical skills and reflection at the beginning of teacher training. In: H. Voorbach and L.G.M. Prick (eds), *Teacher Education,* 4, SVO, Den Haag, pp.188-204.

Veldman, D.J. and R.F. Peck (1963)
Student teacher characteristics from the pupils' viewpoint. In: *Journal of Educational Psychology,* 54, 6, pp.346-355.

Wragg, E.C. (1979)
Interaction analysis as a feedback system for student teachers. In: Bennett, N. and D. McNamara, *Focus on teaching.* New York.

Wubbels, Th., M. Brekelmans and H. Hooymayers
To be published in: B.J. Fraser and H.J. Walberg (eds). *Classroom and School Environment.* London, Pergamon Press.

Wubbels, Th. and J. Levy (1989)
A comparison of Dutch and American interpersonal teacher behavior. Paper presented at the Annual Meeting of the American Educational Research Association, San Francisco (ERIC ED TM 013384).

Wubbels, Th., H.A. Créton and H.P. Hooymayers (1985)
Discipline problems of beginning teachers. Paper presented at the Annual Meeting of the American Educational Research Association, Chicago. (ERIC Document 260040).

Zeichner, K.M. and B.R. Tabachnick (1985)
The development of teacher perspectives : strategies and institutional control in the socialisation of beginning teachers. In: *Journal of Education for Teaching,* nr. 1, p.125.

APPENDIX 1

Points for interview with teacher educators

I   *Questions on the program set-up*

    1.   In which department do you work?
    2.   How long does the course last?
    3.   What is the course set-up practical period, theory etc.

II   *Content*

    1.   What particular emphases are stressed in the theory offered?
    2.   What emphases and aspects are stressed in the practical?
    3.   (What kind of approach does this involve?)
    4.   What criteria are used when evaluating the students' practical period?
    5.   To what extent is specific attention paid to the relationship teacher and pupil behaviour?

III   *Pupil Feedback*

    1.   Should a student teacher be able to involve pupil behaviour which occurs in the learning process? and how?

    2.   Is it for you a requirement that this involvement leads the student teacher to reflect on it and provides a stimulus for altering teacher behaviour?

    3.   If we describe pupil behaviour in its broadest sense as pupil feedback, and if we want the student teacher to involve this in his learning process, what conditions and restrictions should we then introduce into pupil feedback: what should or should not be included by the student teacher?

APPENDIX 2

| | Requested Feedback | | Spontaneous Feedback | |
	Teacher Education	Literature	Teacher Education	Literature
self [own functioning]	almost entirely as part of evaluation	Freiberg and Waxman	1 — 1 tapes reflection	? Wubbels "interaction"
the pupils	mother tongue and mathematics	Paul Burden	1 — 1 tapes (school) supervisor	pré-conception and informal knowledge

stages of concerns [Fuller]
zone of nearby development[(Vygotsky]

teacher development

From 1990 ATEE paper on Pupil-feedback Harrie Broekman and Peter Bannink

FROM THE SCIENCE OF LEARNING
TO THE PERSONAL ART OF TEACHING :
THE USE OF A "TRANSLATOR PARADIGM"
WITH STUDENT TEACHERS

O'Sullivan, M., Williams, K., and McGrady, A.G.

Mater Dei Institute of Education, Dublin

The paper reports on eighteen years experience of using teaching strategy type approaches with student teachers at the Mater Dei Institute of Education, Dublin. It discusses the use of a "translator paradigm" which enables student teachers to link the underlying theory provided by educational psychology with personal growth in the artistry of planning, teaching and debriefing an individual lesson or series of lessons. The "translator paradigm" relates classical learning theory to the actual classroom practice of experienced teachers and it consists of two elements. Firstly, a lesson is conceptualised as a series of episodes each of which is characterised by a distinctive interaction between the teacher and the pupils, an interaction occurring within the context of the demands imposed by the nature of the subject-matter content under consideration. Secondly, each episode is structured as an interplay between four movements, initiation, elaboration, response and closure. Experience has shown that the use of the "translator paradigm" enables student teachers to master "classical" teaching strategy approaches (such as concept formation, problem solving, reception learning and interpretation of data), to integrate these into a personal teaching style, and to generate new strategic approaches (such as concept extension or response to narrative). The paradigm also minimises the difficulties often experienced by student teachers in mastering teaching strategy type approaches, in particular the problems of relating theoretical models to actual classroom practice, and of responding to the distinctive demands of specific subject-matter.

In recent years teaching strategy type approaches have become increasingly popular in teacher-training. Historically such approaches arose not from the area of educational methodology but from educational psychology and from instructional design. Teachers often found it difficult to relate the language of research to the real business of the classroom. The resultant teaching strategy approaches sought to develop a repertoire of teacher skills that were adaptive to the demands of a range of learning and teaching situations.

An important distinction must be drawn between the use of teaching strategy approaches with experienced teachers as part of inservice or continuing education programmes and their use with student teachers in training. In practice many student teachers experience difficulty in mastering teaching-strategy type approaches as they find problems both in relating theoretical models to actual classroom contexts, and in recognising the distinctive demands of specific subject-matter. Their difficulties frequently find expression in two main ways, a tendency to teach the strategy rather than the subject matter, and difficulty in matching the pedagogic structuring of the theoretical models with the rhythm of the classroom interaction. Thus, although one of the aims of teaching strategy type approaches is to enable the student-teacher to function flexibly in the classroom situation, in practice a high level of synthesis and experience is required before the teacher can do this. By definition the student-teacher lacks such experience. Furthermore, individual strategies, such as reception learning, based upon the work of Ausubel 1963, 1968 or interpretation of data, based upon the work of Taba 1962, or problem solving, based upon Dewey 1910, or discussion, based upon Hyman 1974, construe the flow, pace and climate of a lesson in different ways. Student-teachers frequently find it difficult to relate these models to classroom practice because they do not have a wider sense of the whole to which these approaches can be related. What is needed, therefore, is a simple, "user-friendly" translator paradigm, a simple model of what constitutes a lesson, which can be used as a master structure allowing individual teaching strategies to be integrated by the student teacher into a wider framework of the art of teaching.

The lesson as a series of interactive episodes

In response to these concerns a "translator paradigm" is proposed consisting of two elements. Firstly, a lesson is conceptualised as a series of episodes, each of which is characterised by a distinctive personal interaction between the teacher and the pupils, an interaction occurring within the context of the demands imposed by the nature of the subject-matter under consideration. Sensitivity to the mutually interdependent and interactive nature of this triadic conversation determines the quality of the learning/teaching situation. Secondly, each episode itself is structured as an interplay between four movements, initiation, elaboration, response and closure.

A lesson may be seen as consisting of a number of episodes, each structured on the four movements, (see figure 1). Episodes constitute a pattern of concurrent, ordered sequences which knit together into a unified and coherent whole, intentionally and systematically opening-up and illuminating the conversation between teacher, pupils and subject-matter. The purpose and climate of each episode differs according to the planned for, and emerging, educational outcomes. During the planning stage of a lesson the teacher provisionally decides whether a specific topic, or pupil learning need, lends itself to two, three or four episodes, and retains a willingness to adapt these in purpose, scope and number as the lesson is implemented.

The episodic paradigm offers itself to student teachers as a translation device encouraging a movement from a concern with the mastery of a range of discrete component teaching skills to an alternative personal focus on the exercise of the artistry of teaching. It forms the basis of the practical aspect of teacher education at the Mater Dei Institute of Education, Dublin. (Students follow a four year concurrent degree programme incorporating Religious Studies, Education, and an elective Arts Subject). The paradigm is initially presented in first year as part of an introductory Microteaching programme and provides a wider framework to which individual skills such as stimulus variation, lower and higher order questioning, reacting, use of a textbook and teacher exposition are related. It is further developed in both second and third year by Foundational and

Advanced Teaching Skills programmes. It also forms the basis for the Systematic Observation Instruments used during teaching practice and completed by both the student teachers and the teaching practice supervisors.

The application of the translator paradigm to teaching strategy approaches

In applying the episodic paradigm to microteaching and teaching strategies programmes it is useful to identify three broad groups of teacher skills; expository skills, experiential skills and heuristic skills. In each of these the episodic interaction between the teacher, pupils and subject-matter takes a particular shape with a distinctive classroom climate and the assumption of varying roles.

Expository skills of teaching are used by the teacher in systematically presenting subject matter. Most lessons include at least one such episode. The teacher overviews material, explains an important concept, examines a principle or generalisation, interprets important data. Related skills include teacher exposition and concept extension. While such expository teaching skills draw upon some of the classical and traditional approaches to classroom learning, the focus with experiential skills shifts away from the systematic examination of content to the life-experience of the pupils. Such skills enable the teacher and pupils to enter into the important experiences that are central to any unit of work. While the focus during expository skills is often highly cognitive, experiential skills also encourage effective and physical participation. Approaches taken within experiential episodes include using audiovisual media, simulation, role-play and response to narrative. Every subject area has its own characteristic methods and approaches. The emphasis in the final grouping, heuristic skills, is in enabling the teacher to develop in the pupils the skills of analysis, judgement and synthesis. Such skills encourage personal reflection, decision making, critical thinking, interpretation of data and balanced judgement. Since they involve guided discovery learning, such approaches to teaching are often highly motivating. Approaches to such heuristic episodes include group work, discussion and problem solving.

638

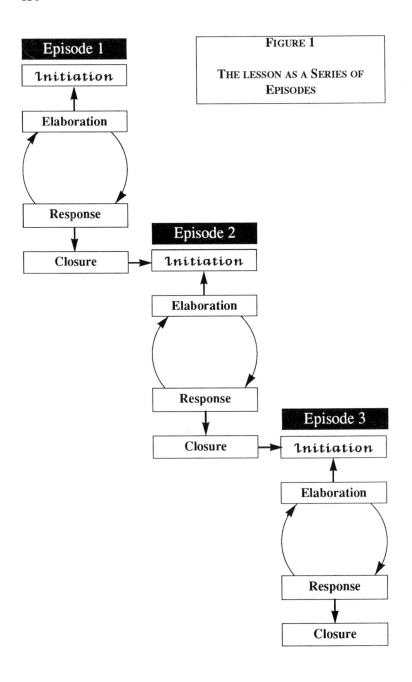

Episode 1

Initiation

Elaboration

Response

Closure

FIGURE 1

THE LESSON AS A SERIES OF EPISODES

Episode 2

Initiation

Elaboration

Response

Closure

Episode 3

Initiation

Elaboration

Response

Closure

**The Application of the Episodic Framework
to Teacher Exposition**

The notion of a teaching episode can now be illustrated with reference to the skill of teacher exposition, which provides the teacher with a means of structuring the input of important subject mater. Most lessons will in practice include a teacher exposition type episode. For instance a consideration of the topic pollution easily lends itself to a lesson structured in three episodes. Episode one would revise the definition of the concept pollution and formalise this in terms of the pupils' initial understanding. A second episode, based on teacher exposition, would allow for the explanation of the common causes of river pollution, while episode three would use problem solving to address the issue of the pollution of a local river. We can explore the second episode based on teacher exposition in greater detail as follows:

Phase 1 : Initiation

The teacher begins the episode by introducing the subject-matter to be covered. A broad framework of types of pollution (including the superordinate class, water pollution) is provided.

Phase 2 : Elaboration

The pupils attend as the material is presented by the teacher in a systematic, challenging and thought-provoking manner aimed at extending their cognitive structures, (this process is well explained by Piaget's notions of assimilation and accommodation). The summary outline presented at the initiation phase is expanded, explained and extended. For example the teacher explains what river pollution is and how it relates to water pollution, how effluent from a factory pollutes a river, and why fish die in polluted water.

Phase 3 : Response

This phase of the episode is aimed at promoting the personal understanding of each pupil. One is mindful of the statement of Dewey 1910, "nothing is really known except in so far as it is understood." Pupils, therefore, respond to the presented subject matter concerning the causes and effects of river pollution. They may be questioned by the teacher about the accuracy of their understanding of the presented subject matter and encouraged to interpret its implications. Pupils interact with the teacher and with each other. New insights evolve through such articulation. The teacher keeps the conversation developing, promoting continuity with previous learning and introducing additional detail as appropriate. Pupil contributions are accepted, redirected, modified or expanded. Follow up tasks may be set.

Phase 4 : Closure

The final stage of a teacher exposition episode involves the drawing together of the material covered so far, for example, the teacher reviews the causes of river pollution. This is the time for consolidating learning both within and between the episodes of the lesson, and often requires the redirecting of the pupils' attention to chalkboard summaries or to the text book. Summarising the content covered during the episode often necessitates the redefinition of an important concept. Given the cyclic nature of the episodic paradigm, the closure of one episode frequently merges into the initiation of the next (in this case to the setting of a problem solving task relating to the effects of greed, ignorance and inertia on the pollution of a local river).

Each episode of the lesson on pollution is terminated by a very definite closure movement which focuses attention on the key elements of the topic being explored, and leads into the next episode. In addition, the final episode of the lesson, in this case the exploration of the options available for dealing with the pollution of a local river, provides an overall summary to, and consolidation of, the learning experience.

**The Application of the Episodic Paradigm
to Classroom Discussion**

Let us now examine how the episodic paradigm might be applied to a different kind of classical teaching skill, taking as an example the heuristic strategy of discussion. There are several reasons for choosing to apply our framework to this strategy. In the first place, discussion is of central relevance not only in much moral education but also in the teaching of many subjects across the curriculum. And it is important to bear in mind that the use of discussion as a teaching strategy is not limited to its role in facilitating the articulation and clarification of values. Discussion can be a fruitful strategy in promoting understanding within the major school subjects and is an essential feature of the teaching of literature, history, geography, economics, social studies and religion (McKernan, 1990; Hyman, 1974).[1] Secondly, discussion is often a feature in the use of other teaching skills, such as problem solving or group work. Thirdly, discussion is a skill which can very easily be used ineffectively and in inappropriate circumstances. Teacher educators hardly need to have their attention drawn to the manner in which discussion can degenerate into a desultory conversational exchange. It is especially important, therefore, that students be given a tight framework within which to conduct discussions whether on moral issues or in teaching more traditional school subjects. Moreover, student teachers find that the treatment of discussion as a teaching strategy in the standard texts (Hyman, 1974; Joyce and Weil, 1980) needs a translator paradigm to convert the strategy into a form sensitive to the reality of the classroom. In particular, they need such a paradigm to adapt the strategy to the constraints of the time frame of a lesson period. Otherwise they are unable to convert the science of learning into the personal art of teaching. Another reason for the choice of discussion to illustrate the episodic framework is the opportunity it provides to make use of the skills of role-play and simulation.

The context of this example is taken from a unit of a series of lessons on the theme of "work." This theme has been chosen because it has rich multidisciplinary and interdisciplinary possibilities across the curriculum. One of the lessons in the series deals with the subject of strikes. The overall aim of the lesson is to alert pupils to the practical and moral complexity of strike situations

---

[1] McKernan gives an excellent account of the central role of discussion in moral education as well as a contemporary statement of the classical approach to the use of discussion as s teaching strategy. Hyman (1974) (especially) and Joyce and Weil (1980) give accounts of the use of discussion in other subjects. Hyman's (1974) extensive treatment of discussion in this book also confirms the importance of the skill.

and, in particular, the difficulty of applying one's principles in concrete situations. Discussion is, therefore, to be used both in the promotion of understanding as well as in facilitating the articulation and clarification of values. As it is proposed to provide pupils with an experiential base for their work, role-play/simulation will also be used as a strategy within the lesson.

The lesson (45 minutes) consists of three episodes. In the first episode (5 minutes) the teacher reviews and revises the work of the previous lesson and relates the theme of the day's lesson to the work already done. The second episode (15 minutes) makes use of role-play to present the subject for discussion and to provide relevant factual background. (The situation involves a strike at the local cafe which the pupils have been requested to support by refusing to pass pickets. Role-play, with two class members chosen in advance to represent the points of view of strikers and management, is used to present this situation).

Episode three (the discussion episode) (25 minutes).

Phase 1 : Initiation

During this phase the climate of the lesson is established and the agenda for the discussion is set. Pupils are invited to give their pre-critical stance to the request to respect the picket. A vote is taken at this point.

Phase 2 : Elaboration

Pupils are invited to contribute to the discussion on whether the class should support the strikers and sign the petition.

Phase 3 : Response

The key issues are identified and explained as they emerge from the discussion. Pupils are invited to re-consider their stances and a second vote is taken. A brief survey may be conducted of the numbers who have changed their point of view as a result of the discussion.

Phase 4 : Closure

The group stance is adopted.   Assignments are set and related to the next day's activity.

This then is a lesson plan for a class period of some forty five minutes in which the central episode (episode 3) is based on the skill of discussion.   What the episodic framework offers here is a structure whereby the teacher can plan his lesson in self contained units.   As the two principal movements in the lesson are dealt with as discrete units, the teacher is enabled to exploit the teaching moments which may arise in the first movement without feeling that he must get through all of his material in order to teach a coherent lesson.   In particular, the response phase of the second episode (role-play/simulation) may develop into a fruitful lesson on economics in which the teacher facilitates the pupils in arriving at an understanding of the economic and social aspects of running a small business.   The episodic framework allows the teacher to make of the second phase a single extended unit of one entire lesson.   The third (discussion) episode would then become the principal element in the subsequent lesson.   Specifically regarding the skill of discussion, the framework can be seen to offer a structure capable of translating the classical treatment of the skill (for example, Joyce and Weil, 1980, pp.226-34) into a tightly structured form sensitive to the demands of the classroom and to the time frame of a lesson period.

Conclusion: The usefulness of the episodic translator paradigm

We can say that the episodic translator paradigm provides for the conversion of the science of learning into the art of teaching in the following ways:

1.   Perhaps the main advantage of the episodic paradigm is that student teachers quickly identify it as being based upon good common sense.   It thus provides a familiar, easy to grasp framework that clearly relates to the behaviour of experienced teachers.

2.   It provides a permanent structure for envisaging the nature of the teaching act to which other aspects can gradually be

related. Here the simplicity of the paradigm is its greatest strength. On the one hand, it is capable of being grasped and used by the novice teacher, while, on the other hand, it forms a schema to which more advanced notions of teaching can be easily assimilated. Thus it becomes progressively elaborated and differentiated as the student-teacher grasps more advanced pedagogic approaches and gains broader classroom experience.

3.   It insists on a view of teaching and learning which stresses human interaction between the teacher, the developing pupil, and a significant body of content, promoting and sustaining a meaningful and on-going conversation between these three elements. It seeks to integrate a component skills model with a view of teaching as a personal synthesis more akin to the activity of the artist than to that of the technician. It thus emphasises the need for student teachers to master "classical" teaching strategy approaches (such as concept formation, problem solving, reception learning, discussion, and interpretation of data), within the context of developing a personal teaching style.

4.   It provides a way of structuring the progressive organisation of subject-matter for both an individual lesson and a sequence of lessons. It lends orderliness to a class period by enabling the student teacher to combine aspects of several teaching strategies into a single lesson, (for example by combining role-play with discussion as two episodes of a single lesson).

5.   It enables the concerns of the Humanities and Arts to be more adequately catered for within teaching strategy type approaches. For example teachers of religion or teachers of literature have often found that the classical "interpretation of data" model does not fit well with biblical or poetic material. Based upon the episodic paradigm it has been possible to evolve strategies such as "response to narrative" or "concept extension" which deal more adequately with human experience or with symbol and metaphor as modes of articulation.

6. Of particular importance to curriculum areas such as religious education, it enables a balance to be effected between valid expository concerns and experiential or heuristic approaches. It stresses the need for purposeful sustained input by the teacher and encourages the judicious selection of significant subject-matter.

7. The application of the episodic paradigm enables the varying concerns and descriptive devices of various classical strategies to be translated into a common frame of reference, that of initiation, elaboration, response and closure. An individual teaching strategy is thus seen not as a substitute for lesson planning but as a classical way of structuring a single teaching episode (among others in the lesson).

8. Finally the paradigm provides a common reference point for both student teachers and those involved in tutoring and supervising their classroom based experience. It promotes good time-management and provides a basis for adaptive decision-making. It thereby constitutes a stable focus for lesson preparation, implementation and assessment.

REFERENCES

Ausubel, D.P. (1963). *The Psychology of Meaningful Verbal Learning.* Holt, Rinehart and Winston.

Ausubel, D.P. (1968). *Educational Psychology, a Cognitive View.* Holt, Rinehart and Winston.

Dewey, J. (1910). *How we Think.* Boston : Heath.

Eggen, P., Kauchak, D. and Harder, R. (1979). *Strategies for Teachers.* Prentice Hall, 1979.

Hyman, R. (1974, 2nd Edition). *Ways of Teaching.* New York : J.B. Lippincott.

Joyce, B. and Weil, M. (1980, 2nd Edition). *Models of Teaching.* Englewood Cliffs, New Jersey : Prentice-Hall.

McKernan, J. (1990). *Health Education and Lifeskills in the Curriculum.* In McNamara, G., Williams, K., Herron, D (eds). Achievement and Aspiration : Curricular Initiatives in Irish Post-Primary Education in the 1980s Dublin : The Drumcondra Teachers' Centre.

Stones, E. (1979). *Psychopedagogy.* Methuen & Co. Ltd.

Strong, R.W., Silver, H.F., and Hanson, R. (1985). *Integrating Teaching Strategies and Thinking Styles with Elements of Effective Instruction.* Educational Leadership, Vol.42, No.8, pp.9-15.

NAMES AND ADDRESSES OF AUTHORS

Pieter Licht
Department of Science Education,
Vrize Universiteit Amsterdam, De Boelelaan 1081,
H.V. Amsterdam, The Netherlands.

H.M.C. Eijkelhof, C.W.J.M. Klaassen and P.L. Lijnse
Centre for Science and Mathematics Education,
University of Utrecht, The Netherlands.

Sheila Turner
University of London, Institute of Education,
20 Bedford Way, London, WC1H OAL.

Pinchas Tamir
Hebrew University Jerusalem,
P.O. Box 12, Rehouot 76100, Israel.

Sarah Berenson and Ann C. Howe
Centre for Research in Mathematics and Science Education,
Box 7801, Poe Hall, North Carolina State University, Raleigh,
NC27695—7801, U.S.A.

Dr. Charly Ryan,
King Alfred's College, Winchester SO22 4NR, England.

Ana Maria Onorbe de Torre and Jose Maria Sanches Jimenez
Escuela Universitaria de E.G.B., Guadalajara,
University of Alcala de Henares, Spain.

Lillian Greenwood
Institute of Informations, University of Ulster, Jordanstown,
Northern Ireland.

Leslie Caul
Education Faculty, Stranmillis College, Belfast, BT9 5DY.

A. Cachapuz, el. Malaquias, Maríla F. Thomaz and N. Vasconcelos
Departmento de Didactica, Universidade de Averico, 3800 Aveiro,
Portugal.

Maria de Fatima Choräo Sanches
Faculty of Science, University of Lisbon, Edificio C130 Andav, Rue
Eunesto, Vasoncelos, 1700 Lisboa, Portugal.

Kauko Hämäläinen, Armi Mikkola
Helsinki University, Vantaa Further Education Institute,
Unikkotie 5 B SF—01300, Vantaa, Finland.

Inge Carlström and Lena-Pia Hagman
Kristianstad University College, Box 59,
S—291 21 Kristianstad, Sweden.

Gerard M. Willems
Institute for Teacher Education, Postbus 30011,
NL6503 HN, Nijmegan, Netherlands.

Gertrand Havranek
Institut für Anglistik und Amerikanistik, Universität für
Bildungswissenschaften, Universitsstrase 65, A—9020, Klagenfürt.

Cveta Razdevsek Pucko
Pedagoska Akademija, Kardeljeva PL.16, 61000 Ljubljana,
Yugoslavia.

Dietland Fisher
Wiengarten 43, D—4400 Münster, Germany.

John Coldron and Pam Boulton,
Sheffield City Polytechnic, 36 Collegiate Crescent,
Sheffield, S10 23BP., England.

Claire Lane,
Thomond College of Education, Plessey, Limerick.

I. Bordas and M. Montané
Facultad Pedagogía, Université, Barcelona.

Teresa Levy
Dept. de Educacoa, Block C.1., 1700 Lisboa, Portugal.

Ciarian Sugrue
St. Patrick's College of Education, Drumcondra, Dublin, 9.

Gerry McNamara
145 Stiles Road, Clontarf, Dublin, 3.

Harrie G.B. Broekman and Peter Bannink
IVLOS Inst. of Education,
University of Utrecht, Heidelberglaan 2, Post Box 80120, 3508
Utrecht, The Netherlands.

M. O'Sullivan, K. Williams, and A.G. McGrady
Mater Dei Institute of Education, Clonliffe Road, Dublin, 9.